The Chiropractic Neurological Examination

Joseph S. Ferezy, DC
University Chiropractic Consultants
Minneapolis, Minnesota

AN ASPEN PUBLICATION®
Aspen Publishers, Inc.
Gaithersburg, Maryland
1992

Library of Congress Cataloging-in-Publication Data

Ferezy, Joseph S.
The chiropractic neurological examination / Joseph S. Ferezy.
p. cm.
Includes bibliographical references and index.
ISBN: 0-8342-0256-5
1. Chiropractic—Diagnosis. 2. Neurologic examination. I. Title.
[DNLM: 1. Chiropractic—methods. 2. Neurologic Examination—methods. WB 905.8 F349c]
RZ250.F47 1992
615.5'34—dc20
DNLM/DLC
for Library of Congress
91-22236
CIP

Editorial Services: Ruth Bloom

Library of Congress Catalog Card Number: 91-22236
ISBN: 0-8342-0256-5

Printed in the United States of America

1 2 3 4 5

Table of Contents

Contributors

A.V. Anderson, MD, DC
Medical Director
Pain Assessment and Rehabilitation Center Ltd
Edina, Minnesota

Thomas F. Bergmann, DC
Editor-in-Chief, *Journal of Chiropractic Technique*
and Private Practice
Mendota Heights, Minnesota

Ronald J. Berk, MEd
Biofeedback and Psychological Services Director
Neurophysiological Institute
Edina, Minnesota

Leo J. Bronston, DC, FACO, CCSP, DABCO
Diplomate Chiropractic Orthopedist
Certified Chiropractic Sports Physician
Board Eligible Chiropractic Neurologist
Private Practice
LaCrosse, Wisconsin

David Hinz, DC
Clinical Coordinator
Pain Assessment and Rehabilitation Center Ltd
Edina, Minnesota

Steven A. Mickelson, DC
Board Eligible Chiropractic Neurologist
Fall Creek Chiropractic Center
Fall Creek, Wisconsin

Preface

With the advent of new and superior "high-tech" diagnostic techniques, the art of the neurological examination appears to be going the way of the saber-toothed tiger. It is certainly easier to order a broad battery of diagnostic tests than it is to spend the time necessary to arrive at a diagnostic impression, and use the advanced testing procedures only to rule in or out possibilities that might alter therapy.

Overutilization of high-tech diagnostic procedures, including imaging studies, almost always carries with it an inherent risk of unnecessary short- and long-term damage to your patient. Additionally, it feeds the upward spiral of health care costs. On the other hand, failure to use available diagnostic studies when indicated might lead to an incorrect diagnosis, which is equally capable of causing damage to your patient. It may also constitute malpractice.

The neurological examination is therefore actually more important than ever. It provides information about the location, type, and extent of neurological disease, in a fashion unrivaled by any other clinical discipline. Only in neurology is the relationship between function and structure, symptom, and pathology consistently clinically proven. Performance and interpretation of the neurological examination is a requisite first step toward the practice of chiropractic. This text offers a concise, basic neurological guide for the doctor of chiropractic and the chiropractic student. Emphasis is given to accurate neurological examination performance and neurodiagnosis.

The Chiropractic Neurological Examination includes chapters on pain, postmanipulative stroke, the chiropractic spinal examination, and documentation, as well as a glossary of neurological terms for assistance in the day-to-day practice of chiropractic.

My most sincere thanks to my wife, Kathleen, and sons, David and Jacques, for their sacrifices during my preparation of this manuscript. Also, I must commend my contributors for their first-class handling of their respective subjects.

chapter **1**

The Patient Interview

PRINCIPLES OF THE PATIENT INTERVIEW

Interviewing the potential patient is difficult to learn. Indeed, the techniques involved cannot really be mastered at all, only continually sharpened by years of clinical practice. It is not the intention of this chapter to exhaustively discuss each detail of the patient interview but merely to outline key areas of consideration from a primarily chiropractic/neurological viewpoint. Additionally, hysteria and malingering are discussed in Chapter 9.

USE OF HISTORY QUESTIONNAIRES

Many practice management groups recommend the use of a list of predetermined questions. This may be good or even essential for the student doctor, as he or she has no foundation of knowledge or experience on which to base the substance and direction of questioning. Ultimately, however, use of such forms will cause the doctor to overlook many specifically directed questions that may further elucidate the diagnosis, such as asking patients with suspected Parkinson's disease if they have noted difficulty getting in and out of chairs, making rapid turns, or cutting their food, or if they have noticed any changes in their handwriting. Conversely, forms may also cause the doctor to waste time and even diminish the patient's confidence by leading the doctor to ask useless and even stupid questions relative to the patient's illness. I vividly recall reviewing a patient's chart that included a "History Questionnaire." The patient had injured his ankle playing tennis, and in the space next to the question "When was the last time that you felt really good," the doctor had actually written "Just before I sprained my ankle." Clearly, questions designed to detect one illness may be completely irrelevant in another. Questioning the above patient regarding his ability to cut his food or changes in his handwriting would be unnecessary and unproductive.

The consummate history elicitor must make the patient completely comfortable. Many features of illness, such as impotence or bladder incontinence, are exceedingly personal issues and may be embarrassing for the patient to discuss. A patient may withhold vital pieces of information if she or he feels in any way ill at ease with the clinician. Thus it is the responsibility of a doctor to make the patient feel completely uninhibited. This can best be accomplished by, first, fitting into the patient's preconception of how a doctor should look and behave. Obviously, patients' different cultural and socioeconomic backgrounds dictate specifically what this entails. For some, a doctor should wear a clean, pressed, white clinic jacket and a tie; for others, a gold ring through the nose is acceptable. Your personal setting will prescribe the specifics. Minimally, one would expect that rigid standards for personal and general office hygiene would be established.

To further ensure complete candor, it is of paramount importance that the atmosphere be unhurried and that the patient be allowed sufficient time to answer all of the questions completely. If rifling through a predetermined list of questions and pressing for answers were the goals, this chapter would be titled "The Patient Interrogation." This is not to say that the patient should be allowed to ramble endlessly on about useless details, such as what he or she had for breakfast the week before the car accident. Here, the doctor's social skills determine the ease with which the patient can be gently guided along the historical pathway the doctor deems most significant. Too much history may be as bad as too little, by clouding the diagnostic issue with useless detail. Knowing what one needs to know is a skill that is constantly being improved and separates the accomplished practitioner from the novice (see Figure 1-1).

Patients themselves may or may not be good historians. I have found that basically there are two different types of difficult history givers, impartors and extractees. Impartors are those who will give you all of the necessary information and more, if allowed to do so. They usually only need to be properly directed during the history. They will usually cite events out of sequence. I have found it especially useful to simply inform these patients that time will be provided at the end of the interview for them to add to or amplify anything they feel we have not sufficiently covered. A well-performed history should cover all of the bases, and most patients have little, if anything, to add. Those who do feel that it is necessary to elaborate sometimes come up with important tidbits of information that may help one arrive at a diagnosis, or may just give one further insight into the patient's personality. Extractees, on the other hand, are those who will only offer basic yes and no answers. These patients are by far the minority, which is fortunate since they are also the most frustrating to deal with (see Figure 1-2).

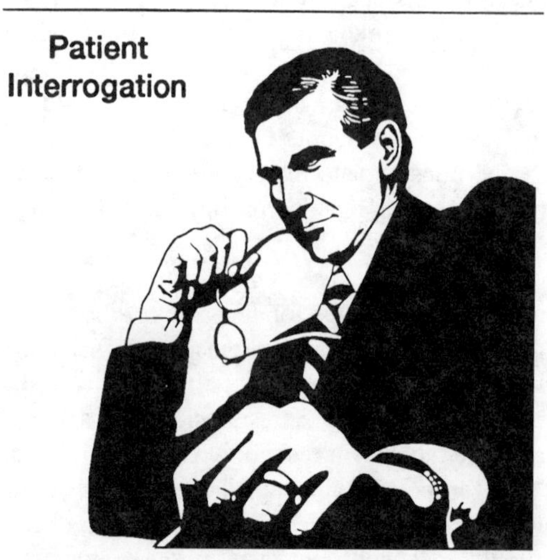

Figure 1-1 A threatening doctor will not get accurate responses.

While a proper patient interview may well be the most difficult task facing a physician, the information it yields is almost always clinically vital.

INITIAL MEETING

General biographical data should be the first sort of information obtained about a patient. This is most commonly accomplished by having the patient fill out an office questionnaire upon first entering the office (see Figure 1-3). Minimally, full name, date of birth, sex, race, occupation, marital status, home address, and social security number should be recorded. Some of this information, such as name and address, has general utility, while other parts of it are important diagnostic considerations, such as age, sex, race, and occupation. For example, a complaint of recent onset of severe headache will have different diagnostic implications for a 19-year-old white female, a 60-year-old white female, and a 35-year-old black male.

Once the forms are completed, the doctor will usually meet with the patient. There is no replacement for the attending doctor when it comes to history taking. Even the most well-trained assistants simply do not have the clinical

Figure 1-2 The two types of poor historians.

experience to know what questions to ask, nor are they qualified to make observations concerning personality, cranial nerve function, or mental state, which are commonly assessed during the history. An assistant might be useful in doing a preinterview, but ultimately the doctor must perform the task.

Prior to the formal history-taking procedure, much information may be gleaned by observation of the posture of the patient. Antalgia, or leaning away from pain, is extremely common in lumbar and even cervical discopathies. Some patients will prefer to stand while waiting for the doctor, and this too may be due to discopathy, as there is less intradiscal pressure in the standing posture than in the sitting posture. Similarly, patients who support their weight with their upper extremities, so that they are almost dangling in the chair, or who sit on the very edge of the chair, leaning backward, may be suffering from lumbar disc involvement. On the other hand, a patient who sits cross-legged is probably not experiencing discal or hip joint pathology, at least not on that side (see Figure 1-4).

Observation of patient behavior and shaking the patient's hand may yield invaluable information regarding personality, central and peripheral motor function, coordination, and autonomic function. A firm handshake is associated with confidence and personability; a weak or flaccid handshake may indicate introversion, or motor impairment. Inaccuracy reaching to the doctor's hand may indicate dysmetria and be a sign of cerebellar dysfunction. A cold, blue, and clammy hand may indicate increased sympathetic tone, whereas a hot, flushed, and dry hand might indicate sympathetic paralysis. Adduction of the thumb into the palm may be an early sign of upper motor neuron involvement or a late sign of extrapyramidal disease. Radial nerve damage causes weakness of the wrist extensors. Ulnar nerve involvement may cause a loss of hypothenar and intrinsic hand muscle mass, and,

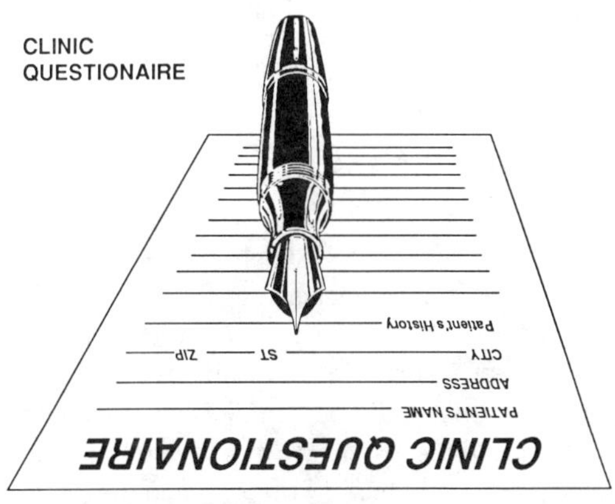

Figure 1-3 The patient should fill out a biographical questionnaire on the first visit.

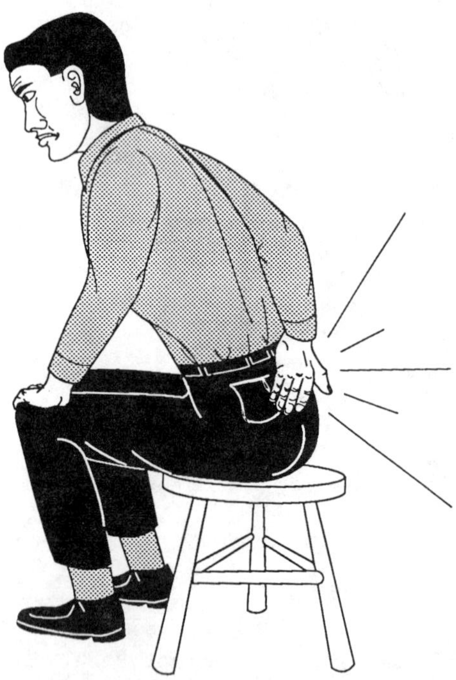

Figure 1-4 Observe patient position for clues about the presenting complaint.

later, a flexion contracture of the fourth and fifth digits, which may result in the "claw hand" deformity, while median nerve involvement causes thenar atrophy and a characteristic "ape hand" deformity. A contracture in the palm causing flexion of one or more fingers may be a sign of Dupuytren's contracture, and pain in the area of the radial styloid that is exaggerated by volar flexion might indicate de Quervain's disease (stenosing tenosynovitis of the abductor longus and extensor brevis).

PATIENT HISTORY

Normally, it is a good idea for the patient to be sequestered from any friends or family members who come to the office with him or her, in order to obtain an accurate history. An obvious example where this would be beneficial is a 16-year-old female who presents with headaches, accompanied by her mother or father. When the doctor inquires about whether or not she is currently taking oral contraceptives, the answer may well be unreliable with a parent in the room. Another instance is the case of a malingerer who requires coaching from another person. In other instances, having a friend or relative in the room is extremely useful or absolutely essential. A patient with impaired communicative skills or a very young child is an example. Additionally, a patient's parent or spouse may be quite put off by an office policy that completely excludes his or her presence. I recommend that interested friends and family be allowed, not invited, into the history-taking area but asked to wait outside during the formal examination. This affords the doctor ample opportunity to add a private history session with the patient. Subsequent to the exam, or during a report of the findings procedure, any person who may be able to contribute to the history's accuracy should be invited into the room.

A good patient history must at least be able to answer the who, what, when, where, and how of an illness. Who is this person (biographical data)? What exactly is his or her complaint? When did it first occur? Where exactly is it located? How did it occur? With luck the answer to why will be provided by the diagnosis. Specific areas to cover usually include

1. the chief complaint
2. the present illness
3. past history
4. family history
5. occupational history
6. review of systems

Chief Complaint

The chief complaint should appear in the first sentence or two of the history. It will immediately tell the reader why the patient has presented himself or herself for examination. It should include all of the patient's complaints that are directly related to his or her coming to see a doctor. It should be simple and brief and always in the patient's own words. Too often the doctor prejudices the entire history by writing a medical term or even a diagnosis based on the patient's use of medical terminology to formulate the complaint. If the patient states a diagnosis, ask the patient where he or she heard that and what it means. For example, the patient tells you that he is having "sciatica" in his right leg. You ask him to clarify, and he tells you that he is experiencing right lower extremity pain that his grandmother told him was sciatica. Your sentence should read, "His chief complaint is that of right lower extremity pain." The statement "His chief complaint is that of right sciatica" would be inappropriate. Patients experience symptoms that eventually lead them to seek care. The chief complaint is nothing more than a list of related symptoms experienced by the patient prior to seeing a doctor. As simple and basic as that sounds, failure to actually understand a patient's complaints can and does often lead to many an erroneous diagnosis.

History of Present Illness

The history of present illness is probably the single most important portion of a new patient work-up. It is essential that the doctor elicit a factual recreation of the events leading up to the patient's presentation. Most important is the chronological sequencing of events. It is imperative that the doctor guide the patient into a detailed description beginning with the first onset or exacerbation of symptoms that led to this visit. If a patient has had back pain on and off for 20 years, the doctor would begin with the most recent exacerbation that led the patient to the office on this particular occasion. After a detailed account of the date and mode of onset, factors such as the specific location and character of the complaint, its course and duration, things that exacerbate or alleviate it, and its relation to any other body systems should be explored.

Specific Location

In chiropractic practice it is exceptionally important for the patient to be specific about the location of his or her complaint. At some point the doctor should have the patient actually attempt to point with one finger to the exact location of the complaint. Radicular versus plexus versus peripheral nerve distributions of pain and paresthesia are invaluable diagnostic aids in determining the exact site of a lesion. Pain sensation arising from the scleratome distribution is "achey," deep, and poorly localized. When the pain begins in one location and radiates to another, as is commonly encountered in spinal complaints, it is useful to have the patient actually point out the entire pathway.

Date and Mode of Onset

It is important to note the date of onset. This should always be recorded as a calendar date such as January 30, 1990, and not as "about 6 weeks ago" or "over the holidays." Dates of other important factors should also be recorded as calendar dates, except where a specific reference point is present. For example it may be acceptable to say that the patient's neck pain began following a motor vehicle accident on January 30, 1990, and "the next morning" the patient awoke with low back pain as well.

The specific mode of onset is important in determining the system involved, as well as the ultimate diagnosis. Sternal pain experienced during exertion is more indicative of cardiac disease than is sternal pain associated with a punch in the chest!

Character of the Complaint

If the patient complains of "dizziness," the doctor must inquire as to what that means. Different terms mean different things to different people. Pain should always be graded as mild, moderate, or severe and described as sharp, dull, achy, burning, shooting, etc. Since pain is not the only problem a patient may present with, it is particularly important for the neurological history to include the exact nature of the symptoms. Dizziness may actually be lightheadedness, fainting, vertigo, disequilibrium, or dystaxia. The patient who complains of "numbness" may be referring to paresthesia, dysesthesia, or hypesthesia. Additionally, a temporal (time) profile of the illness must be distinguished, as this may aid in the ultimate diagnosis. Is the problem continuously progressive, as in degenerative or neoplastic disease? Is it intermittent or relapsing, with or without progression, as in multiple sclerosis or immunological disorders? Or does it have an acute onset followed by gradual recovery, as one might expect with an infectious or vascular disease?

Course, Duration, and Effects of Treatment

Dates and modes of improvement or worsening of a condition must also be explored to give a clearer understanding of the entire situation of the particular patient. Beginning immediately after the onset, the patient should be asked to discuss the details of any factors that alter the course of the disease. Is the condition better after a night's sleep? Does lifting at work exacerbate the problem? Does aspirin or hot baths relieve the pain? If the patient has seen any other physicians, records from those offices should be requested. That is not to eliminate the need to arrive at one's own diagnosis but to avoid repeating unnecessary tests, as well as to see if the patient has reported a similar history in the past. A good diagnostician will never assume a previous diagnosis is correct.

Relationship to Other Symptoms and Pre-Existing Illness

Patients are allowed to suffer from more than one illness. A doctor who is always trying to string complaints together may become involved with a great deal of unnecessary work. However, certain seemingly unrelated symptoms might dramatically change the diagnostic or therapeutic options available to the doctor. For example, in regard to lower back pain, it is essential that the doctor inquire specifically about radiation of pain and lower extremity and bowel or bladder symptoms.

Pre-existing illness may have a direct bearing on the current problem, but the patient may not see the relationship. This is true in cases of carpal tunnel syndrome secondary to hypothyroidism, back pain associated with genitourinary disease, headache secondary to hypertension, and myriad other conditions.

Past History

Dates and descriptions of prior major illnesses or hospitalizations should be recorded, along with recent visits to physicians and current medications or known allergies. This often yields enlightening information. What are the patient's exercise and personal hygiene habits? Does he or she use tobacco, alcohol, or street drugs? If so, how much?

Family History

Inquiries regarding the health of close family members (grandparents, mother, father, spouse, siblings, children) might yield the sister and mother who have identical headaches, the brother who died of a massive coronary, etc.

Occupational History

So often overlooked, a complete occupational history is often of unrivaled importance. For obvious reasons the occupation of the patient may be directly or indirectly related to the presenting complaint: wrist pain in the factory pieceworker or typist, chronic headaches in the interior room painter or high-powered executive—the list is endless. It is vital to uncover the specifics of what a job entails. A "warehouse worker" may be continually lifting heavy objects or may be driving a forklift. The doctor needs to be aware of many details, not only to help determine the cause of the complaint but also to impose intelligent job restrictions when necessary.

Review of Systems

A careful review of all of the body systems may well reveal a symptom or disease that the patient has omitted from the history. It may become evident that apparently unrelated symptoms have a common cause. Weight gain may be related to carpal tunnel syndrome by uncovering hypothyroidism. Back pain and urinary incontinence may reveal discopathy; visual complaints and numbness may have their origin in demyelinating disease. Areas to review include

1. body weight
2. skin and skin appendages
3. eyes, ears, nose, and throat
4. cardiorespiratory system
5. gastrointestinal system
6. genitourinary system
7. reproductive system (including menstrual and obstetrical history)
8. psychiatric state

Common pitfalls experienced by the beginning clinician include failure to gather all of the facts and putting words in the patient's mouth. Remember, the patient should tell the story, with the doctor serving as a guide; questions that only require a yes or no answer should generally not be asked.

There is no shortcut to the development of a good history. It is a painstaking process that, when properly performed, will usually reduce the diagnostic possibilities from a list of dozens to a list of but one or two. It should not be looked upon as a time-consuming procedure but as a time-saving procedure. It takes much more time to do physical, chiropractic, neurological, and orthopaedic testing when one has little or no idea of what one is looking for.

RECORDING THE PATIENT HISTORY

It is most beneficial for the doctor to learn or invent a system of shorthand so that the history can be recorded as it is delivered by the patient. This enables a detailed account to be given in the record, or to be dictated for transcription at a later date. Many common medical terms have standardized abbreviations. It is a good idea for the doctor to become familiar with those commonly used and incorporate them into the recording process. It is good practice to keep notes as legible as possible so that other doctors can work from them if the need arises, though this is not as important in an office as in a hospital setting; and indeed, as long as one can interpret them, that may be all that is absolutely necessary. For a list of common medical abbreviations, see Appendix A.

chapter 2

Head and Neck Examination and Mental Status Examination

GENERAL HEAD AND NECK ASSESSMENT

Prior to proceeding with the formal neurological examination, a general physical examination of the head and neck is in order, since this is the protective housing of the central nervous system, and findings can account for, or reveal clues regarding, disease anywhere in the body. It is particularly important should the patient's complaint involve neck/head trauma or pain.

Aside from the information obtained regarding the cranial nerves (see Chapter 3), a great deal of information may be gleaned by spending a few minutes assessing the head and neck. It is not the intent of this chapter to provide an exhaustive listing of all possible physical findings involving the head and neck, but simply to concentrate on those areas that may reveal primary or secondary neurological disease. Techniques for head/neck physical/neurological examination include

- inspection (observation)
- auscultation
- light palpation
- deep palpation
- percussion

Inspection

Inspect for and document any obvious evidence of trauma, such as deformities, lacerations, contusions, etc. This is useful both in identifying certain diagnostic signs of disorder and in documenting injury for future legal purposes. The tissues around the eyes, cheekbones, ears, and nose readily display the results of trauma; for example, Battle's sign (black and blue discoloration of the area behind the ear, above the mastoid) and the raccoon or panda bear sign (bilateral black-and-blue eyes, or "shiners," without conjunctival hemorrhage; see Figure 2-1) are associated with basilar skull fracture. Inspection of the scalp usually necessitates parting the hair in several locations. Lacerations of these areas tend to bleed profusely. Clear, sparkling fluid (cerebrospinal fluid) draining from the ear (otorrhea) or nose (rhinorrhea) should arouse a suspicion of basilar skull fracture as well. Cauliflower ear, caused by subchondral bleeding, is a widely known sign of trauma to that area. Obviously, any area of the head or neck may be involved in trauma, and therefore both head and neck should be thoroughly inspected in cases of recent trauma.

Inspection may also yield clues regarding other aspects of craniocervical disease. Various skin lesions have diagnostic significance, such

Figure 2-1 Raccoon or panda bear sign.

as the spider angioma, which may be associated with liver disease or intracranial aneurysms, and the café au lait spot, which suggests the peripheral or central nervous system tumors of neurofibromatosis. Observations should include noting the size and shape of the head, changes in which might represent congenital abnormalities, hydrocephalus, osteitis deformans (Paget's disease), acromegaly, skull tumors, or metastasis.

The facies and/or postures of various neuroendocrine diseases may be evident, such as the mask facies and stooped posture of parkinsonism, or the moon facies and buffalo hump of Cushing's disease. Corresponding changes in skin appearance and texture, as well as hair texture, quantity, and distribution, may be noticed and may be significant signs of neuroendocrine disorders. A strong jaw line (prognathism) with widely dispersed teeth on the lower jaw of a tall person might alert you to acromegaly, which causes back pain in many such afflicted individuals. The true beauty of observation is that once seen and registered, a simple look will often diagnose a complex problem faster and more accurately than any other examination procedure.

Auscultation

Auscultation of the blood vessels of the head and neck may be useful in assessing certain vascular phenomena. An abnormal vascular noise, or bruit, may be caused by vessel stenosis, external compression, or normal anatomical variants, or the etiology may remain unknown. These sounds must be considered carefully, as some signify disease while others are quite benign. Far too often they are indicative of large-vessel pathology.

Auscultation of the supraclavicular area, as well as over the anterior neck and temples bilaterally, and even over the eyes, spine, and skull, may reveal bruits (see Figure 2-2). In relation to skull auscultation, the presence of a bruit may be the only evidence of a dangerous intracranial arteriovenous malformation or aneurysm. Auscultatory fremitus, or vibrations, may be detected by a change in the sound usually heard when auscultating the patient's skull while the patient is making a resonant vocal sound. This may signify abnormal bony skull architecture, as noted in Paget's disease, or osteomalacia or metastatic disease.

Suggestions for stethoscope bell placement for various arteries are listed below:

1. Carotid: Place at the anterior sternocleidomastoid muscle, superiorly. Bruits are usually found at and are loudest at the bifurcation of the common carotid into the internal and external carotids.
2. Vertebral artery: If indeed one may auscultate this vessel, it would best be accomplished by listening at the point where it comes off of the subclavian, near the supraclavicular fossa. However, a bruit in this location would be of questionable vessel origin and significance.
3. Temporal: The temporal artery can be palpated and auscultated beginning just anterior to the tragus of the ear. The signifi-

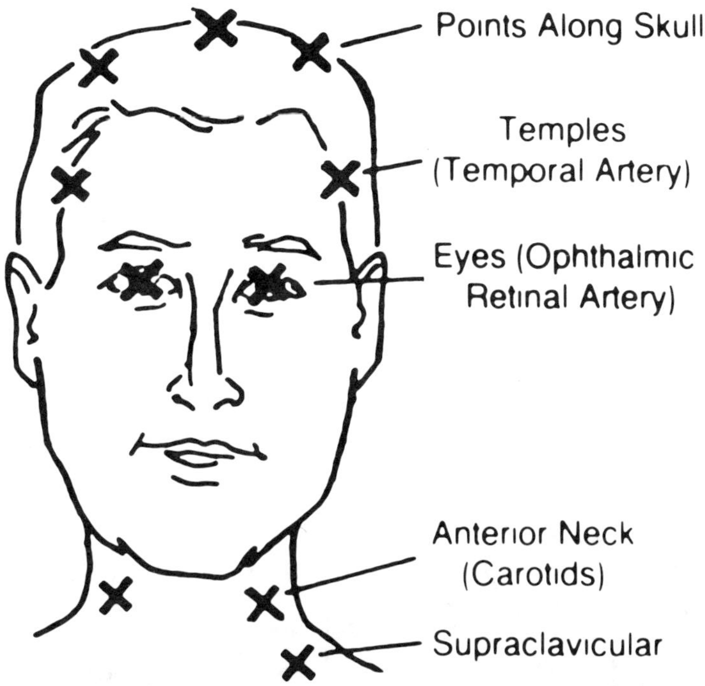

Figure 2-2 Points of auscultation on the head and neck.

cance of abnormal auscultatory findings lies in the predilection of this artery to become inflamed, a condition known as temporal arteritis.

4. Ophthalmic artery: The ophthalmic artery may, though it is difficult at best, be auscultated by placing the stethoscope bell directly over the eyes. Stenosis of this artery often causes transient ipsilateral monocular blindness, described by the patient as a "curtain coming down" over the sight in the affected eye. This type of transient ischemic attack is termed amaurosis fugax.
5. Suboccipital artery: This artery may be auscultated along the occipital nuchal line. This vessel is rarely involved but may become inflamed; such a condition would need to be differentiated from suboccipital neuralgia.
6. Skull: Several locations should be auscultated if bony cranial disease is suspected.
7. Spine: Vascular abnormalities may rarely be auscultated by placing the stethoscope over the spine itself. In cases of recurrent, severe spinal pain or spinal pain accompanied by complaints or signs of transient neurological dysfunction, it may be a good idea to auscultate.

Palpation and Percussion

Palpate the head and neck for signs of trauma or metastasis, as well as the face for temperature, and the hair for texture. This may reveal significant clues toward your diagnosis. Palpation of the spine and paraspinal musculature may reveal tenderness, chiropractic subluxation (see Chapter 9), and/or local or diffuse paraspinal muscle spasm. Use the fingertips of digits 1, 2, and 3, and roll the skin and superficial tissues over the paraspinal muscle tissues. Palpation of the skin and hair may also prove useful when noting trophic disturbances resulting from nervous system disorders.

Percussion of the skull is of no clinical use, but gentle percussion of a single finger over the spinous process of a specific vertebra may reveal disease by causing radiation of pain in fracture, chiropractic subluxation, or other lesion producing radiculopathy. Additionally, direct percussion of the maxillary and frontal sinuses leading to discomfort in those areas may be indicative of related sinus disease.

Other Techniques

Valsalva's maneuver is a simple but highly useful test; localized pain felt during its execution is often indicative of a craniospinal space-occupying lesion such as a neoplasm, disc bulge, or osteophyte. Extending the head slightly and asking the patient to cough is another way to reveal space-occupying lesions in the head and neck, as pain may be elicited by this maneuver. Large anterior osteophytes may occasionally cause difficulty with swallowing.

Mental Status Assessment

Aberrations of mental status can signal the onset of a wide variety of maladies, and it behooves chiropractors, as primary caregivers, to recognize this variety of neurological abnormality as quickly as any other type. Certainly Alzheimer's disease (or dementia of Alzheimer's type, as it is more properly referred to) will be at the top of any list of diseases brought to early light through mental status assessment, as it is the most common and significant variety of dementia.[1] The prevalence rate of this condition is reported to be as high as 10% for those aged 65 and older and 20% for those aged 80 or older[2] (though other reports give slightly lower figures[3]), so it is important for all primary contact physicians to be acutely aware of any subtle mental changes in their patients that may indicate onset of dementia of Alzheimer's type. Initially, these patients do remarkably well at hiding the cognitive defects associated with the disease. Good mental status assessment will reveal them, however, and their detection may even enhance a patient's confidence in your management of the problem. On other occasions, potentially curable or reversible causes of dementia may be identified and treated.

You must remember that the mental status examination can add as much to your patient diagnosis as any other part of the formal neurological exam, and in many cases it is the only area of examination to be markedly abnormal. It begins the instant you lay your eyes upon the patient. Whether you are aware of it or not, you automatically assess all individuals who come into contact with you. As a trained observer of the new patient and a longtime confidant of the existing patient, you should note many aspects of behavior that may be invisible to the casual

Exhibit 2-1 The Mini–Mental State Exam

Orientation: (10 points maximum)
Inquire about date, time of day, current location.

Registration: (3 points maximum)
Have patient repeat 3 words which you have previously stated. Repeat if necessary; count the trials.

Attention and Calculations:
(5 points maximum)
Spell a word backwards (5 or 6 letters).
Subtract 7s from 100 (stop after 5 answers).

Recall: (3 points maximum)
Have patient recall the 3 words from the registration above.

Language: (9 points maximum)
Show the patient 2 common objects and have them identify them aloud.
Have the patient repeat a simple phrase after you.
Have the patient perform a three-stage command (i.e., "take this paper in your right hand, fold it in half, and put it on the floor").
Have the patient perform a written command (e.g., print "close your eyes" on a piece of paper and ask the patient to do what it says).
Ask the patient to write a sentence.
Draw two intersecting pentagons and ask the patient to copy the design.

Level of Consciousness:
Assess whether the patient is alert, drowsy, or in a stupor.
Remember—a score below 23 signifies disease.

Source: Adapted with permission from *Journal of Psychiatric Research* (1975;12:189), Copyright © 1975, Pergamon Press.

observer or that evolve so slowly that they go unnoticed by family members. Typically, patients have dementia of Alzheimer's type for 8 to 12 years[4] before it is identified. Minor observations, such as failure to remember simple names or dates, or current events, should lead to a mental status assessment, which may reveal enormous defects, often to the surprise of both doctor and patient.

While a thorough case history-taking procedure may be all that is required to sum up the normal patient's mental status, a mental status screening examination is invaluable in those cases where some question of mental disorder may arise. Proper technique for this examination begins with an unhurried atmosphere. You will not get reliable responses if you rifle questions or push for answers. If you suspect a problem, use the Mini–Mental State Examination[5] later described to help qualify and quantify it. The examination takes only 5 to 10 minutes.

The areas immediately following are generally accepted as notable for expression of mental aberrations, during the history-taking process. It is always important to know the patient, or to interview family members and/or friends, so that you may first determine what is "normal" for that particular patient. A change in previous personality or habits is far more revealing than is just the absolute value arbitrarily assigned to any specific area.

The easiest, most statistically validated, and most widely used tool to help gauge disease in patients who may have mental state abnormalities as determined by clues related to the above categories, or in those who you otherwise feel may have mental status defects, is the Mini–Mental State Exam. A score below 23 (30 possible) indicates enough impairment to warrant further investigation. Of course, these values are not absolutes. Your decisions will be based on the overall clinical picture. An adaptation of this exam may be found in Exhibit 2-1.

REFERENCES

1. Katzman R. The prevalence and malignancy of Alzheimer's disease. *Arch Neurol*. 1976;33:217.

2. Kay DWK, Bergmann K, Foster EM, McKechnie AA, Roth M. Mental illness and hospital useage in the elderly: a random sample followed up. *Compr Psychiatry*. 1970; 11:26–35.

3. Jarvik LF, Ruth V, Matsuyama SS. Organic brain syndrome and aging: a six year follow-up of surviving twins. *Arch Gen Psychiatry*. 1980;37:280.

4. Cummings JL, Benson DF. *Dementia: A Clinical Approach*. Boston, Mass: Butterworth; 1983.

5. Folstein MJ, Folstein SE, McHugh PR. Mini-mental state: a practical method for grading the cognitive state of patients for the clinician. *J Psychiatr Res*. 1975;12:189.

SUGGESTED READING

Arnold LE. *Chiropractic Procedural Examination*. Seminole, Fla: Seminole Printing, Inc; 1979.

Bates B. *A Guide to the Physical Examination*. Philadelphia, Pa: JB Lippincott Co; 1983.

Prior JA, Silberstein JS. *Physical Diagnosis*. St. Louis, Mo: CV Mosby Co; 1977.

Strub RL, Black FW. *The Mental Status Examination in Neurology*. 2nd ed. Philadelphia, Pa: FA Davis Co; 1985.

chapter 3

The Cranial Nerve Examination

Twelve pairs of cranial nerves emerge from the brain and brainstem. Broadly speaking, the cranial nerves control all motor and sensory functions involving the head, face, and neck, including the special senses. These nerves mediate the senses that allow us to constantly interact with our environment. Damage to the cranial nerves often results in disorders that impair this link to the outside world, evidenced as disorders of vision, speech, and hearing, as well as movement disorders of the head and face. As a clinician, one cannot overlook inherent sensitivity to communication impairments as a tool for diagnosing cranial nerve disease. The most important component of a cranial nerve screening examination may well be the doctor's assessment of the patient's ability to engage in normal conversation, noting facial and eye movements, as well as listening to the patient's articulation.

Aside from cranial nerve VII, which has contralateral innervation in the lower part of the nuclei, nerve fibers mediating volitional movement of cranial nerve-innervated musculature arise bilaterally from the precentral gyrus of the cerebral motor cortex and descend along the corticobulbar tract (or pathway) of the brain. (In the word "corticobulbar," "cortico" refers to the cortex and "bulbar" to the brainstem. "Bulb" was the original name of the medulla oblongata, as it describes its shape. It has since been used to refer to the entire brainstem.) Due to this bilateral innervation both the right and left hemispheres have control over the right and left sides of the body. The neurons of the corticobulbar tract are also termed upper motor or supranuclear neurons, as the entire nerve cell resides in the central nervous system to terminate in different cranial nerve motor nuclei in the brainstem. Here they synapse with the lower (or alpha) motor neurons forming the synaptic link to the peripheral cranial nerves, which go on to innervate specific muscles. Links between vestibular cranial nerve nuclei, cervically innervated muscle and joint proprioceptors, as well as trigeminal (cranial nerve V) nuclei exist. These interconnections have long been thought to be responsible for the clinical relationships between headache and dizziness and the neck. Indeed, it appears that cervicogenic pain may be the greatest cause of headache while cervicogenic vertigo may be the greatest cause of dizziness.

An important anatomical feature to keep in mind during diagnosis is the bilateral innervation of cranial nerves. With bilateral innervation, relatively equal distributions of right and left brain hemisphere innervation govern the function of a specific body part. As a rule, movements performed in bilateral synchrony, such as swallowing or moving the forehead, are bilaterally innervated. Movements that are mainly unilateral, such as fine movements of the face, receive primary innervation from the contralateral hemisphere. This explains why lesions of only one cerebral hemisphere will not usually permanently paralyze normally bilateral symmetrical movements.

CRANIAL NERVE I

Anatomy and Function

The first cranial nerve is really not a peripheral nerve but a central nervous system tract terminating in the olfactory bulb. Special second-order ganglion nerve cells—true olfactory nerves in the stricter sense—pierce the cribriform plate of the ethmoid bone and terminate in the mucous membranes that line the nasal cavity. In order to perceive a particular smell, certain molecules must dissolve into the mucus overlying the cribriform plate and supply chemical stimulation of the nerve endings there (see Figure 3-1).

Disorders

Anosmia or the complete loss of smell is usually not indicative of a cortical lesion. The pathways are complex, and perversion, hallucination, or diminution of smell would be far more likely in cortical lesions. Complete loss of the sense of smell is more commonly associated with viral infections, allergic rhinitis, aging, or head trauma causing a basilar skull fracture and fracture of the delicate, wafer-thin cribriform plate. (In the latter event, CSF rhinorrhea and backwash meningitis are possible and should be investigated.) Even without fracture, neck and head injuries can cause the cribriform plate to shear off neurons descending from the olfactory bulb. In all of the above conditions but aging, the sense of smell may eventually return, but it often does not.

Lesions of the uncinate gyrus of the anterior temporal lobe may cause hallucinations of smell associated with strong feelings of deja vú, termed uncinate fits or seizures, causing hyposmia (a decrease of smell), hyperosmia (an

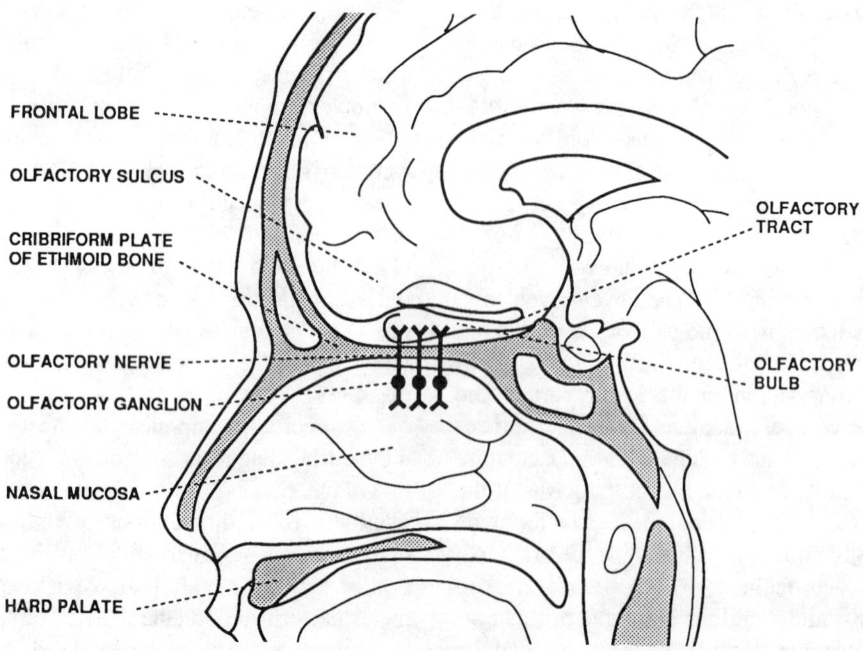

Figure 3-1 Basic anatomy of the olfactory apparatus.

increase of smell), parosmia (a perversion of smell), or cacosmia (abnormally disagreeable smell). Additional but less frequent causes of disorders of smell include frontal lobe tumors, which may compress the olfactory tract, and tumors involving the structures surrounding the olfactory tract, such as meningiomas.

Examination

The sense of smell is not routinely tested. It may be tested when complaints include changes in smell and/or taste. One nostril must be occluded by asking the patient to apply external pressure to close it or by packing it with cotton. The patient is asked to close his or her eyes. To verify that the patient will not be guessing at the smells, it is prudent to ask the patient what he or she smells prior to placing any substance near the patient. A substance producing a nonirritating smell such as peppermint, coffee, or lemon should then be placed under the patient's nose and another inquiry made regarding what the patient smells. A different smell should be used for the other nostril (see Figure 3-2).

Figure 3-2 Conducting a test of the sense of smell.

CRANIAL NERVES II, III, IV, AND VI (THE VISUAL SYSTEM)

Normal Ocular Anatomy

The anatomy of the eye includes the bulbar and palpebral conjunctivae, the medial and lateral canthi, the limbus, the cornea, the ciliary body of the iris, the lens, the retina, the choroid, and the sclera (see Figure 3-3). Other structural features are described in other sections of this chapter.

Anatomy and Function

Like the olfactory nerve, the optic nerve (cranial nerve II) is not a true cranial nerve but rather a central nervous system tract terminating in a specialized sensory ending, in this case the retina. Exposure of the terminal structures of the optic nerve, the rods and cones of the retina, to light is responsible for our ability to see. Central vision refers to the retinal area upon which the visual image is focused, the fovea centralis of the macula lutea. It provides our color vision and corresponds to the area of the retina with the greatest concentration of cone receptors. Damage of this area results in a corresponding decrease in central visual acuity. Retinal rod receptors are responsible for black-and-white peripheral vision. These receptors function in very low light conditions; pathology affecting their numbers may be responsible for night blindness or tunnel (gun barrel) vision.

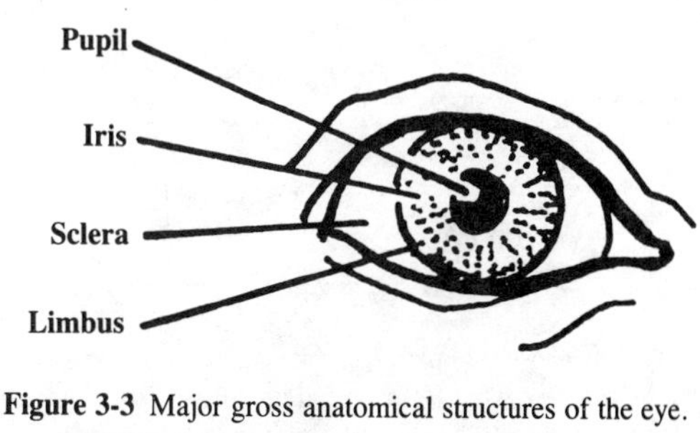

Figure 3-3 Major gross anatomical structures of the eye.

A clear understanding of the pathways along which retinal impulses travel is essential to clinical interpretation of visual field defects and eye light reflexes. Fibers from the lateral portion of the retina pass through the optic nerve without synapsing or decussing at the optic chiasm. Fibers from the medial retina cross at the optic chiasm without synapsing. They then travel posteriorly, with the lateral fibers ipsilateral and the medial fibers contralateral, as the optic tract and synapse in either the pretectal nucleus (for bilateral distribution to the Edinger-Westphal nuclei, ultimately resulting in reflex pupilloconstriction) or the lateral geniculate body (in the thalamus). From the lateral geniculate body, fibers travel through the optic radiation to the calcarine fissure of the occipital lobe (see Figure 3-4). This area is referred to as the striate or primary visual cortex. A strict laminated organization of fibers is maintained from the retina to the primary visual occipital cortex. In fact, even the firing pattern of neurons in the striate cortex of the occipital lobe after visual stimulation maintains the physical characteristics of the shape of the stimulus.

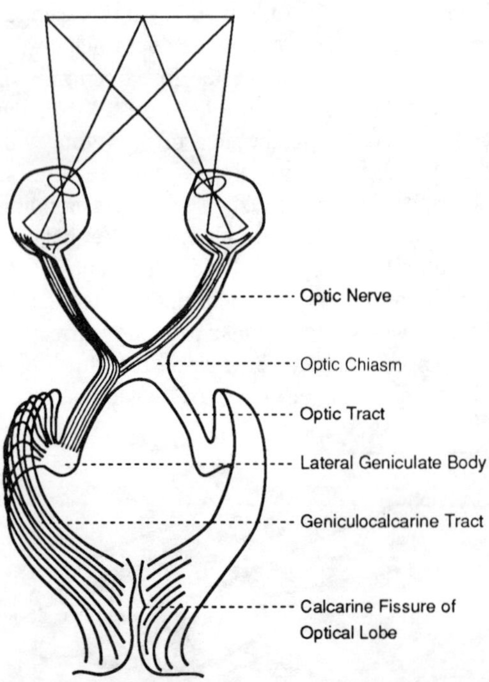

Figure 3-4 The visual path from the retina to the occipital lobe. *Source:* Adapted from *Technique of the Neurological Examination*, ed 3 (p 111) by W Demyer with permission of McGraw-Hill Book Company, © 1980.

The oculomotor (III), abducens (IV), and trochlear (IV) nerves are associated with extraocular muscular control. Corticobulbar (supranuclear) fibers descend to midbrain and pontine nuclei, which in turn activate the lower motor neurons innervating the extraocular muscles:

1. superior oblique (trochlear)
2. lateral rectus (abducens)
3. medial rectus (oculomotor)
4. superior rectus (oculomotor)
5. inferior rectus (oculomotor)
6. inferior oblique (oculomotor)

Stimulation of cranial nerve IV causes the eye to move down when it is internally deviated, stimulation of cranial nerve VI causes it to move laterally, and stimulation of cranial nerve III causes it to move in all the other directions.

Other ocular muscles associated with these cranial nerves are the levator palpebrae (oculomotor) and the superior tarsal muscle (receiving sympathetic autonomic innervation via the superior cervical sympathetic ganglia).

Cranial nerve III is also associated with pupil constriction through its involvement in the direct and consensual eye light reflexes. Impulses generated by the stimulation of photosensitive retinal sensors in a given eye travel back through the optic nerve. After passing through the optic chiasm, impulses travel along the optic tract (the segment of the pathway of the optic nerve fibers from the chiasm to the midbrain). Impulses pass back to the pretectal nucleus, in the midbrain, for equal distribution to the ipsilateral and contralateral Edinger-Westphal nuclei. There the impulses stimulate parasympathetic fibers that travel along cranial nerve III to the episcleral ganglion behind the eye and then to the pupilloconstrictor muscle (see Figure 3-5). Therefore, light perceived in any quadrant of the visual field of one eye will cause constriction of the pupil of the eye receiving the stimulus (direct reflex) and also constriction, to an equal extent, of the pupil of the other eye (consensual reflex). Cranial nerve II is the sensory arc of this reflex, and the parasympathetic fibers traveling along cranial nerve III comprise the motor arc.

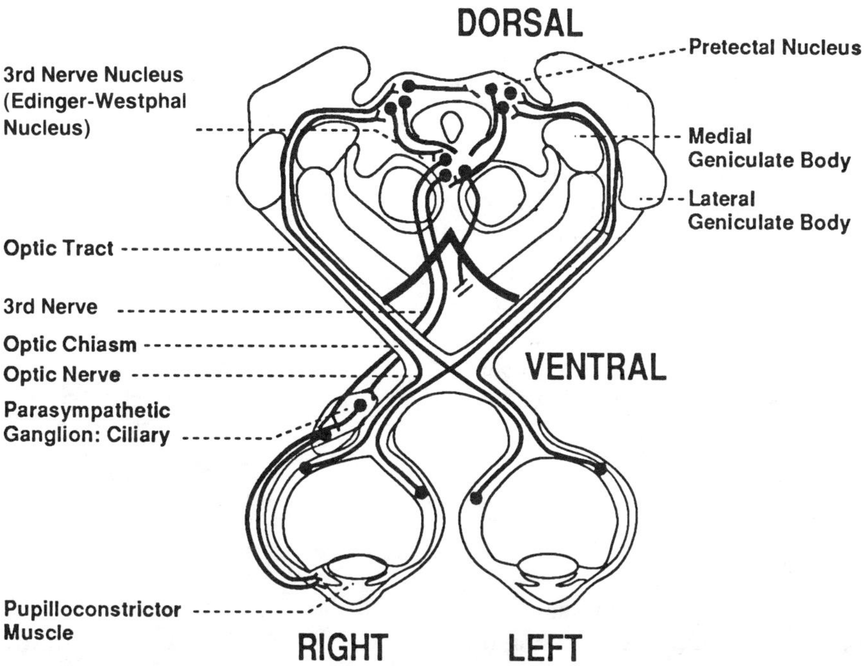

Figure 3-5 Parasympathetic innervation of the eyes. *Source:* Adapted from *Anatomy of the Nervous System* by E Crosby et al., Macmillan Publishing Company, 1962.

The sympathetic nervous system is also responsible for the regulation of pupil dilation. Sympathetic motor fibers exiting from the upper thoracic region of the spinal cord ascend the paravertebral sympathetic ganglion chain to the superior cervical ganglion. From there, some of them ascend along the internal carotid arteries and go on to innervate the pupillodilator muscle (causing pupillodilation). Some go to the superior tarsal muscle (see Figure 3-6). (The other fibers ascend along the external carotid arteries to innervate the sweat glands and control vasoconstriction for the face; this has important implications in the genesis of Horner's syndrome, discussed below.)

Disorders

Visual Field Deficits

Objects situated in the nasal (medial) half of the visual field are projected onto the temporal

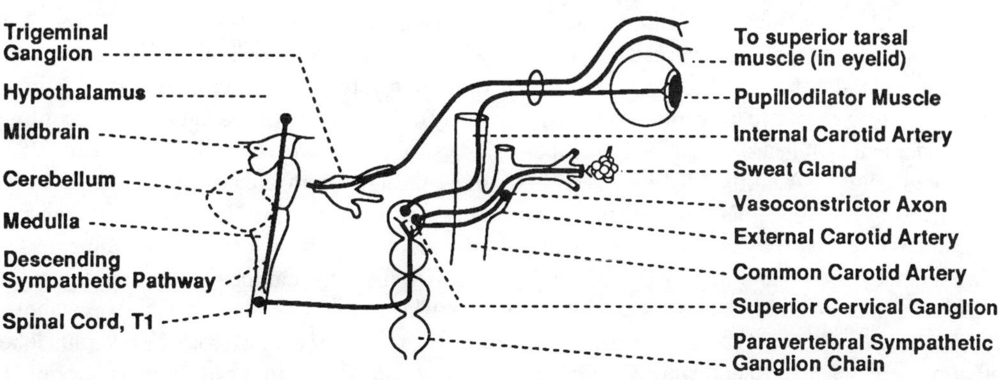

Figure 3-6 Sympathetic innervation of the eyes and face. *Source:* Adapted from *Technique of the Neurologic Examination*, ed 3 (p 103) by W Demyer with permission of McGraw-Hill Book Company, © 1980.

retinal surface, and objects in the temperal (lateral) half are projected onto the nasal retinal surface. Likewise, objects in the upper visual field are projected onto the surface of the lower retina, and vice versa. It is thus possible to relate a specific area of visual field deficit to pathology in a specific portion of the retina, and in turn to pathology in a specific portion of the optic nerve, chiasm, tract, etc. This is of obvious value in diagnosing problems of cranial nerve II function. A disturbance at a given point in the pathway can cause a characteristic visual defect. Specific terminology exists to exactly describe visual field defects (see Figure 3-7).

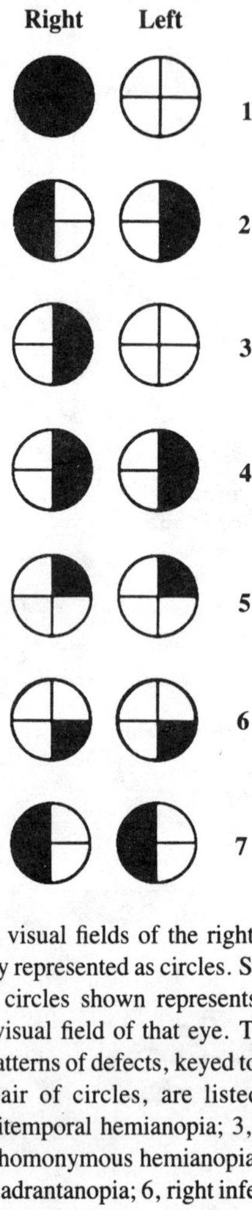

Figure 3-7 The visual fields of the right and left eyes are diagrammatically represented as circles. Shading of portions of the different circles shown represents defects in those portions of the visual field of that eye. The terms used for these different patterns of defects, keyed to the number to the right of each pair of circles, are listed below: 1, right amblyopia; 2, bitemporal hemianopia; 3, right nasal hemianopia; 4, right homonymous hemianopia; 5, right superior homonymous quadrantanopia; 6, right inferior homonymous quadrantanopia; 7, left homonymous hemianopia.

Deviations of Eye Alignment

Deviations of bilateral eye alignment, termed heterotropias ("hetero," different; "tropia," place), are named for the direction of the ocular deviation present when the patient's eyes are focused straight ahead in the distance. The modifiers ''left,'' ''right,'' ''alternating'' (when the deviating eye changes from left to right), or ''intermittent'' (not always present) are attached to the following terms (see Figure 3-8):

1. exotropia: outward/lateral
2. esotropia: inward/medial
3. hypertropia: up
4. hypotropia: down

Disease of the cranial nerves is sometimes responsible for deviations of eye alignment. Disorders involving cranial nerves III, IV, and VI or their central connections can cause heterotropia, cranial nerve IV disease can cause hypertropia, and cranial nerve VI disease can cause esotropia. In the case of eye movement, we must also consider bands of neurons, for example, the medial longitudinal fasciculus (MLF) whose primary function is to coordinate eye movements (also known as yoked movement) by interconnecting the nuclei of cranial nerves III, IV, and VI. Disease of these interconnecting pathways may produce a characteristic internuclear ophthalmoplegia. The most noteworthy example is the MLF. A lesion in this area (often caused by multiple sclerosis) causes paralysis of lateral gaze, so that whichever direction the patient is instructed to look toward, neither eye can deviate nasally. However, both eyes will converge when testing accommodation. (Convergence requires only function of cranial nerve III bilaterally). This is due to the lateral gaze requiring the use of two separate cranial nerves, III and VI, to move the left eye inward and to move the right eye outward, respectively. There are two separate supranuclear pathways for eye movement. The first (from the frontal lobe) is thought to control mostly saccadic (rapid or darting) eye movements, while the second (from the occipital lobe) controls mostly smooth or following eye movements. In fact, nystagmus (involuntary eye

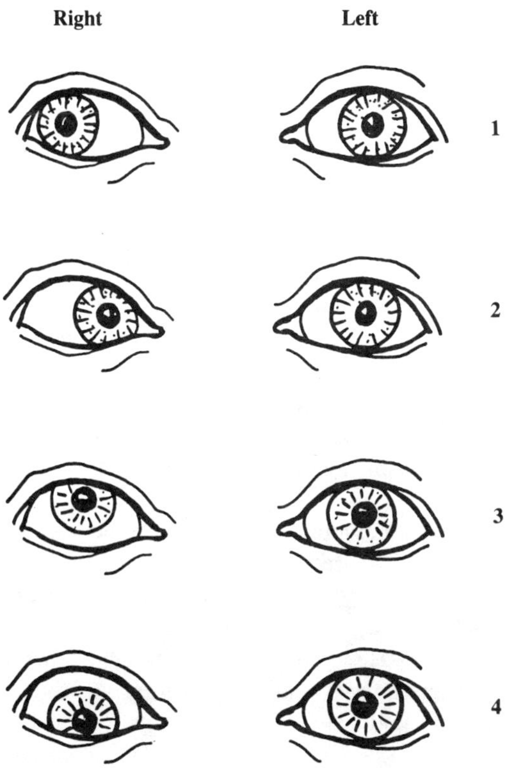

Figure 3-8 1, Right exotropia; 2, right esotropia; 3, right hypertropia; 4, right hypotropia.

oscillations) is the result of uncoordinated attempts at controlling eye movement, with the fast component representing saccadic movement and the slow portion representing following movement. At the nuclear or peripheral level, disease results in characteristic ophthalmoplegias. With disease of cranial nerve IV, the patient is unable to laterally deviate the eye on the side ipsilateral to the lesion. Cranial nerve VI disease causes difficulty for the patient when looking down and in. Disease of cranial nerve III is usually more obvious due to the accompanying parasympathetic manifestations (eyelid ptosis and corectasia).

Disorders of Pupil Function

Disease of cranial nerve II will diminish pupilloconstriction with bilateral symmetry due to decreased sensory perception, associated with visual loss. However, exposure of the uninvolved side should cause brisk bilateral pupilloconstriction. Pathological involvement of the motor arc of the eye light reflex (cranial nerve III) results in a decreased ability to carry out the act of pupilloconstriction in the ipsilateral eye. Loss of diencephalon or midbrain function results in unopposed sympathetic (pupillodilator) dominance; light as a stimulus causes no pupilloconstriction, and the pupil is fixed and dilated.

Adie's pupil (tonic pupil) is a pupil that reacts to light very slowly, remains constrieted longer, and then dilates slowly. It is considered a benign condition and occurs most often in young women. The Argyll Robertson pupil reacts only to accommodation; it has neither a direct nor an indirect reaction to light. It was once considered pathognomonic of tabes dorsalis (neurosyphilis), but it has now been found to occur as a diabetic complication.

Disorders due to Sympathetic Pathology

Sympathetic hypofunction, often due to lesions of the neck proximal to the carotid artery bifurcation that compress ascending sympathetic fibers, is termed Horner's syndrome. This condition causes mild or moderate ptosis due to paralysis of the superior tarsal muscle, pupilloconstriction (cormiosis) due to unopposed cranial nerve III pupilloconstriction, facial anhydrosis (i.e., lack of sweating) due to denervation of the sweat glands in the ipsilateral side of the head, and ipsilateral facial vasodilation, causing a red or flushed look and a palpable increase in skin temperature.

Lesions along the sympathetic pathway distal to the bifurcation of the common carotid arteries will cause only pupilloconstriction and ptosis, if occurring along the internal carotid path, or only vasodilation and anhydrosis, if occurring along the external carotid pathway. Enophthalmos, an inward sinking of the eyeball in the eye socket, is theoretically a part of sympathetic paralysis due to disruption of sympathetic contractile impulses to the small muscle of Müller. It has been suggested that it is the enophthalmos which causes the characteristic "pseudoptosis" of Horner's syndrome and not the superior tarsal paralysis ptosis.

Examination

You must first ask yourself three questions in order to fully evaluate the visual system: (1) What do the eyes look like from the outside? (2) How do the eyes function (what can the patient see)? (3) What do the eyes look like on the inside?

Optimal test performance will be obtained if all procedures requiring introduction of a light source (ophthalmoscope, penlight, etc.) are performed after testing for central and peripheral vision. This principle is honored in the organization of the discussion that follows.

Observation—What Do the Eyes Look Like from the Outside?

Inspection for eyelid ptosis, pupil asymmetries, and ocular deviations is a first, painless step in performing a visual system examination. Remember, something as slight as eyelid ptosis might indicate a lesion involving hypothalamic, brainstem, spinal cord, peripheral cranial nerve III, peripheral sympathetic, and neuromyal pathways, as well as muscular and local causes.

It is simple and useful to observe the patient's ocular alignment to detect pathological deviation of normal gaze due to disease of the visual system. Additionally, head tilting due to ocular deviation or paralysis can cause significant cervical spine somatic dysfunction. The patient is instructed to keep the eyes focused straight ahead in the distance. Note whether the upper eyelid covers the superior aspect of the iris, without covering any part of the pupil. The lower eyelid should form a tangent with the limbus or outer edge of the iris. This is referred to as the limbus-to-lid distance. The same amount of scleral tissue should be visible both medial and lateral to the iris (from limbus to canthi), and none should be visible above or below it (see Figure 3-9). With complete abduction or adduction of the eye during testing of ocular motility, no scleral white should be seen on the side of the iris in the same direction as the patient's gaze.

A number of conditions, some normal and some abnormal, can cause erroneous diagnosis of eye deviation, such as canthus dystopia, epicanthal folds, hypertelorism, hypotelorism, enophthalmos, micro- and macrophthalmos, and micro- and macrocornea (see Figure 3-10). It is best to follow up an abnormal observation of limbus-to-lid and limbus-to-canthi distances with a more objective testing procedure. A quick and simple method is to compare the relative positions of the reflection of light off of the cornea during the ophthalmoscopic examination (discussed below).

While the sympathetic system does not readily lend itself to direct in-office testing, a satisfactory way to assess sympathetic function in the head and face is to elicit the ciliospinal reflex. This test is accomplished by pinching the skin on the patient's neck and observing for brisk bilateral pupillodilation.

Assessment of the Visual Fields—What Can These Eyes See?

Central Vision. Central vision is classically tested in the office of a primary contact practitioner by way of the Snellen eye chart. A rating system has been established whereby the first number represents the 20-foot distance between the patient and the chart, and the second number represents the distance in feet at which a "normal" individual can correctly read a given line of the chart. If an individual can read the line of the chart determined to be readable by the normal eye at 20 feet, that person is said to have

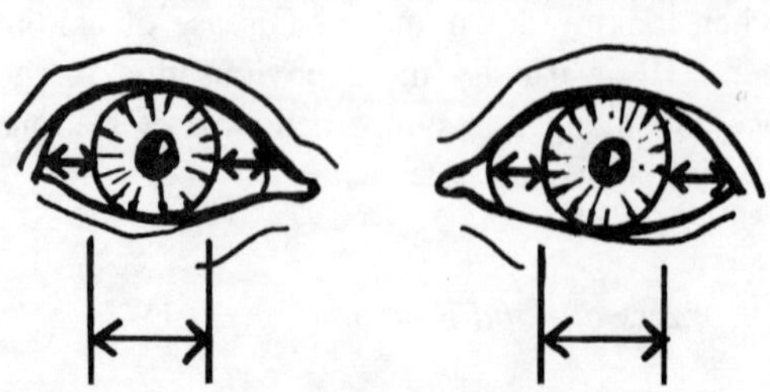

Figure 3-9 Normal limbus-to-lid and limbus-to-canthi distances.

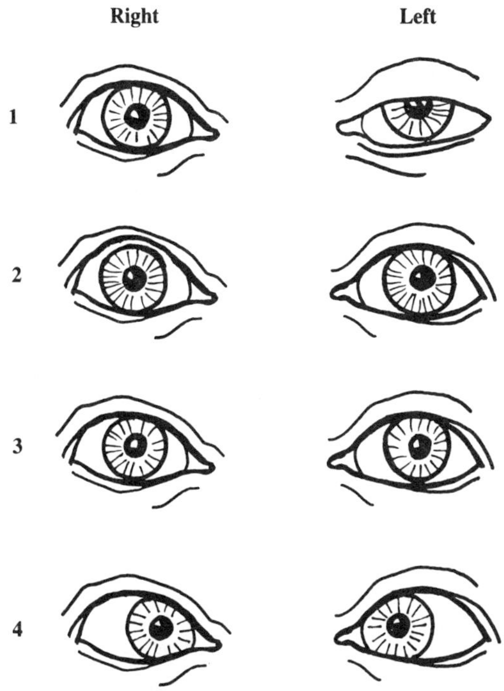

Figure 3-10 Conditions causing a false appearance of ocular deviation. 1, left eyelid ptosis; 2, right exophthalmos; 3, normal; 4, canthus dystopia.

20/20 vision. The wider the gap between the two numbers, the poorer the person's vision. Though this chart was meant to be used at a distance of 20 feet, a 25% reproduction of the chart used at a distance of 5 feet, or newsprint held at arm's length, may suffice for practical clinical purposes. Questions regarding central visual function may warrant patient referral to an optometrist or ophthalmologist.

The patient is given an object suitable for occluding vision in one eye. Corrected vision is tested using one of the above-discussed methods, and accuracy is noted. Each eye is separately tested. Legal blindness is a legal issue, but medical blindness is failure to perceive light stimulus.

Peripheral Vision. Clinical testing for peripheral vision is accomplished via a technique known as confrontation. This is not to suggest that you should shout "what do you know about your peripheral vision" at your patient, but to describe the physical position that you take with your patient. Strict directions are usually given regarding various aspects of this test, such as the exact number of centimeters to establish between the examiner and the patient and exact titration to the examiner's vision, but they are impractical. A modified version of this test may be performed by occluding one of your patient's visual fields and imagining the other to be broken into four equal quadrants—medial and lateral, superior and inferior. The patient is instructed to fix the gaze of the unoccluded eye on your nose and not to deviate from this point. The eyes of the patient must always be in plain view. The urge to deviate the eyes as one waits to see an object in the periphery is very great, but peeking voids the test. The patient is instructed to point to any object you bring into his or her visual field. Preferably, the object will have a red tip, such as a pencil with an eraser, but for general practical purposes your fingertips may be used. The object is brought from some point outside of vision into the center of one of the four quadrants of vision. Unless you can drag your knuckles when you walk upright, it will be necessary to come from behind the lateral visual field of the patient. Test at least the center of each of the four quadrants for each eye.

As the patient points to an object in the visual field, note the accuracy of pointing and the absence of eye deviation from the midline. As a supportive measure and reliability check, ask the patient to say "moving" immediately if he or she sees that the object is moving or spinning; further refinement may be made by placing two or three fingers in the visual field being tested and asking the patient to tell how many fingers he or she sees. Note the patient's accuracy, as well as any temporal delay between the stimulus and the response, as you bring stationary objects into the visual quadrants and arbitrarily move some of them. Be sure that you cast no shadows that could alert the patient as to your movements.

To test for certain cerebral lesions that suppress vision but do not alter classic visual pathways, use tests for visual inattention or extinction. A patient suffering from inattention will not attend to a visual stimulus on one body side; it will be detected only if it is accompanied by a simultaneous stimulus on the opposite side.

Parieto-occipital lobe lesions may yield contralateral inattention.

Assessment of Extraocular Movement

In cases where there is no visual complaint or obvious ocular deviation, or in cases where movement of the neck is painful or otherwise ill-advised, one will use the customary method of examining extraocular movement. This is done by asking the patient to keep his or her eyes on your finger without moving the head. Your finger should be several feet in front of the patient's eyes; if you are too close, nystagmus may result from supra- and internuclear interaction. Move your finger through the six cardinal fields of gaze. Be sure to hold up the eyelids of the patient when testing downward gaze, or you will not be able to visualize the eye. Also, remember to cause enough eye movement as to approximate eye limbus to the canthus, both medially and laterally. Bring your finger slowly to within 6 inches of the patient's nose and note accommodation. Accommodation is a reflex that occurs when one voluntarily focuses the eyes on an object moving nearer. It consists of three components: convergence, pupilloconstriction, and lens thickening. Convergence of the eyes is accomplished by the medial recti muscles and is therefore also dependent on cranial nerve III function. Pupilloconstriction is also accomplished through parasympathetic fibers traveling within cranial nerve III. An unnoticeable change in the thickness of the lens is accomplished by the action of the ciliary muscles, also innervated by cranial nerve III, and allows the patient to see in focus. Failure to accomplish any of these three things may be due to a cranial nerve III or higher center disorder. An excellent supplemental or selective replacement method of performing this type of testing is described below under "Ophthalmoscopy and Related Procedures."

There are two main objectives when assessing extraocular movement. First, you should look for full, concomitant movement of both eyes; second, the movement should not include nystagmus. Even though ocular deviation may be observed, it is essential that the patient report any diplopia. Only millimeters of ocular duration can cause diplopia, whereas a far greater defect would be required for doctor objectification. If an ocular deviation is detected, it is essential to note whether or not ocular movement is the same in both eyes. If it is, then the likelihood of extraocular muscle paralysis is small. If eye movement through the fields of gaze is clearly not concomitant, then extraocular muscle paralysis should be suspected. In most cases, concomitant eye movement along with ocular deviation is caused by a disturbance of image formation due, for instance, to a cloudy cornea, refractory error, cataract, or macular lesion. Nonconcomitant eye movement results in diplopia due to the brain's inability to resolve the images.

Nystagmus is involuntary to-and-fro eye oscillation. It is thought to be caused by several factors, most notably conflicting proprioceptive input from cranial nerve VIII and cervical and cerebellar sources. This input is distributed to many brainstem nuclei involved in the coordination of reflex and volitional eye movement. It is important to remember that a certain amount of nystagmus is physiological (nonpathological) in certain patients. Physiological or "end-point" nystagmus is common. Pathological nystagmus usually begins well before the patient is at the visual end-point. Nystagmus may also be congenital and benign. The typical clinical picture accompanying nystagmus of recent onset includes nausea, vertigo, vomiting, and ataxia.

Nystagmus may be described as being jerky or pendular. The side toward which the quick component of the nystagmus travels is the side that bears the name. For example, a right jerky nystagmus tells you that the eye quickly jerks to the right, followed by a slower return to the left. Nystagmus usually occurs in both eyes but may occur in only one, especially in intranuclear ophthalmoplegias. Eye movement may be on a horizontal plane or a vertical plane. It may even occur in a rotary fashion.

Ophthalmoscopy and Related Procedures—What Do the Eyes Look Like on the Inside?

Corneal Light Reflex. Prior to performing the classic ophthalmoscopic examination, several other procedures using the ophthalmoscope may be first attempted. To verify any suspicion of ocular malalignment, the corneal light reflection test may be done. This test does not examine a reflex but simply observes the relative position of the two points of reflection of the ophthalmoscope's light, one in each eye, on the patient's corneas. With the patient's eyes focused straight ahead, the reflection from a light source shined directly into both eyes should be located slightly medial to the corneal center (see Figure 3-11). The patient's ability to look in the distance may be significantly diminished by the confines of a typical office exam suite, so it is important to observe the relative symmetry of position of the light reflections, as opposed to their absolute position on a map of the patient's cornea.

A modification of this test may supplement or even replace the classic examination for extraocular movement, in selected cases. It is recommended only if full, pain-free, non-symptom-provoking cervical ranges of motion are obtainable, and nystagmus does not become evident. The test is accomplished by placing a weakly lit ophthalmoscope in front of the patient and instructing him or her to look directly into the ophthalmoscope light. At this time, gently direct active movement of the patient's head, sufficient to test the cardinal fields of gaze and, therefore, the extraocular muscles under finer and more objective scrutiny (see Figure 3-12). Do not forget to test accommodation without using the ophthalmoscope light.

Eye Light Reflexes. Light introduced into the pupil of one eye will cause reflex constriction of both pupils, equally, assuming intact neural pathways, as discussed above. The patient is instructed to look forward into the distance directly. Carefully observe the size of one pupil—shall we say the right one. Introduce through that pupil at a distance of 2 to 6 inches a beam of light from the ophthalmoscope. Note the degree and speed of right-sided pupilloconstriction. Remove the light source without taking your eye off of the right pupil, and observe for right-sided pupillodilation. Now, observing the left pupil, shine the light into the right pupil again. It is difficult to accurately shine the light in the patient's right pupil, while not taking your eye off of the patient's left pupil, but avoid looking away. Observe for left pupilloconstriction, of equal degree and speed to the previous right pupilloconstriction. Remove the light source, and observe for pupillodilation. You can and should repeat the test three to four times to recheck any questionable or presumed abnormalities. Repeat the above procedure for the

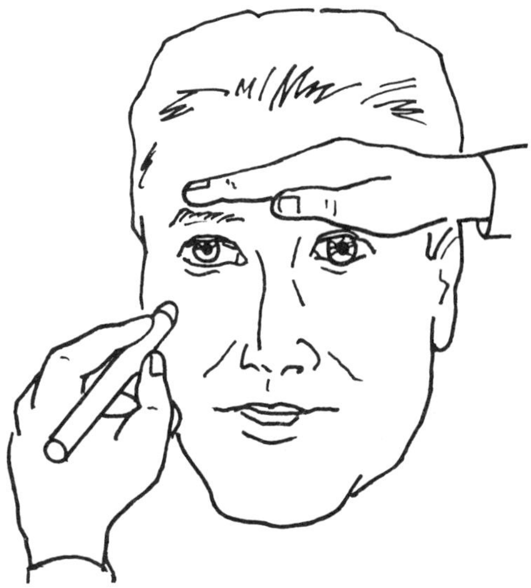

Figure 3-11 Testing the pupillary light reflex in a brightly lit room.

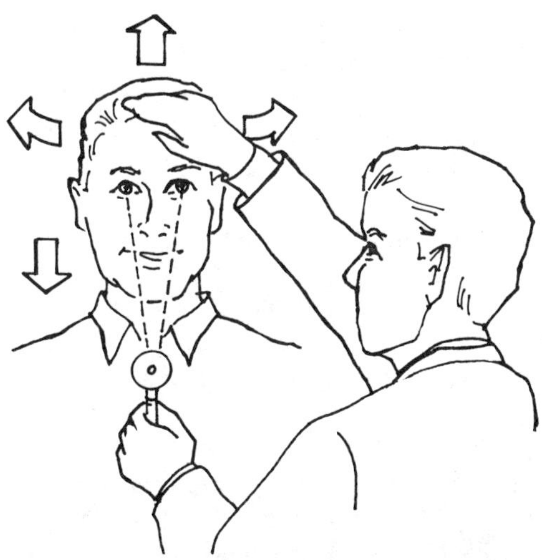

Figure 3-12 Alternative method of assessing extraocular muscle function.

other (left) eye. If a cruder source of light, such as a penlight, must be used, it is a good idea to use your hand or another object to block the possible spillover of light into both pupils simultaneously during testing.

The swinging flashlight test is a simple and sensitive method to test equal pupil constriction. The apparent pupillodilation with light introduction is known as the Marcus-Gunn phenomenon. The light source is introduced into one pupil and then the other pupil in continuous succession. The patient's pupil does not dilate when light is introduced but constricts slightly less than when the light was introduced to the other pupil. This phenomenon indicates a retinal or cranial nerve II lesion with the sensory arc decreasing the amount of pupillary (motor) response. Optic neuritis, often an early sign of multiple sclerosis, is the most frequent cause.

The so-called red reflex is not a reflex. This term refers to a yellow-orange-red light reflection seen through the ophthalmoscope when it is held at distances greater than about 6 inches from a patient's pupil. Any partial or complete blocking of this reflection indicates disease of the translucent structures of the eye, such as the cornea, lens, or vitreous, or of the retinal pigment.

Funduscopy. The ophthalmoscope is held in your right hand and placed firmly against your right eyebrow when examining the patient's right eye (see Figure 3-13). You may wear your glasses or contact lenses, but the patient's glasses or tinted contact lenses should be removed. Your head and right upper extremity move as one with the ophthalmoscope as you peer through the tiny aperture. The diopters on the instrument should be set to zero and the small white light beam selected. The patient is instructed to look straight ahead in the distance.

Visualizing the patient's pupil, move to within about 3 to 6 inches of the patient, at an angle so as not to obstruct the visual field of the patient's other eye. In the undilated pupil good funduscopic examination is challenged by variable pupil size; getting close as though peering through a keyhole helps. You may want to hold your breath while performing funduscopy to aid in steadiness and avoid offending the patient.

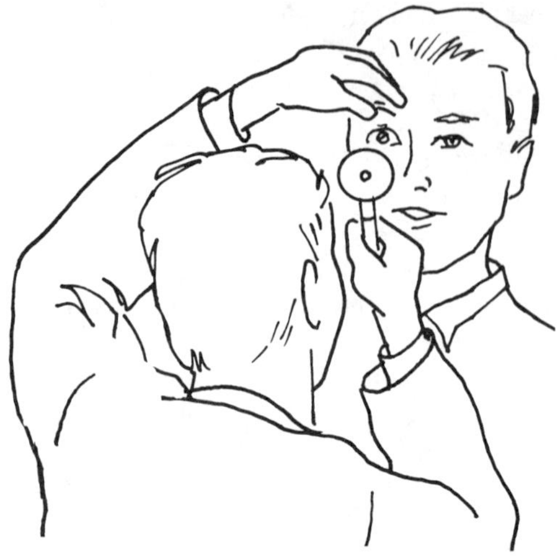

Figure 3-13 Conducting the ophthalmoscopic examination.

When seen, a blood vessel should be brought into focus using appropriate diopter adjustments. Negative (red) numbers on the ophthalmoscope focus further back and are used for myopic (nearsighted) patients. The number of diopters necessary to focus on that blood vessel represents the degree of nearsightedness. Hyperopic (farsighted) patients may require focusing in the range of the positive (black) numbers.

Once in focus, slowly follow the vessel in the direction that causes it to enlarge. Follow it back to the optic disc. Four basic areas of the fundus should be examined for pathological changes: the optic disc, the vessels, the macula, and the general background (see Figure 3-14).

Disc margin clarity, color, and cup-to-disc ratio should be observed. The margins between the optic disc and the fundus should be sharp temporally and less so medially. The size of the physiological cup in the center of the disc ranges from congenitally absent to about half the size of the disc itself. If it is greater than about half the size of the disc, increased intraocular pressure, such as is due to glaucoma, is suspected.

In papilledema (swelling of the optic disc), the disc appears blurred with jagged edges. This is due to nerve fiber edema and backup of venous blood. It usually results from increased intracranial pressure or a compressed retinal or ophthalmic vein. Findings include

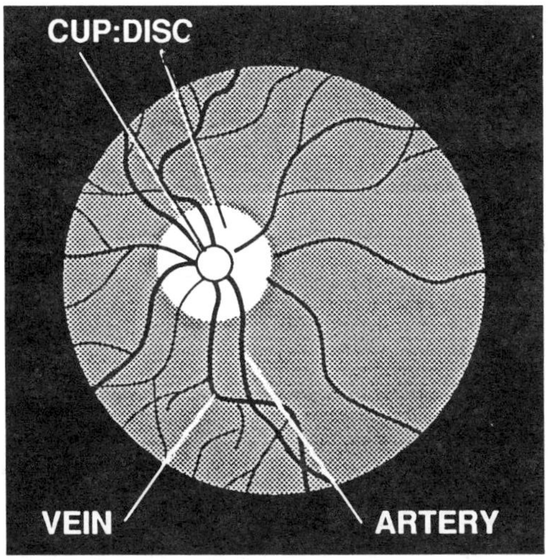

Figure 3-14 The optic fundus.

- blurred nerve fibers and cup
- tortuous, engorged veins and loss of venous pulsations at disc margins
- obliteration of physiological cup
- disc elevation and edema

A pseudopapilledema has been described in up to 5% of the normal population (usually in blond whites), especially with predisposing hyperopia. It is thought to be hereditary and is benign.

The apparent color of the disc is actually produced by the capillary vessels supplying the nerve fibers, as retinal fibers are translucent. If primary optic atrophy occurs (not secondary to another process), the optic disc has a dead white color, and there is associated visual loss. Optic atrophy secondary to another pathological process such as glaucoma reveals a gray, ragged disc, the result of long-standing retinal disease.

Inflammation of the optic nerve (optic neuritis) or disc (papillitis) has similar ophthalmoscopic characteristics to papilledema; however, a distinct visual complaint and sometimes pain are experienced by the patient, sharply contrasting papilledema. It is usually benign and self-resolving, without apparent cause. It may predate the onset of signs of multiple sclerosis. If the inflammation is behind the portion of the optic disc that can be visualized during funduscopy, it may be referred to as acute retrobulbar neuritis. In this case the fundus looks normal but the patient has visual loss.

Observe normal course, caliber, and crossings of vessels at about half the distance of a disc diameter outside of the disc. Vessels should gradually taper as they travel distal to the optic disc. Arteries should be between one half and two thirds the size of their accompanying veins. Venous engorgement distal to a point of arterial crossing is abnormal and a possible sign of arteriosclerosis. Another sign of arteriosclerosis is a light reflection off of the artery which is larger than the middle one third of the artery, or that is unusually shiny (silver-wiring).

The general background around the fundus is observed, and the macula is checked by asking the patient to look directly into the light, thereby aligning the macula for you. Any increase, decrease, or clumping of pigment distribution should be noted. A collection of pigment at the disc margin, known as a pigment crescent, is very common. Remember that pigment levels vary from none, in the albino, to high levels, in black patients. What is normal for a particular patient should be gathered from bilateral observation and clinical experience. Local changes in pigment distribution are almost always abnormal. Drusen are collections of degenerative deposits that often appear in the fundus of elderly people. They are not considered to have any clinical significance.

CRANIAL NERVE V

Anatomy and Function

Cranial nerve V is the great sensory nerve of the face, but it also serves the muscles of mastication with motor fibers. There are three peripheral sensory divisions whose cells have their nuclei in the Gasserian (semilunar) ganglion: the ophthalmic, maxillary, and mandibular divisions (see Figure 3-15). An important clinical note is that this cranial nerve's sensory distribution spares the cutaneous area over the angle of the jaw, which is innervated by the great auricular nerve of the cervical plexus (C-2, 3 dermatome). A knowledge of this anat-

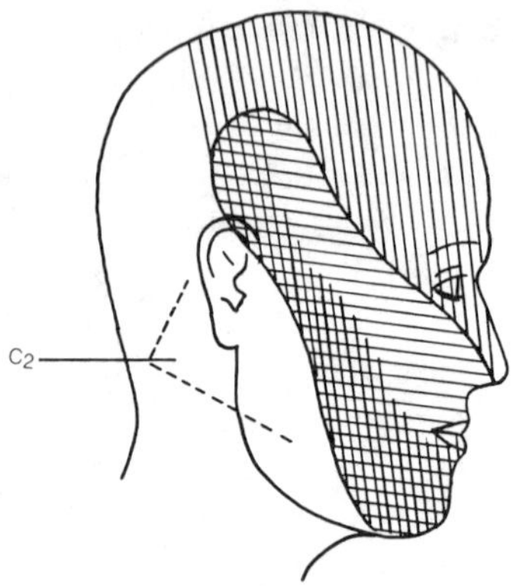

Figure 3-15 Distribution of cutaneous innervation of cranial nerve V.

omy allows the clinician to appreciate that a peripheral lesion of cranial nerve V causing complete loss of facial sensation will usually follow a relatively strict anatomical pattern, that is, it will spare the cutaneous area over the angle of the jaw. It is equally important to note that poorly localized sensations, including diffuse pain, will usually show no such anatomical distribution, due in part to cervical afferent input into the spinal (pain and temperature) nucleus of cranial nerve V. The input from cervical afferents to facial nerve nuclei provides clear support for cervically referred facial pain.

Another note of clinical interest is that the mandibular branch of cranial nerve V has a recurrent or meningeal branch that innervates the dura of the middle and anterior cranial fossae. This pathway may also account for cervical influence on head pain. The relationship is manifest clinically as headache and nuchal rigidity in meningitis, and possibly with traction on the dura associated with upper cervical subluxations. The mandibular division also supplies fibers to the temporomandibular joint.

The motor portion of the nerve supplies the muscles of mastication, including the temporalis, masseter, and medial pterygoid, all of which function to close the jaw. Cranial nerve V also innervates the lateral pterygoids, which either open the jaw (when used bilaterally) or cause lateral movements (when used unilaterally) (see Figure 3-16). The primary action of the right lateral pterygoid muscle is to move the jaw (tip) to the left side. The primary action of the left lateral pterygoid is jaw deviation to the right. When functioning together, they tend to aid in jaw opening.

Disorders

As you might suspect, upper or lower motor neuron disease can cause jaw paralysis. Each lateral pterygoid muscle receives equal supply from upper motor centers of the right and left hemispheres. For this reason, bilateral corticobulbar lesions (often from hypoxic insult) are usually required to permanently paralyze volitional jaw movement. An acute unilateral corticobulbar lesion or a lower motor neuron lesion involving cranial nerve V may also account for jaw paralysis, and the presentation may be confusing for the unprepared practitioner.

Peripheral nerve or brainstem disease is usually responsible for sensory impairment. This impairment is often accompanied by atrophy of the temporalis and masseter muscles resulting in a ''hollowing out'' of the temples and zygomatic

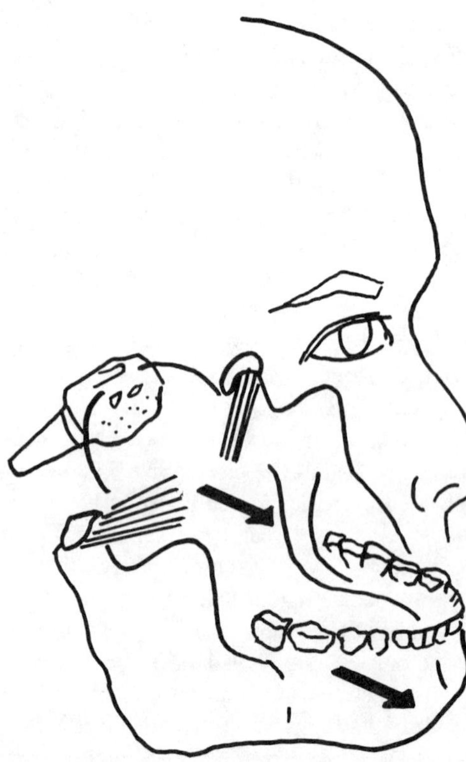

Figure 3-16 Action of the lateral pterygoid muscles.

arches. If the ophthalmic division is involved, there may be corneal inflammation and ulceration, which is termed neuroparalytic keratitis. Referred pain in the trigeminal distribution also frequently occurs. Cervical somatic dysfunction, oral and dental problems (including temporomandibular joint syndrome), glaucoma, or sinus disorders may be uncovered in the investigation of referred facial pain. Central causes of facial paresthesias are not uncommon and should always be considered.

Trigeminal neuralgia (also known as tic douloureux and Fothergill's neuralgia) is a common disorder of cranial nerve V. It is an idiopathic syndrome of recurrent, usually sharp, painful facial sensations in the clear distribution of the ophthalmic, maxillary, or mandibular divisions of cranial nerve V. It commonly follows herpetic facial infections in the elderly.

Examination

Motor Examination

The motor examination of cranial nerve V is just as simple as testing the muscles that move the jaw. Observation for normal temporalis and masseter muscle volume, along with no jaw deviation on forced opening, followed by opposition of jaw closure and lateral jaw movements, provides for a complete exam. Palpation of the masseter and temporalis muscles while the patient clenches his or her teeth is an acceptable substitute for opposing jaw movements, especially in cases where temporomandibular joint disease makes jaw injury an unacceptable risk of opposition testing. Lower motor neuron lesions of cranial nerve V may occur anywhere from the nerve cell body in the pontine nucleus to the peripheral cranial nerve. It usually results in paralysis and denervation atrophy of the mastication muscles.

Sensory Examination

The sensory examination of cranial nerve V is normally performed simultaneously with the somatic sensory examination and does not differ in examination technique except for location. Light touch may be tested bilaterally with the fingertips. One must remember to test all three sensory divisions bilaterally. Pinprick sensibility, alternating pin with blunt for continued reliability checks, should be tested as well.

Reflex Examination

The corneal reflex may be elicited by touching a clean wisp of cotton to the cornea, being careful to move the cotton in from outside the patient's visual field. Additional care must be exercised so as not to touch the eyelashes, eyelids, or conjunctivae. Cranial nerve V carries the sensory arc of the corneal reflex, synapsing directly on cranial nerve VII's motor nuclei, ultimately causing eye blinking. This is an important reflex to test when facial paresthesias are complained of, especially with a questionable or abnormal sensory examination. Absence of this reflex is strong evidence of pathology involving cranial nerve V or its central connections. This reflex may be absent in early cases of multiple sclerosis.

CRANIAL NERVE VII

Anatomy and Function

Cranial nerve VII supplies motor innervation to all of the muscles of facial expression, as well as taste sensibility to the anterior two thirds of the tongue. It is important to note that descending upper motor neurons (corticobulbar tract) controlling volitional movement of forehead musculature are equally distributed from each cerebral hemisphere. All the rules of bilateral innervation apply. Since forehead movement is not finely controlled but usually moves with bilateral symmetry, it is normally spared in unilateral lesions involving corticobulbar pathways. The lower face requires unilateral movements; it therefore receives a greater percentage of contralateral innervation, and contralateral lesions may have long-term effects. One interesting clinical note is that often it is possible for a central lesion to cause an initial facial paralysis, followed in the chronic phase by exaggeration of involuntary emotional movements of the face with paralysis of volitional movements. This underlines the different pathways involved in voluntary and emotional (involuntary) movement.

Corticobulbar fibers synapse in cranial nerve VII motor nuclei in the brainstem, where the peripheral cranial nerve VII arises. Sympathetic and parasympathetic fibers are also carried by the peripheral nerve. In the substance of the parotid gland the nerve divides into the temporofacial (temporal, zygomatic, and upper buccal branches; see Figure 3-17) and cervicofacial (lower buccal, mandibular, and cervical branches) divisions. Cranial nerve VII also innervates the stapedius, a small muscle in the ear that functions to damp movement of the tympanic membrane. The so-called nervus intermedius supplies sensory and parasympathetic fibers to cranial nerve VII and is considered by some to be a separate nerve. Distally, the chorda tympani nerve carries taste and general visceral afferents as well as preganglionic parasympathetics that synapse in the geniculate ganglion. In addition to supplying taste sensation to the anterior two thirds of the tongue, the chorda tympani supplies parasympathetic secretory and vasodilator impulses to the submaxillary and sublingual salivary glands and to the lacrimal glands, as well as to the mucous membranes of the mouth and tongue. Stimulation of these parasympathetic fibers causes increased secretion of thin and watery saliva. Sympathetic stimulation, by contrast, causes a scant supply of thick, turbid saliva.

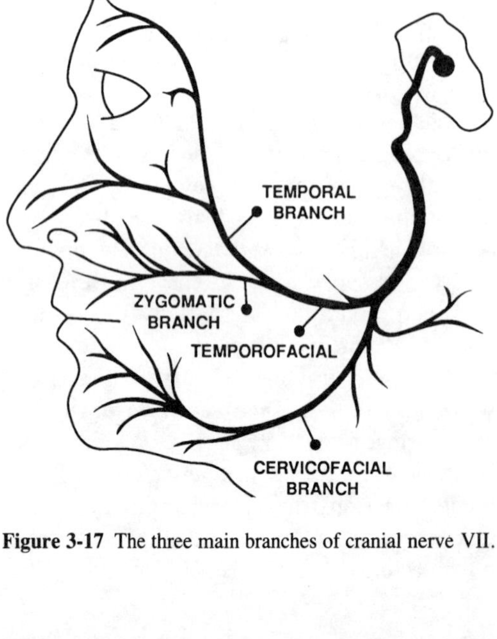

Figure 3-17 The three main branches of cranial nerve VII.

Disorders

Facial muscle paresis or paralysis can be of peripheral (nuclear) or central (supranuclear) varieties. Peripheral facial paralysis, or prosopoplegia, is a common condition, often seen by the doctor of chiropractic. The peripheral lesion may be located in the pontine nuclei, peripheral to the pons, in the facial canal, in the geniculate ganglion, peripheral to the geniculate ganglion but central to the stapedius branch, peripheral to the stapedius branch but central to the chorda tympani nerve, peripheral to the chorda tympani, or in the body of the parotid gland. In the type of facial paralysis known as Bell's palsy, the lesion is peripheral to the geniculate ganglion. All of these varieties of peripheral cranial nerve VII paralysis have one common factor: a flaccid (i.e., lower motor neuron) paralysis involving all ipsilateral facial muscles distal to the lesion site. By contrast, in the central type of facial paralysis there is a gradient of facial weakness due to bilateral innervation; the forehead is spared, the eyes are only partially involved, and the mouth and neck are fully involved. Central and peripheral facial paralysis may thus be readily differentiated.

Examination

Motor Examination

Observe for facial asymmetry manifest during active movement. The patient is instructed to look up and must usually be coached and coaxed into giving full effort on this, and on each of the subsequent commands. See that there is symmetry in the forehead wrinkles. Remember, eyelid elevation is primarily controlled by cranial nerve III. Therefore, when the patient looks up, the eyelids will elevate, even if there is a cranial nerve VII lesion. Note the nasolabial folds when telling the patient to "give a big smile"; coaxing for more effort will usually cause the patient to laugh, and laughter is an excellent condition under which to test facial symmetry. Other tests, such as asking the patient to hold air in his or her cheeks and not let you squeeze it out, may be performed. Note any drooling, dysarthria, or dysphagia.

Sensory Examination

While taste is carried by cranial nerves VII, IX, and even X, the anterior two thirds of the tongue is generally accepted as the territory of cranial nerve VII. Central lesions affecting cranial nerve VII pathways rarely, if ever, cause complete taste loss (ageusia) but are more likely to cause spontaneous or perverted tastes. These findings may be present with lesions of the geniculate ganglion or of the insular portion of the frontal lobe. Peripheral lesions (proximal to the stylomastoid foramen) will cause taste loss, but only ipsilaterally, and this will not usually be immediately noticeable to the patient. It is therefore the case that complete loss of taste is a rare complaint, and one should immediately consider olfactory function and non-neurological causes such as viral infection, aging, and toxic/metabolic disease. It is important to remember that a peripheral lesion must be proximal to the stylomastoid foramen to affect taste. Therefore, a complete hemifacial paralysis without loss of taste on the ipsilateral anterior two thirds of the tongue confirms a diagnosis of Bell's palsy, which responds excellently to chiropractic therapy.

The sense of taste can be examined by placing a dissolved solution of sugar, salt, lemon, etc., on one half of the tongue and asking the patient to identify the taste without closing the mouth or smacking the tongue. The mouth should be rinsed with water prior to testing the other side. The nostrils may need to be occluded prior to testing substances that might be easily identifiable by smell.

CRANIAL NERVE VIII

Anatomy and Function

Cochlear Division

The receptors are the auditory cells within the organ of Corti, inside the cochlea. Impulses travel to the bipolar cells of the cochlear ganglion. The emerging fibers travel as the cochlear nerve through the internal auditory meatus to the cochlear nuclei. From there fibers pass to the ipsilateral lateral lemniscus. They then ascend to the inferior colliculus and the medial geniculate body. Finally, as auditory radiations they terminate on the cortex of the transverse temporal convolution (Heschl's gyrus) (see Figure 3-18). The cochlear division of cranial nerve VIII's sole function is to provide hearing.

Vestibular Division

The receptors are situated in the semicircular canals, the utricle and the saccule of the middle ear. Impulses are carried to the vestibular ganglia, from which fibers pass as the vestibular nerve. This nerve travels through the internal auditory meatus to enter the brainstem. There the fibers either terminate on the four vestibular nuclei or pass through the inferior cerebellar peduncle as a part of the vestibulocerebellum. These pathways are connected to cranial nerves III, IV, and VI and are therefore important in regulating movements of the eyes, head, and neck in response to stimulation of the semicircular canals. A "short circuit" or abnormal or conflicting impulses from any of these areas may result in nystagmus. The canals are excited by movement in space as well as by direction and velocity of movement, especially rotatory motions. Even the slightest change in the position of the head is picked up by the vestibular system, and a motor correction is activated automatically (via the kinetic labyrinthian reflex).

Disorders

The patient who presents with a diminution or loss of hearing (hypoacusis), with or without

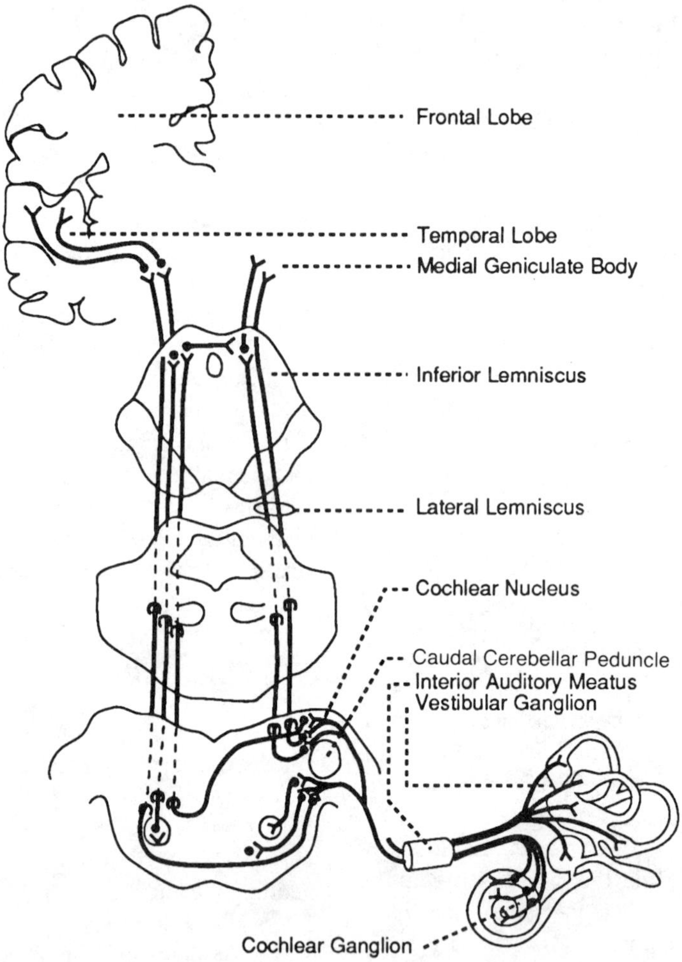

Figure 3-18 Pathway of the cochlear nerve.

tinnitus, is probably suffering from a conduction loss, receptor disease, or lesion affecting cranial nerve VIII. Central lesions are not often associated with loss of hearing, but more commonly with hallucinations of hearing. An increase in intensity of hearing (hyperacusis) may be due to a cranial nerve VII disorder or a centrally located problem. There are two major varieties of hearing loss, conductive and sensorineural.

Conductive loss usually refers to some kind of physical blocking of the sound (vibration) transmission. Typical areas involved in conduction loss and common etiologies involved are as follows:

1. Auditory canal: Cerumen deposits are the most common cause; other obstructions from debris (cigar butts) should be considered, especially in children.
2. Tympanic membrane: Direct or indirect trauma to the tympanic membrane may result in conductive hearing loss. Long-term exposure to loud noise, such as that to which a rock musician or fan, a rifleman, or an industrial factory worker may be exposed, may cause sclerosis, seen as silvery-white deposits on the tympanic membrane. In some cases a single exposure to loud noise can rupture the membrane and cause similar scarring. A slap on the ear or sudden pressure changes might also be responsible.
3. Ossicles: Damage to or sclerosis of the ear ossicles might cause immobility

(ankylosis), which is considered to cause a type of conduction loss. This difficult-to-treat cause of hearing loss is usually associated with advancing age, or, rarely, with chronic middle ear infections.

4. Middle ear: Accumulation of fluid in the middle ear, as in acute or chronic otitis media, will cause conductive hearing loss.

Sensorineural (nerve or perceptive) hearing loss is usually attributed to disease of the end organ (organ of Corti) or the auditory nerve. Other related problems include presbycusis, or the typical hearing loss associated with advancing age, and tinnitus aurium, or ringing in the ear.

Examination

Testing of the Cochlear Division

If a patient has no subjective complaint of hearing loss, only a minimal screening procedure may be necessary during the cranial nerve exam, especially if you notice no communication problems during the history-taking process. As a matter of fact, it is useful at least once during the history to be certain that the patient cannot see your mouth moving and to speak in soft tones, to specifically screen hearing during the history-taking process.

Another useful test is the finger rustle. Here you ask the patient to close his or her eyes while you place your hands about 6 inches from the patient's ears. The patient is instructed to raise his or her hand on the same side as the ear that perceives some sound. You may then proceed to rustle your fingers first on one side, then on the other, repeating in random fashion five or six times. The patient's response should be 100% accurate and quite immediate. Similarly, you may use the watch tick test, which is performed the same as above, only asking the patient to identify the tick of a watch. (Of course, not many of us have watches that tick these days, and there is no corresponding "quartz buzz" test.)

More refined and reliable testing may be accomplished with the aid of a tuning fork. The fork should vibrate at 256 or 512 Hz. Three separate tests are generally described: the Rinne test, the Weber test, and the Schwabach test.

In the Rinne test the buzzing tuning fork is placed upon the mastoid, and the patient is instructed to tell you when he or she can no longer hear or feel it. At the time when the patient reports that he or she can no longer perceive the buzzing, the tuning fork (still buzzing) is placed in front of the ipsilateral external auditory meatus (air conduction). The patient is asked if he or she can now hear the buzzing. The patient should continue to hear the buzzing, and some texts say that it should be heard twice as long as was the ipsilateral bone (mastoid) conduction. This "twice as long" rule is impractical since it is dependent upon how vigorously the fork was initially struck and requires some kind of timing device, thereby complicating the test. The test is useful, however, because the patient should definitely hear via air conduction after bone conduction has ceased. If the patient cannot hear, or if he or she only hears the air conduction for a fraction of the expected time (compared to your own experience as well as the other side), then there is a strong possibility of a conductive hearing loss.

The Weber test is accomplished by placing the buzzing tuning fork on the vertex of the patient's skull. Normally, the patient will hear the sound equally in both ears. To be certain that the patient understands the instructions, is cooperating, and knows what to listen for, it is advisable to ask him or her to occlude one ear and tell you if the buzzing changes. The patient should respond by saying that the buzzing becomes louder in the occluded ear. If the tuning fork is initially heard louder in one ear (without occluding either ear), this is known as lateralization. It usually represents a conductive loss in the ear toward which the sound lateralizes. The rationale is that the sound is heard better through bone conduction (nerve hearing) because air conduction (conductive hearing) is decreased on that side. Remember, lateralization may also occur opposite from a side stricken with nerve hearing loss (nerve deafness), due to frank deafness on that side. A correlation between Rinne and Weber tests usually clearly answers the question of nerve versus conductive hearing loss.

The Schwabach test simply asks that you place the buzzing tuning fork in front of a patient's external auditory meatus and instruct him or her to notify you when the buzzing can no longer be heard. At that moment, place the tuning fork in front of your own ear, and compare the patient's hearing to your own (see Figure 3-19). This is a simple test, hardly deserving of an eponym, but very useful (assuming your own hearing is normal).

A helpful procedural suggestion is that you perform the Schwabach test immediately following the Rinne test. In other words, after placing the tuning fork in front of the patient's ear and having him or her report when it can no longer be heard, the final portion of the Rinne test, quickly bring the fork to your own ear and compare your hearing (Schwabach). This actually eliminates several minutes from the exam procedure, as you do not have to restrike the tuning fork and wait for the patient to report no longer hearing it.

Another test, seldom used but having its place in certain situations, is termed the auditopalpebral reflex. A loud noise from out of sight should cause a patient to blink. In very young children and infants, this is a reasonable test of noise perception. In the malingering patient who claims deafness, dropping a book on a hard floor or clapping together the hands might elicit a blink and therefore prove noise perception.

Otoscopy should be performed as a physical part of the neurological exam of cranial nerve VIII. Pulling slightly up and back on the adult ear tends to straighten out the canal somewhat, allowing better observation. Congenital variations make some canals more difficult to visualize, but usually adequate visualization is not a problem. Pain accompanying manipulation of the external ear (auricle) should be noted as it may be indicative of acute external otitis or otitis media. The auricle and external canal should be inspected for signs of inflammation, and the ear speculum (sized only just large enough to fit snugly) gently inserted into the outer third of the canal. Going past this cartilaginous outer third places your speculum into the bony inner two thirds, which can be excruciatingly painful to the patient. Tell the patient to tell you if it hurts, and if it does, back out slightly, and go in no further during the exam. To avoid painful damage to the inner portion of the external auditory meatus by sudden head movements of the patient caused by painful ear canal entry, hold the otoscope like a pen, and loosely. This will minimize pressure in the ear caused by head movement. Otoscopy is an important step in differentiating hearing loss due to primary neurological disease and that due to local ear disease.

Finally, one may test for auditory inattention or extinction. In this instance the patient can hear stimuli applied to either ear separately but will not hear in one ear when simultaneous bilateral stimuli are applied.

Testing of the Vestibular Division

Vestibular disease is always accompanied by vertigo, or the sensation of movement. Other symptoms of vestibular disease include nausea,

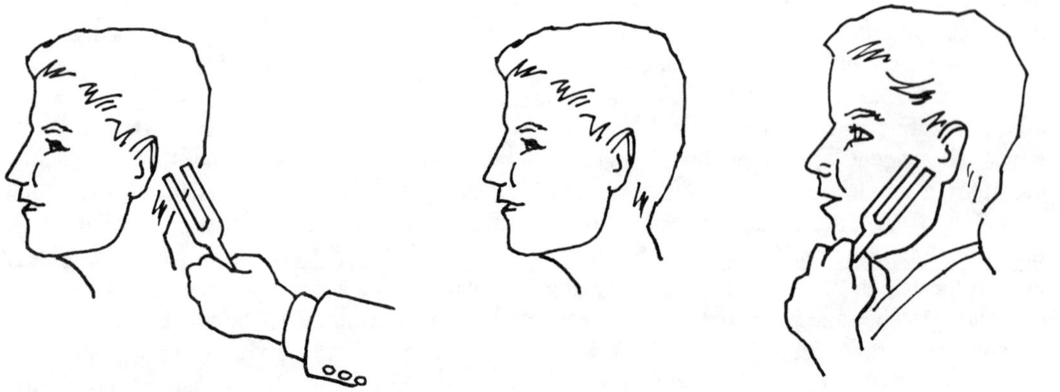

Figure 3-19 The Schwabach test.

anxiety, and oscillopsia (the visual perception of rapid to-and-fro movements often accompanying nystagmus). Signs of vestibular disease include unsteadiness with or without falling, nystagmus, and autonomic signs such as pallor, sweating, vomiting, and hypotension.

Observation for nystagmus is of paramount importance in detecting vestibular disease. Nystagmus is labeled in descriptive terms, as it might oscillate in a horizontal (most common), vertical, or rotatory fashion. If it is horizontal (moving left to right) it may move more quickly toward one side and then more slowly back the other way. The side toward which the fast movement occurs is the side for which the nystagmus is named. If there is no fast component, the nystagmus is termed pendular.

Most often discussed as a test of vestibular function is caloric irrigation. In the chiropractic office, this is an impractical test, as it is time consuming and extremely uncomfortable for the patient, who may vomit. Additionally, results of the test must be very carefully and quickly observed, leaving the doctor who only rarely performs this procedure in a difficult position.

First, you must syringe the external auditory canal with either warm (103° to 110°F) or cold water (a few drops of ice water will do for the latter). This apparently causes convection currents in the semicircular canals. This unilateral stimulus causes a characteristic nystagmus, the direction of which is usually remembered by the mnemonic "COWS": cold opposite—warm same. The direction "same" or "opposite" refers to the side of the ear stimulated and is labeled according to the fast component of the jerky nystagmus. A difference in reaction between right and left ears, or an absent, reduced, or improper response is suggestive of vestibular disease.

Since movement of the head causes stimulation of the vestibular receptors, an adjunctive or alternative method of testing is to have the patient sit on the examining table and turn his or her head toward you, as you stand at the side of the table. At that time, have the patient lay back on the table, fairly abruptly, allowing his or her head to extend over the end of the table. Observe for nystagmus as well as reproduction of symptoms. It is also a good practice to have the patient hyperventilate some, since so many patients confuse hyperventilation with vertigo. If hyperventilation reproduces the patient's symptoms, vestibular disease is much less likely.

One of the easiest things to confuse with vestibular disease is cervical spinal proprioceptive disease, or so called cervicogenic vertigo. Ataxia and vertigo associated with cervical proprioceptive disease are well documented. It is my belief that cervicogenic vertigo is not well understood by members of the medical community and therefore the symptoms are misdiagnosed as vestibular disease and grossly underreported. It may well be the leading cause of vertigo and explain why doctors of chiropractic have such strong empirical evidence regarding favorable outcome after cervical manipulation of such patients.

Since neck movement normally accompanies head movement, symptoms of "dizziness" associated with head movement are not specific to cervical or vestibular disease. One test is specifically designed to separate head and neck movement.

The patient is seated in a swivel chair. Either you or your assistant should immobilize the head by placing one hand over each of the patient's temples. The patient is instructed to swivel the chair back and forth, but the head is not allowed to move, thereby stimulating only the cervical proprioceptors (see Figure 3-20). Reproduction of the patient's symptoms, sometimes with nystagmus, is suggestive of cervical proprioceptive disease. It has been my experience that this is a very safe and reliable test and that the faster and more the patient's symptoms are approximated, the better the outcome of manual cervical manipulative techniques will be.

CRANIAL NERVES IX AND X

Anatomy and Function

Cranial nerve IX motor fibers originate in the nucleus ambiguus, as do some motor fibers of cranial nerves X and XI. Cranial nerve IX exits the skull through the jugular foramen along with

Figure 3-20 Testing for cervicogenic vertigo with a swivel chair.

cranial nerves X and XI. The innervation is to the stylopharyngeus muscle, which elevates the pharnyx and larynx as well as aids in raising the soft palate.

Disorders

Isolated lesions of cranial nerve IX are very uncommon. There is never any disturbance of speech, and due to bilateral innervation, disturbances in swallowing are very transitory in unilateral cerebral lesions. Due to overlap, the same is true of peripheral lesions.

Cranial nerve X is far more important in deglutition and articulation. Sensory deficits are even less pronounced. Unilateral paralysis of cranial nerve X is followed by transient paresis of the soft palate, pharynx, and larynx on the affected side, along with absent gag reflexes and an absent oculocardiac reflex. Gastric symptoms are slight or absent. More acute lesions bring on more severe symptoms. Complete bilateral cranial nerve X, or vagus, paralysis is not compatible with life. Any branch may become affected, and the paralysis will involve the structure innervated.

The following terms are associated with cranial nerve IX and X disease:

1. aphonia: no phonation
2. dysarthria: faulty articulation
3. anarthria: no articulation
4. dysphagia: faulty swallowing
5. aphagia: no swallowing
6. hypernasal: increased air entering into nasal cavity
7. hyponasal: decreased air entering into nasal cavity

Examination

Cranial nerves IX and X are tested together clinically. Cranial nerve X, along with IX, causes elevation of the palate. This is readily observed by having the patient say ''Ahhh'' continuously while looking at the soft palate under a light source. Many patients must be coaxed to continue to say ''Ahhh'' as they find it amusing and will only say it for a few seconds before laughing. It is helpful to say ''Ahhh'' along with the patient so that he or she does not feel so foolish.

Many authorities recommend noting deviation of the uvula as evidence of asymmetrical palatal elevation. While this is often a useful sign, an asymmetrically shaped or bifid uvula (very common), or the presence of an associated papilloma, can cause a normally elevated palate to look abnormal. It is best to look at either side of the free edge of the soft palate directly for observation of bilateral muscular contraction, which yields symmetrically shaped palatal arches (see Figure 3-21). Cranial nerves IX and X cause pharyngeal movement associated with swallowing. Actually, cranial nerves V, VIII, IX, X, and XII have some function in swallow-

Figure 3-21 Testing the palatal reflex.

ing. Finally, cranial nerve X is tested by having the patient phonate. Remember that hoarseness of the voice, without laryngeal disease, may be caused by paralysis of cranial nerve X origin (recurrent laryngeal nerve). Since this nerve comes in intimate contact with both the arch of the aorta and the thyroid gland, diseases involving these areas should be investigated by methods including laryngoscopy.

The syndrome of pseudobulbar palsy is often confused (hence the name) with disorders of cranial nerves IX and X. It is important to remember that a bilateral cerebral lesion is responsible for pseudobulbar palsy. Bilateral interruption of corticobulbar pathways may mimic brainstem or peripheral cranial nerve IX disease. Signs include slow speaking and swallowing, a peculiar strained pitch and quality of voice, emotional lability, and masked facies with exaggerated emotional movements. Remember, with lower motor neuron (cranial nerve) disease all innervated movements are paralyzed, while with upper motor neuron disease only voluntary movements may be paralyzed. Emotional and reflex movements are often spared.

The K-L-M test helps differentiate the probable cause of faulty articulation. The patient is asked to pronounce the sounds "kuh," "la," and "mi," which each require different movements of the palate, tongue, and lips, respectively. If faulty articulation is noted, have the patient clearly speak each of the above sounds to determine where the fault lies.

Palatal elevation may be achieved both voluntarily and reflexly. If under careful observation the palate fails to elevate symmetrically while the patient says "Ahhh," stimulate the gag reflex by touching the posterior third of the tongue with a tongue depressor. Care must be taken not to strike the buccal mucosa or anterior third of the tongue. Touching these areas should not cause a gag reflex; if it does, the patient may only be reacting volitionally to the stimulus, and the reflex may or may not be present. If the palate still fails to elevate on one side, it is paralyzed both voluntarily and reflexly, and this suggests a lower motor neuron lesion. Should the palate elevate with bilateral symmetry only after reflex testing, suspect an upper motor neuron lesion affecting only voluntary pathways.

CRANIAL NERVE XI

Anatomy and Function

Cranial nerve XI is composed of two parts, the cranial or accessory portion (to the vagus) and the spinal portion, which is by far the larger. Neurons of the spinal portion arise from the ventral horn of the spinal cord. They ascend through the foramen magnum and exit the skull through the jugular foramen. They then pass through and supply fibers to the sternocleidomastoid (SCM) on its way across the posterior triangle of the neck, to end deep in the surface of the trapezius. Cranial nerve XI is primarily motor in function. It supplies the upper trapezius (head extension and lateral flexion), as well as the SCM (head flexion and rotation). The lower trapezius is innervated by the third and fourth cervical nerves.

Disorders

With a unilateral upper motor neuron lesion, paresis will only be partial due to bilateral innervation. Depression of the shoulder and weakness of shoulder elevation and cervical rotation may be present. Irritative lesions are more common and may result in spasmodic torticollis.

Examination

Testing of cranial nerve XI is as simple as examining the upper trapezius and sternocleidomastoid for strength, tone, and volume. Strength may be gauged by opposing the following muscular actions:

- sternocleidomastoid actions
  1. Tilt head to same side.
  2. Turn chin to opposite side.
  3. Flex head when contracted bilaterally.
- trapezius actions
  1. Tilt head to same side.
  2. Turn chin to opposite side.
  3. Elevate shoulders when contracted bilaterally.

CRANIAL NERVE XII

Anatomy and Function

Cranial nerve XII, the hypoglossal nerve, is the motor nerve to the tongue. Fibers originate in the hypoglossal nuclei and emerge at the bottom of the brainstem.

Disorders

Paresis or paralysis of the tongue, as you might have guessed, is the cardinal finding in cranial nerve XII disease. Unilateral supranuclear lesions only reveal diagnostic signs such as slight speaking and chewing difficulties temporarily. Bilateral cerebral lesions, on the other hand, can be responsible for long-term problems with glossal function.

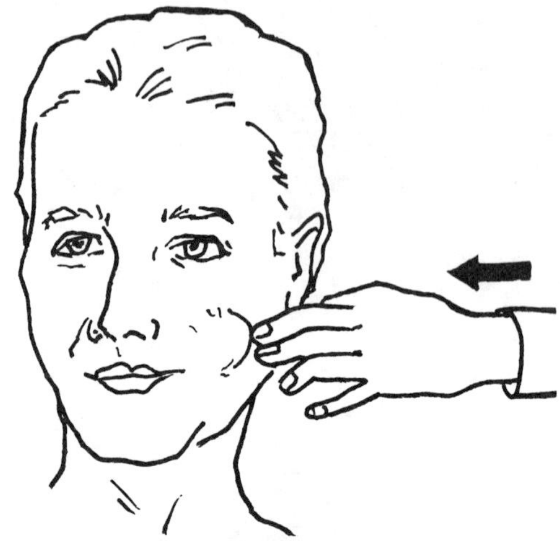

Figure 3-22 Testing lateral deviation of the tongue.

Examination

Cranial nerve XII innervates the genioglossus muscle. Bilateral muscle contraction pulls the tongue forward or sticks it out, and this is the first and most useful test. Right-sided muscular contraction causes the tip of the tongue to deviate to the left, and left-sided contraction causes the tip of the tongue to deviate to the right. You may test deviation of the tongue against resistance by asking the patient to place the tongue in one cheek, while you resist from the outside of the same cheek, the "tongue in cheek" test (see Figure 3-22).

Atrophy of the tongue, observed when the tongue is protruded, may be notable and associated with cranial nerve XII diseases. Fasciculation of the tongue is an unreliable finding, as most tongues do not keep still very well.

SUGGESTED READING

Arnold LA. *Chiropractic Procedural Examination*. 2nd ed. Seminole, Fla: Seminole Printing, Inc; 1979:40,52–53.

Chusid JG. *Correlative Neuroanatomy & Functional Neurology*. 17th ed. Norwalk, Conn: Lange Medical Publications; 1982:195–210.

DeJong RN. *The Neurologic Examination*. 4th ed. New York, NY: Harper & Row; 1979:39–78.

chapter 4

The Voluntary Motor System Examination

It is essential to assess motor function through muscle testing in each patient upon whom you are performing a neurological examination. This is the easiest and most clinically useful way of gauging motor nerve function.

BASIC CONCEPTS OF MOTOR SYSTEM INNERVATION

As you will recall, the voluntary motor impulses are initiated in the cerebral motor cortex, located primarily in the motor cortex of the frontal lobe on the precentral gyrus (see Figure 4-1). Each area of this cortex controls an area of the face and body, and these relationships have been meticulously mapped out and presented in a figure known as the motor homunculus (see Figure 4-2). More recent insights in neurophysiology suggest that there is no rigid organization and that brain plasticity (ability to shift functions to other areas) is considerable. However, this has minimal effect on neurodiagnosis since the general principles of topical localization of brain function remain unchanged. The size of the body part represented in the homunculus is proportional to the concentration of motor neurons (or pyramidal cells, named after their shape) in this area of the cortex. The larger the part represented, the more neurons for that part.

As discussed in Chapter 3, the motor cortex neurons controlling the actions of the cranial nerves descend the corticobulbar tract to the brainstem nuclei, where they synapse on lower motor neurons. Other motor cortex neurons descend along a different tract, the corticospinal, through the brainstem and down the spinal cord, where they terminate at various levels in synapses on their corresponding lower motor neurons (see Figure 4-3). Whatever their origin in the central nervous system, all these lower motor neurons go on to innervate specific muscles. Therefore, testing for muscle integrity supplies information regarding not only the muscles themselves but also the upper and lower motor neurons.

Generally three areas of muscle integrity are assessed for purposes of neurological evaluation: strength, tone, and volume.

GENERAL INSPECTION AND PALPATION

Every good evaluation begins with inspection. Muscle inspection must be performed with the examined areas disrobed. Failure to properly

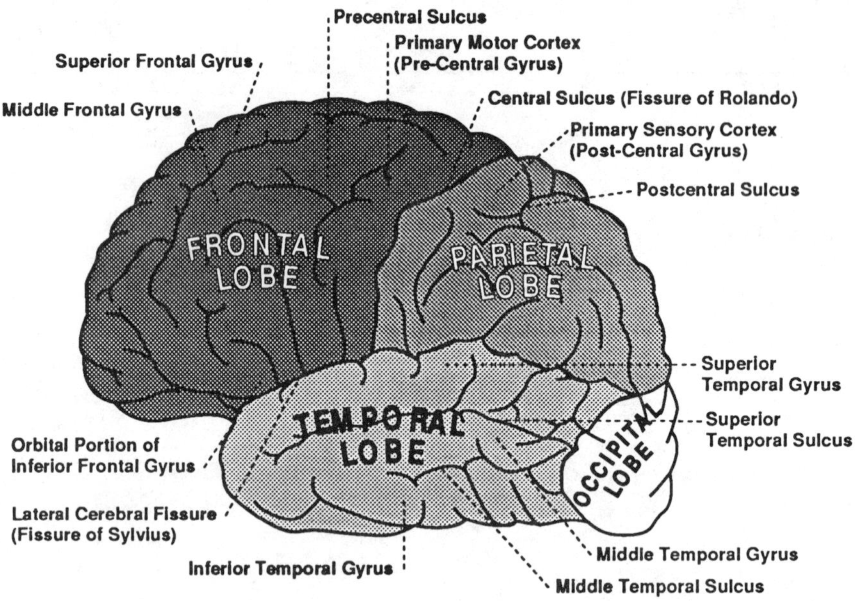

Figure 4-1 Gross anatomy of the cerebrum.

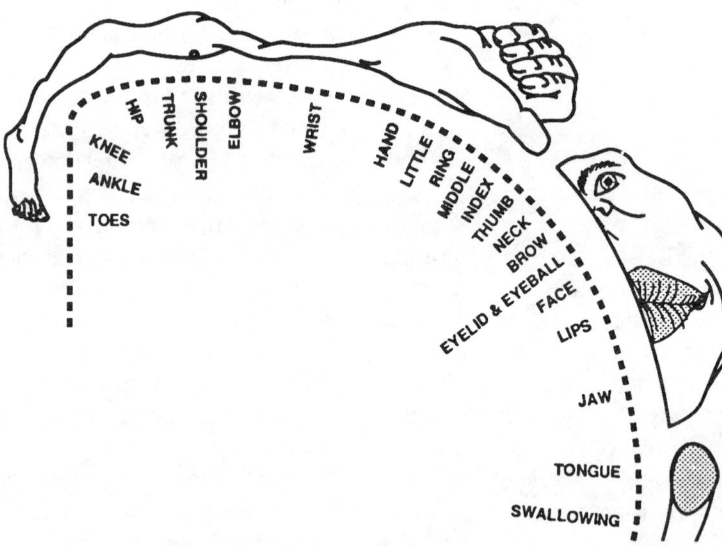

Figure 4-2 Motor homunculus shown overlying a coronal section through the precentral gyrus. *Source:* Adapted from *The Cerebral Cortex of Man* by W Penfield and T Rasmussen, Macmillan Publishing Company, © 1950.

perform this simple and most basic step has probably caused more misdiagnosis of lower motor neuron disease than any other single factor.

Inspection of body contours should be performed with the patient in the standing neutral posture. Note unusual postures or positioning of body parts. For example, scoliosis of the spine may be indicated by a low shoulder or iliac crest height. Such abnormalities as pronation of the hand or flexion of the entire upper extremity may give rise to suspicion of hemiparesis.

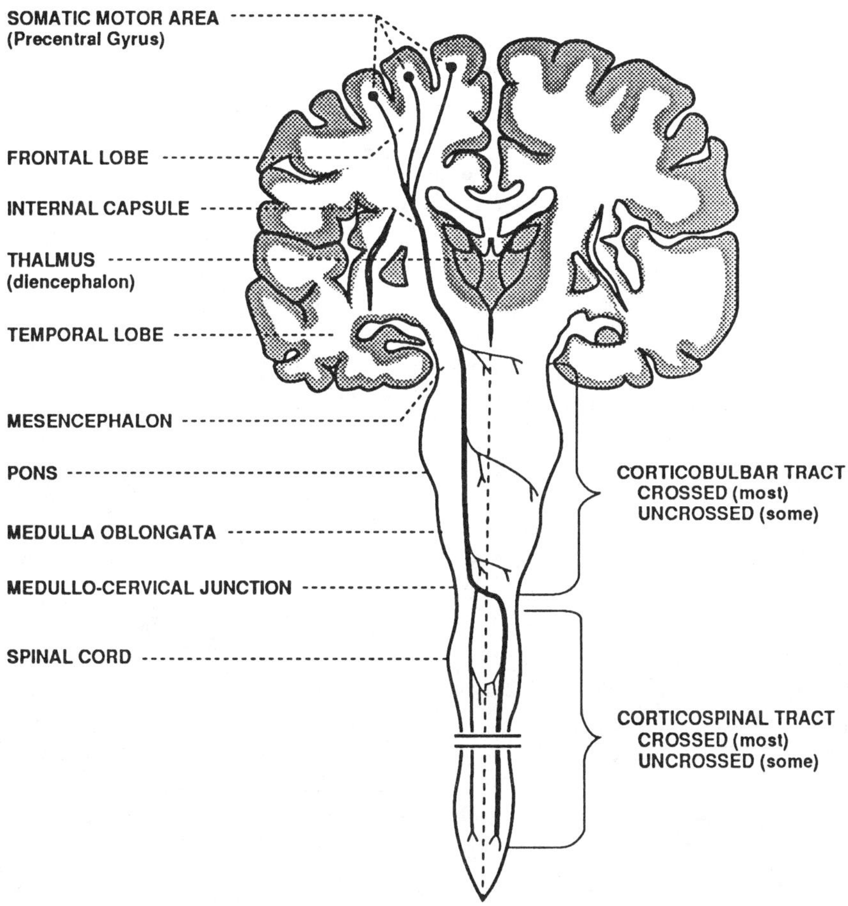

Figure 4-3 Diagram of the descent of upper motor neurons from the somatic motor area.

It is most important to systematically check for atrophy or hypertrophy. This may be performed by careful observation of the size of one extremity, or the appearance of one side of the face, as compared to the other. Slight enlargement of the dominant side extremities and slight facial asymmetries are common. However, excessive differences or recent changes are extremely noteworthy, as they are purely objective. No one can exaggerate or fake a muscle volume asymmetry.

Additionally, one should observe for muscle fasciculation. Fasciculations are discrete, palpable contractions of small areas of muscle. They may or may not be felt by the patient. Fasciculations may become more apparent after gently percussing over the muscle. It is believed that fasciculations are due to spontaneous discharges along specific neurons, leading to contraction of all muscle fibers innervated by that specific neuron. The appearance of such muscular ''twitching'' when continual in one area has been likened to that of a bag of worms. Larger muscle groups have large numbers of muscle fibers innervated by single neurons, whereas small muscles, such as the extraocular muscles, may have nerve:muscle ratios approaching 1:1.

MUSCLE STRENGTH TESTING

The strength of specific muscles gives direct information about nerve integrity. Generally, the examiner will have an idea as to what is the normal amount of strength for a particular sex, age, and build. Right versus left side strength determination is invaluable. Several generally accepted rules for strength testing should be kept in mind during exam performance.

The expected strength of the patient's muscle should be matched by your own. Obviously, some of your patients will have stronger muscles and some weaker muscles than do you, the examiner. This is not a problem, as you should use laws of muscle strength and mechanical advantage to match or exceed the patient's strength. In this way, you can be sure that the patient exerts considerable, if not maximal, effort. Clinically, a muscle's strength increases as its length decreases. An example would be the biceps muscle, which is much stronger, and more difficult to test, when the forearm is flexed on the arm (shortened position) (see Figure 4-4). With the elbow extended (lengthened position), even the biggest biceps muscleman can be easily overcome. Additionally, using a contact point distal to the fulcrum, or joint, gains a mechanical advantage over the muscle and gives you increased ability to overcome the patient's resistance.

It is extremely important that the patient make this kind of maximal effort, as some varieties of weakness, especially of central nervous system origin, can be very subtle and only brought to light by this type of challenge.

This type of muscle testing varies sharply from muscle "locking" used with applied kinesiology muscle testing and therefore requires that neurological and applied kinesiology muscle testing be performed separately.

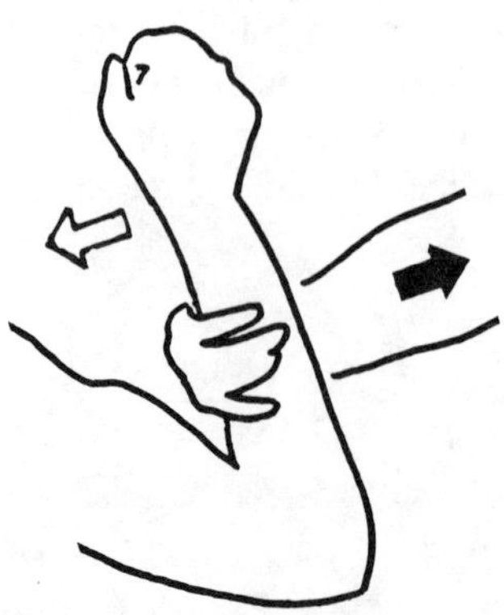

Figure 4-4 Mechanical disadvantage.

The patient should have the body part passively placed into the correct position usually midway between flexion and extension prior to testing. He or she should be instructed thus: "Resist my effort to move your (arm, leg, etc.)." Being careful not to injure the patient, you may then exert your power in a slow crescendo, just until the point at which you begin to defeat the patient's effort. Test the opposite side immediately following (if applicable), while the feeling of that strength is fresh in your mind, and the direction of struggle is still fresh in the patient's mind.

A "give-way" variety of muscle weakness, characterized by strong effort, followed by relaxation, followed by effort, will be noted in the hysterical or malingering patient. It has the feeling of a series of efforts. True weakness is noted by the examiner as a smooth, weakened resistance throughout the range of that muscle's test.

Antigravity muscles, those muscles that hold the body, in the quadruped position (see Figure 4-5), up against gravity, are stronger than their antagonists. Therefore, wrist flexors are stronger than wrist extensors, the triceps stronger than the biceps, trunk extensors stronger than flexors, plantar flexors stronger than dorsiflexors, etc.

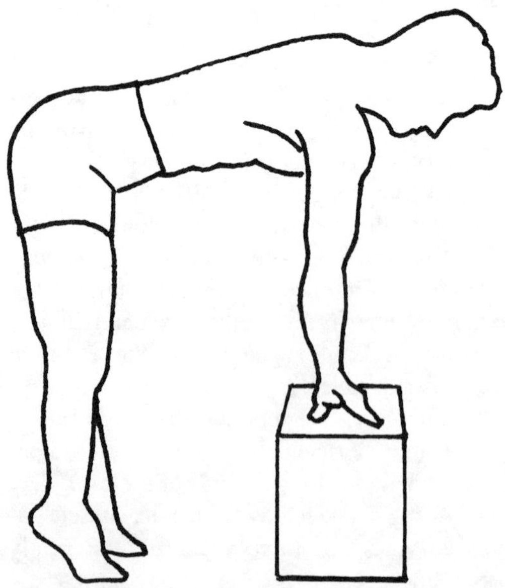

Figure 4-5 The quadruped position.

Remember to develop an organized testing method, and don't forget large muscle groups.

Individual muscle testing is illustrated below (see Figure 4-6). Table 4-1 shows the innervation levels of various muscle groups. Large muscle groups, such as the biceps, triceps, hamstrings, gluteals, and quadriceps, should be tested routinely. Distal muscles of the hands and feet also require routine observation due to the frequency of involvement in central nervous system disease.

To test abdominal muscles for partial paralysis (paresis), the umbilical migration test is performed. The supine patient is asked to perform a partial sit-up. Normally, the umbilicus does not move, but with paresis or paralysis, the umbilicus will migrate toward the side of the stronger muscles (Beevor's sign).

A very useful screening tool for hemiparesis is observation for drift. The patient is asked to extend both arms out in front with the palms turned up (supinated) and the eyes closed. Failure to maintain this position may be due to a unilateral upper motor neuron lesion characterized by pronation and lateral (outward) dropping or drifting of one extremity. In cerebellar disease, the ipsilateral extremity drifts laterally.

Recording muscle strength is extremely important. It will help document normality, as well as progress or deterioration of a particular

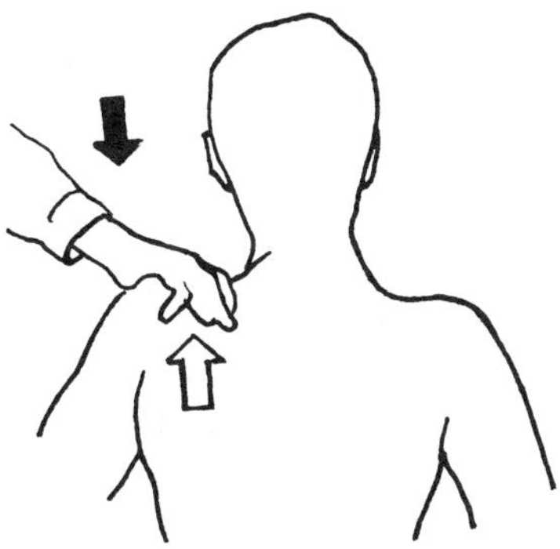

1 Upper trapezius.

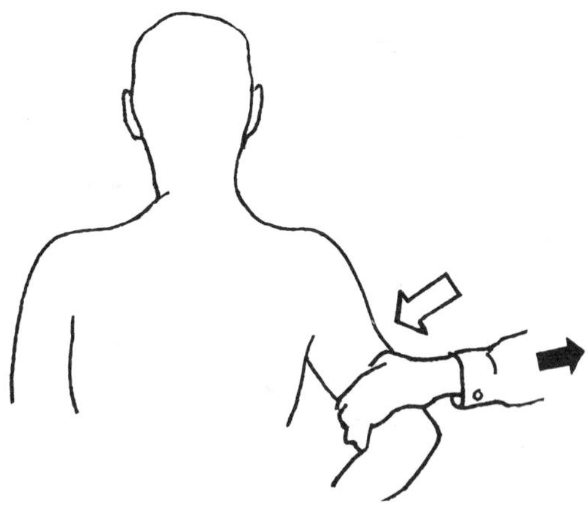

2 Shoulder adductors.

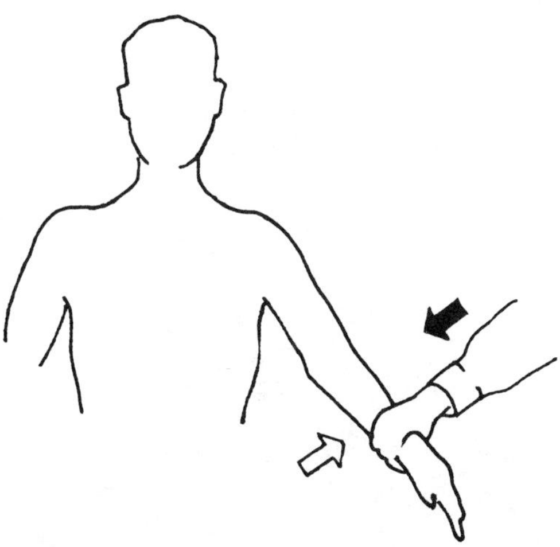

3 Shoulder abductors.

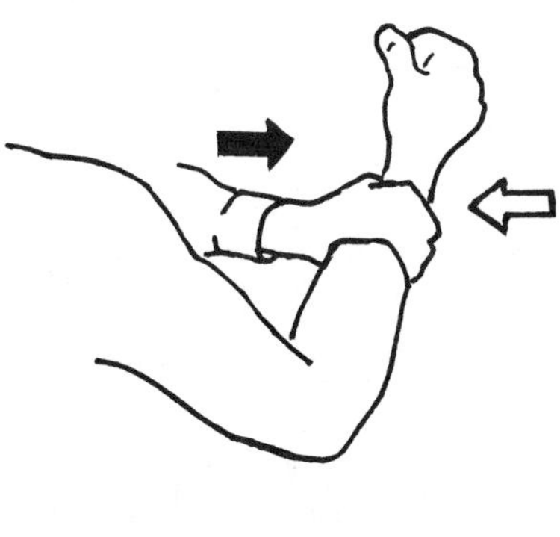

4 Biceps.

Figure 4-6 The sequence of procedures in performing a test of muscle strength.

continues

Figure 4-6 continued

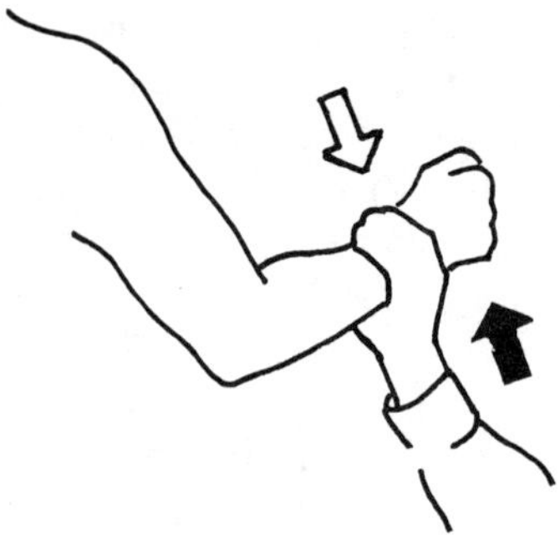

5 Triceps.

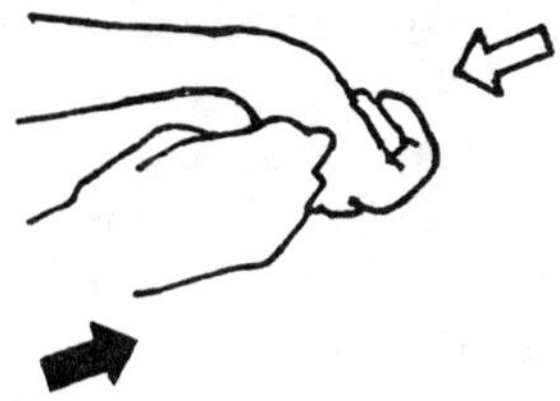

6 Wrist extensors.

7 Finger flexor (alternate to grip strength).

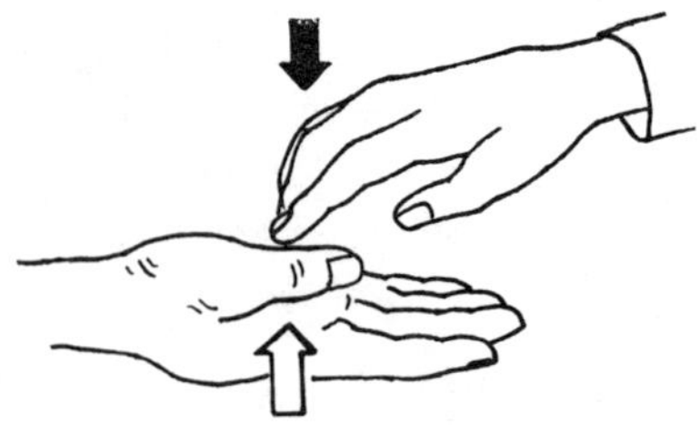

8 Abduction of the thumb.

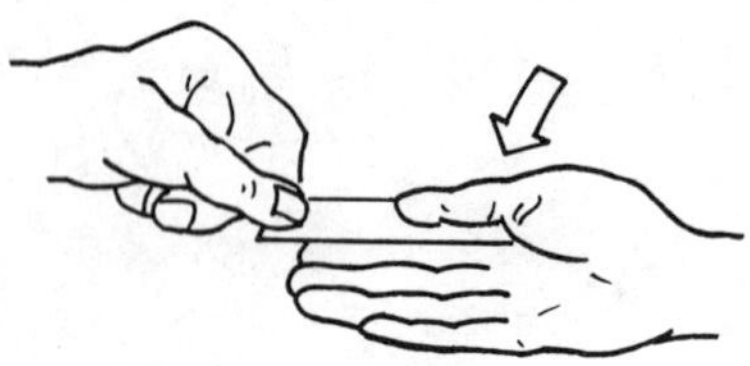

9 Thumb adduction. (If flexion of thumb is substituted by patient, this is known as Froment's sign.)

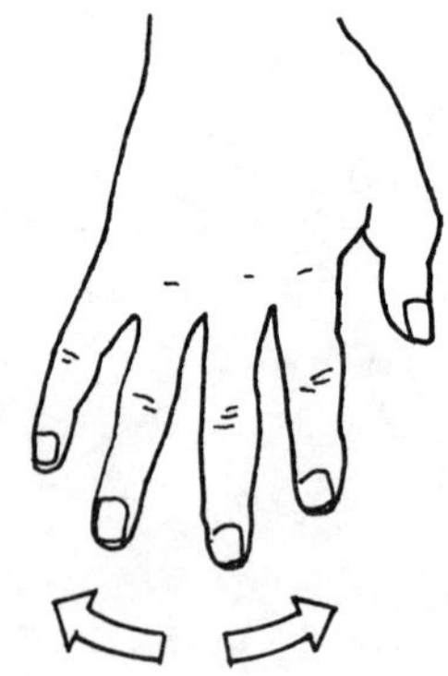

10 Finger abductors.

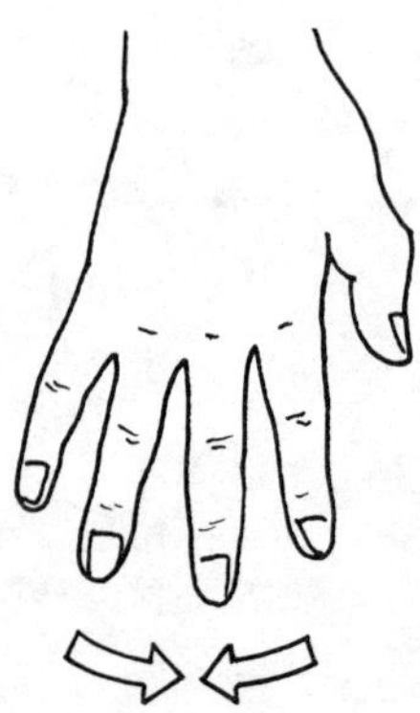

11 Finger adductors.

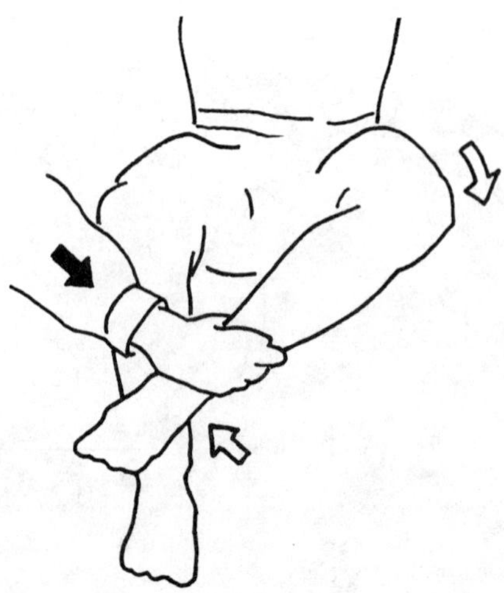

12 External rotators of the hip.

continues

Figure 4-6 continued

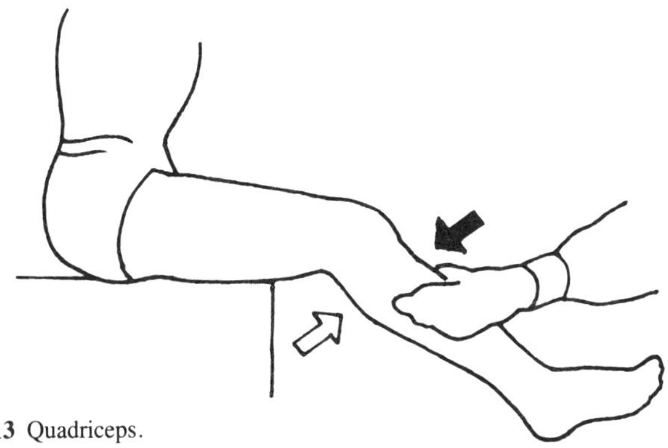

13 Quadriceps.

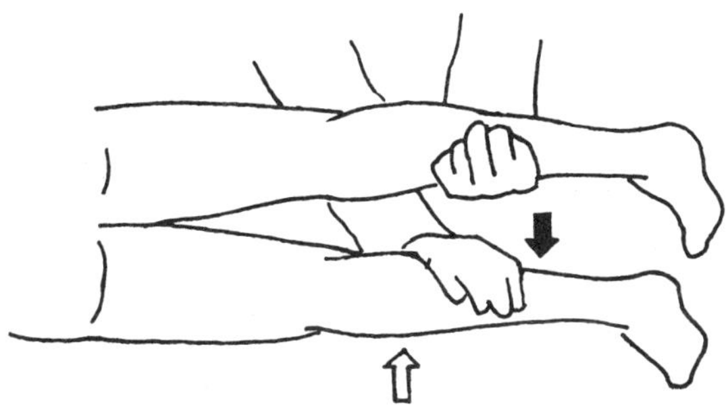

14 Lower extremity adductors.

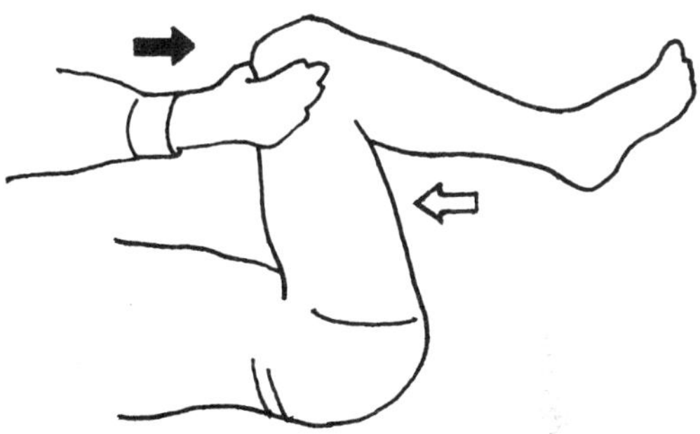

15 Hip flexors.

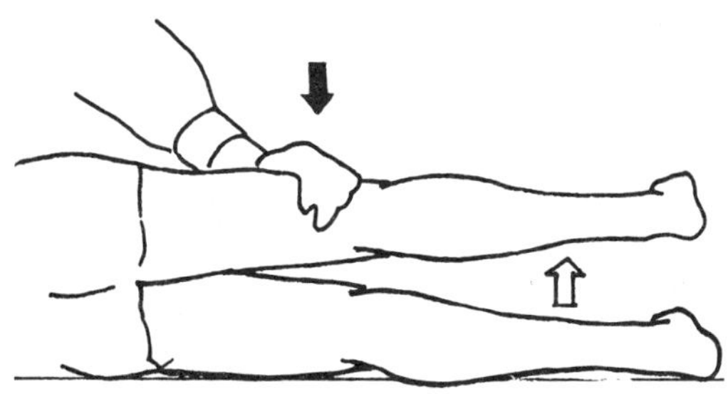

16 Hip abductors.

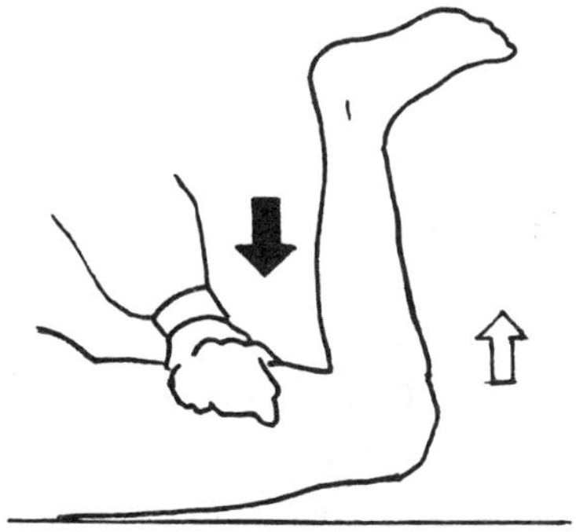

17 Gluteal muscles.

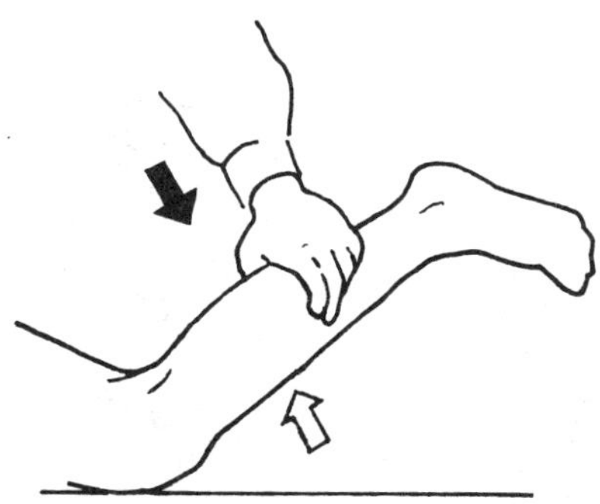

18 Hamstring muscles.

continues

Figure 4-6 continued

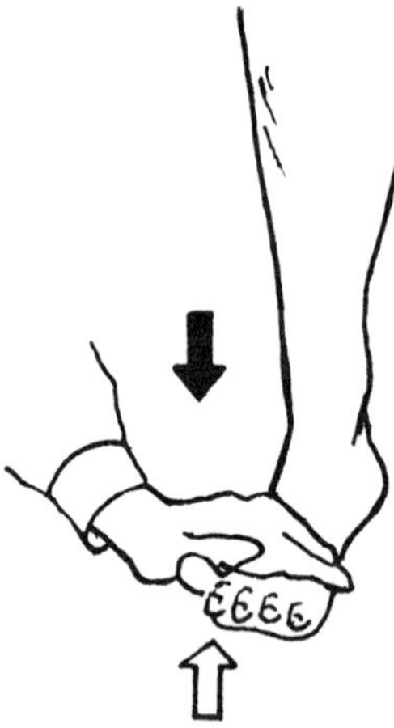

19 Foot and toe dorsiflexors (anterior compartment muscles).

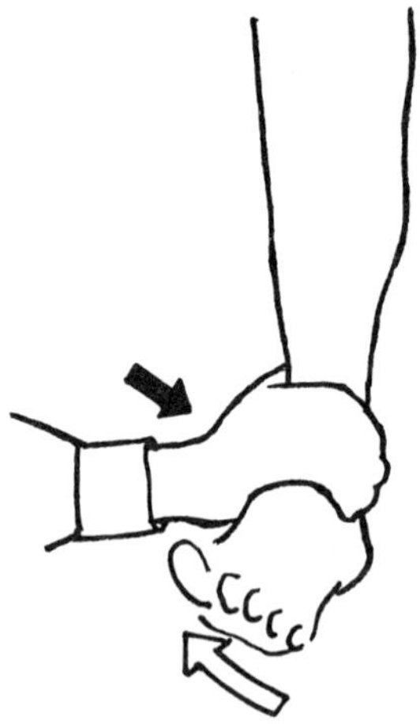

20 Inverters of the foot.

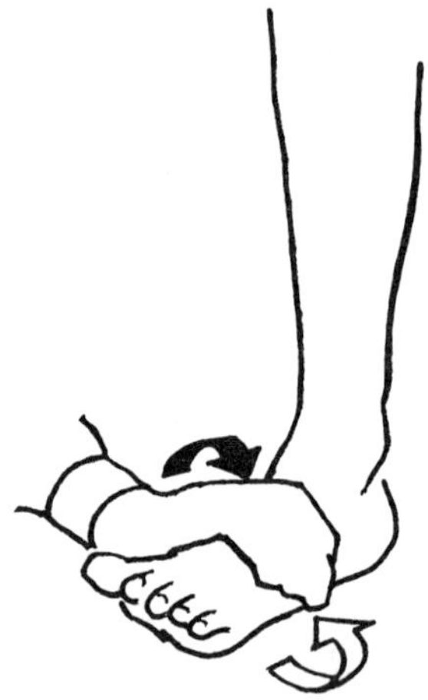

21 Everters of the foot.

condition. For intra- and interoffice consistency, a scale of 0 to 5 should be employed, noted as 0/5, 1/5, 2/5, 3/5, 4/5, or 5/5. The only firm convention is that 0/5 signifies complete paralysis and 5/5 muscle strength that is interpreted as being within normal limits. Generally, 1/5 signifies severe paresis (just a twitch of movement), 2/5 moderate to severe paresis, 3/5 moderate paresis, and 4/5 mild paresis that may be described as just subnormal. Grading muscle movement against gravity has been omitted here due to its limited clinical utility.

Table 4-1 Level of Innervation of Selected Muscles

Muscle	*Level*	*Muscle*	*Level*
Temporal	CNV	Wrist, extensors	C678
Masseter	CNV	Wrist, flexors	C678 T1
Pterygoid	CNV	Digits, extensors	C678
Frontalis	CNVII	Digits, flexors	C78 T1
Orbicularis oculi	CNVII	Thenar	C8 T1
Mouth	CNVII	Hypothenar	C8 T1
Platysma	CNVII	Interossei	C8 T1
Soft palate	CNX	Abdomen	T6 L1
Pharynx	CNX	Iliopsoas	L1234
Sternomastoid	CNXI	Adductors, thigh	L234
Trapezius	CNXI	Abductors, thigh	L45 S1
Tongue	CNXII	Gluteus max.	L5 S12
Neck, flexors	C1-6	Quadriceps, femoris	L234
Neck, extensors	C1-T1	Hamstrings	L45 S12
Scapular	C4-7	Tibialis anterior	L45 S1
Pectoralis major	C5-T1	Toes, extensors	L45 S1
Deltoid	C56	Peronei	L45 S1
Biceps	C56	Gastroc.-soleus	L5 S12
Triceps	C678	Toes, flexors	L5 S12

Note: C = cervical, CN = cranial nerve, L = lumbar, T = thoracic.

PERCUSSION

In some cases, muscle percussion may be performed to assess primary muscle or peripheral nerve disease. Muscle percussion is performed by directly striking the belly of a particular muscle (often the thenar eminence) with the pointed end of a reflex hammer and noting the following possible reactions. Percussion irritability (intrinsic irritability) is simply a focal muscle contraction appearing as a slight transient ripple or dimple at the site of impact to the muscle. This reaction is completely independent of any volitional or reflex activity and is normal in many individuals. After denervation (lower motor neuron) of a muscle, a phenomenon known as Cannon's law of hyperexcitability of denervated structures may occur. This law describes the muscle's increased propensity for spontaneous contraction (or fibrillations) due to a lack of nervous stimuli. Therefore, muscle percussion irritability may be greatly increased in denervated muscles. For this reason, it is improper to directly strike the muscle when attempting to elicit a muscle stretch reflex, as you might encounter increased muscle irritability, which in turn may be interpreted as a muscle stretch reflex. Additionally, increased muscle irritability may cause fasciculation to become more apparent after muscle percussion which is a useful clinical tool in the diagnosis of muscle denervation. The distinction between percussion irritability and muscle stretch reflexes must be clearly understood. Remember, muscle percussion irritability is not a reflex and therefore gives different and limited information about the nervous system.

Another phenomenon that may be observed following muscle percussion is termed percussion myoedema. This is a hump or bump at the site of percussion. While this reaction is sometimes normal, it is usually associated with debilitation, uremia, or myxedema.

Percussion myotonia is a finding that usually signifies a myopathy (primary muscle disease). The patient's palm is placed upward on a table. After percussion of the thenar eminence with a hammer, the thumb may actually rise off of the table due to contraction of the thenar muscles. The test may also be performed on the tongue by placing a tongue blade under the tongue and percussing it with the reflex hammer. If the tongue mounds up, it may indicate myotonia. Myotonia may also be assessed by asking the patient to make a tight fist and then quickly opening it on command. A delayed relaxation may indicate myotonic grip.

MUSCLE TONE ASSESSMENT

Muscle tone is operationally defined as the muscular resistance felt by an examiner when moving a patient's joint without voluntary resistance. Assessing it is the most subtle if not difficult task in neurological muscle assessment.

Normal resting muscle has palpable (albeit minor) tone, caused mostly by lower motor neuron discharges activated by segmental and suprasegmental reflexes. A contribution to muscle tone may also be made by inherent muscular elasticity, especially in fibrotic muscle tissue. Muscle tone may be characterized as normal, increased, or decreased. In clinical practice, generally increased paraspinal muscle tone is an extremely common phenomenon. While it may or may not be a reliable indicator of underlying joint disease, it is rarely indicative of nervous system pathology.

Hypertonia

Generally, two types of hypertonia are described. Spasticity is defined as increased muscular resistance felt by the examiner during quick joint motion, which then rapidly fades away (see Figure 4-7). This is often described as the "clasp-knife" phenomenon since, as in opening out the blade of a pocket knife, there is tension when first moving the joint, followed by a decrease in that tension as the joint is opened. It is clinically accepted that an interruption in the pyramidal (upper motor neuron) pathways is responsible for this type of finding. Scientific studies of experimentally severed pyramidal tracts do not support this, however, leading to

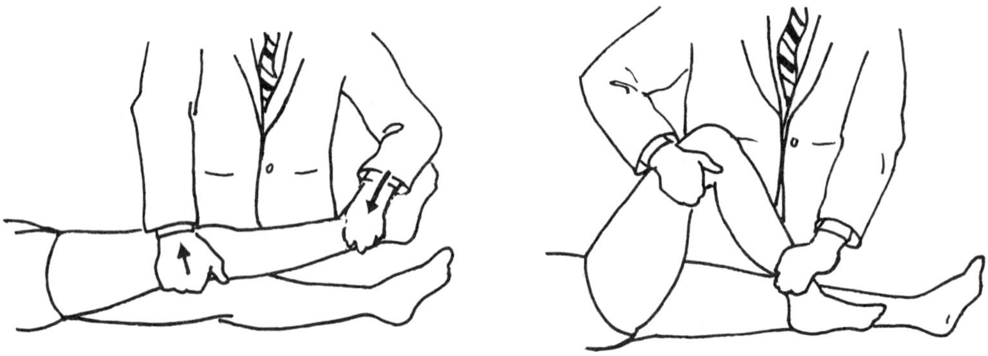

Figure 4-7 Testing for muscle spasticity in the quadriceps.

the belief that some other area(s) (probably extrapyramidal) appear to be necessary to produce this finding. In any event, most clinical circumstances that produce spasticity (head trauma, stroke, etc.) have associated cortical or pyramidal pathway lesions.

When testing for spasticity, it is important to perform the joint movement quickly, as the physiological mechanism behind this reaction is dependent on stimulation of the intrafusal muscle fibers (as described in Chapter 6). Since stimulation of the muscle spindles (intrafusal fibers) is essential for this reaction, the degree of spasticity is often roughly proportional to the degree of hyper-reflexia and muscle clonus. It is also a good idea to attempt to move two or three joints in an erratic and unpredictable fashion, to avoid a patient's inadvertent "help" in moving the body part for you.

The other type of hypertonia, rigidity, is defined as involuntary muscular resistance felt when moving a resting joint, which persists as the joint is moved through its entire range of motion. It is sometimes referred to as "gooseneck" rigidity since, as in bending a microphone holder, resistance is felt in all planes of movement. Usually, this finding is consistent with lesions of the extrapyramidal pathways. It is believed that the mechanism for this may be related to muscle spindle mechanism interference from diseased extrapyramidal structures.

This test is performed in the same manner as the test for spasticity except that brisk stretch is unnecessary. All ranges of joint-muscle range of motion are affected, and generally speaking, all body muscles are involved. This is not to say that rigidity may not be more pronounced in the neck or upper extremities or on the right side as compared to the left. One should note that like spasticity, rigidity will not affect individual muscles without involving the other local muscles or antagonists. Remember, spasticity and rigidity are not mutually exclusive, and combinations or mixtures of these phenomena are common.

Hypotonia

Hypotonia is usually indicative of neurological damage at the level of the reflex arc, though cerebellar disease may cause diffuse hypotonia. Lesions of the motor nerve cell body (in the spinal cord or brainstem), ventral root, motor nerve axon, neuromyal junction, or even of effectors of the sensory arc, including the sensory axon, nerve cell body, and dorsal root, might yield hypotonia. Additionally, primary myopathies, neural shock, and cerebellar disease may also cause hypotonia.

Neural shock is a phenomenon that is in no way related to vascular shock. Neural shock may occur following acute, severe upper motor neuron damage, in either the brain (cerebral shock) or the spinal cord (spinal shock or diatesis), due to such events as cerebral infarction or spinal cord transection. The unique finding here is that a suddenly occurring and severe upper motor neuron lesion, which would (and eventually will) typically cause central nervous system findings, first causes only peripheral type neurological findings.

All neurological signs can be divided into deficit and release phenomena. Deficit phenomena would be defined as a loss of normal neurological function. Reductions in muscle tone, muscle stretch reflexes, muscle strength, and muscle volume would all fall into the category of deficit phenomena. Lower motor neuron lesions produce only deficit phenomena.

Release phenomena would be defined as exaggerations or perversions of normal neurological function and are due to a loss of cortical inhibition. Hyper-reflexia, hypertonia, and pathological reflexes would be considered release phenomena (so named due to the release from descending cortical inhibition). Release phenomena are only associated with central nervous system motor lesions, which may produce both deficit and release phenomena.

Immediately following the appearance of an acute, severe central nervous system lesion, only deficit phenomena may appear (neural shock). It is usually impossible to assess whether or not full or partial function will be regained in this stage. As time passes, release phenomena may or (one hopes) may not appear. If release phenomena appear, functional return will be impaired.

INVOLUNTARY MOVEMENTS

Prior to a discussion of dyskinesias, or disorders of voluntary movement, it should be noted that many actions have both voluntary and involuntary components—posture, breathing, and sphincter action, to name a few. Also, certain individuals possess greater ability to control voluntary and even so-called involuntary muscular actions. With that said, the definition of involuntary movements, for our purposes, will be those that the patient cannot start or stop at the doctor's command.

The involuntary movements characteristic of a given dyskinesia may be caused by a structural or biochemical nervous system lesion. In order to diagnose their presence, first discuss the evolution of the disorder with the patient during the history. You must seek information about when the movements started, when they appear or disappear, and what (if anything) exacerbates them. Physical findings can be noted during the physical/neurological examination. These include the pattern, distribution, rate, amplitude, and force of the movements.

Once observed, most movements will fall into a specific category.

Certain apparently involuntary movements are actually normal. For example, physiological tremor is a shaking noted in the fingers with the arms extended and is merely a manifestation of the alternating contractions of agonists and antagonists required to maintain any posture. Variability of the degree of tremor between individuals is great and ranges from hands that are steady as a rock to hands that are very shaky. The tremors occur at approximately 10 Hz. Physiological synkinesias are involuntary but normal movements accompanying certain voluntary movements. Myoclonic jerks are startle reactions and are usually normal occurrences. The jerks may involve the whole body or just large muscle groups. (Myoclonic jerks occurring regularly while the person is in the state between waking and sleeping, though, are considered to constitute a type of seizure disorder.) Finally, benign fasciculations are twitches within a muscle that often occur after exercise and are not pathological.

Involuntary movements may, of course, also be due to pathological events. For example, pyramidal tract disease will cause paralysis of voluntary movements and deforming spastic postures. Extrapyramidal tract disease will spare voluntary movements but will cause notable slowing of movement, as well as rigid and excessive involuntary movements. The dyskinesias that result from disease may be divided into hypokinesia and hyperkinesia. Hypokinesia is decreased movement, such as is observed in depression or parkinsonism. Hyperkinesia is increased movement; it may be categorized according to the list that follows. It is interesting to note that all of the below-mentioned disorders are exacerbated by emotional stress, and all decrease with repose. Patients can also suffer from any combination of the listed conditions.

- tremor
  1. emotional: A rapid tremor of low amplitude that worsens with volitional movements.
  2. familial: A hereditary tremor that usually affects the hands.
  3. senile: Similar in character to familial tremor, and associated with aging.
  4. parkinsonian: A "pill-rolling" movement of the hands seen when they are at rest that disappears or damps down during volitional movement; due to an extrapyramidal lesion (i.e., basal ganglion lesion).
  5. intention: A tremor that worsens with refined volitional movements; usually due to cerebellar pathology.
  6. postural: A tremor that occurs during maintenance of an intentional posture; disappears with movement.
- nontremorous hyperkinesia or chorea: Random, quick movements simulating fragments of normal movements (fidgets).
- athetosis: Slow, writhing movements of the fingers and extremities that may come and go and are usually associated with pyramidal tract signs.
- dystonia: Slow, alternating contraction and relaxation of agonists and antagonists, with one movement predominating for a long time; causes fixed joint contractures.
- hemiballismus: A violent, flinging movement of half of the body.
- tics: Quick, stereotyped, repetitive movements of the face, tongue, or extremities; usually associated with emotional stress.
- akathisia: Motor unrest manifested as continual shifting of posture and/or movements; associated with Parkinson's disease and psychotropic medication use.
- epilepsy: Tonic or clonic spasms of all or part of the body.
- tardive dyskinesias and other medication-related disorders: See below.

Movement disorders secondary to use of psychotropic medication stand as the largest single category of involuntary movement. A biochemical lesion resulting from long-term exposure to certain agents is responsible for the disorders seen. Most prominent among these is tardive dyskinesia, which is characterized by smacking movements of the lips, jaw, and tongue.

SUGGESTED READING

Arnold LA. *Chiropractic Procedural Examination.* 2nd ed. Seminole, Fla: Seminole Printing, Inc; 1979:40, 52–53.

Chusid JG. *Correlative Neuroanatomy & Functional Neurology.* 17th ed. Norwalk, Conn: Lange Medical Publications; 1982:195–210.

DeJong RN. *The Neurologic Examination.* 4th ed. New York, NY: Harper & Row; 1979:39–78.

Van Allen MW. *Pictorial Manual of Neurologic Tests.* 2nd ed. Chicago, Ill: Year Book Medical Publishers, Inc; 1981:65–83.

chapter 5

The Somatic Sensory Examination

All sensory abnormalities are characterized by an increase, perversion, decrease, or loss of sensation. Consciously perceived sensations lend themselves to sensory testing. It is incorrect, however, to assume that only conscious sensation may be altered by disease. Explanation of testing procedures for the special senses will be found in Chapter 3 on the cranial nerves, as it is the cranial nerve pathways that mediate those sensations. By testing conscious sensation, however, information regarding the level of a neurological lesion can be obtained (see Figure 5-1).

The sensory exam is often the final component of the formal neurological examination. It is often considered to be fatiguing, time consuming, and of limited usefulness, and it is often completely omitted by both the doctor of chiropractic and the doctor of medicine, including the medical neurologist. These beliefs probably arise from the fact that the sensory examination is primarily a subjective one, in that it is dependent on accurate patient responses. Additionally, it requires some special diagnostic materials (pin, cotton wisp, tuning fork, hot and cold test tubes, two-point tester, etc.) and testing of the entire integument, to be complete.

The fact is that the sensory exam can be partially objectified by the use of the reliability checks described below, and that a simple, brief screening of modalities related to specific spinal cord districts may offer considerable information. This is true both in serious neurological disorders noted for their early or profound sensory findings (multiple sclerosis, tabes dorsalis, etc.) and in disorders noted for their complete lack of effect on sensory findings (amyotrophic lateral sclerosis, spinal muscular atrophy, etc.). Detailed and time-consuming sensory testing may be necessary in the presence of frank sensory involvement. The sensory examination may be used to detect the hysterical, somatizing, or frankly malingering patient by testing the accuracy of a patient's responses via reliability checking. In chiropractic practice, another noted use is to detect areas of increased sensitivity to pinprick (i.e., hyperalgesia), which are often dermatomally related to corresponding areas of spinal subluxations.[1]

Some of the terminology involved in sensory assessment can be confusing, so some definitions are provided in Appendix 5-A. When describing findings, one must keep in mind that if the primary sensory modalities of pain, touch, temperature, etc., are not in working order, then the deficit is referred to as an anesthesia or analgesia. The primary modalities must necessarily be intact before the term "agnosia" can be applied.

The sensory exam should be performed in a comfortable setting, preferably with the patient recumbent. This not only puts the patient at ease

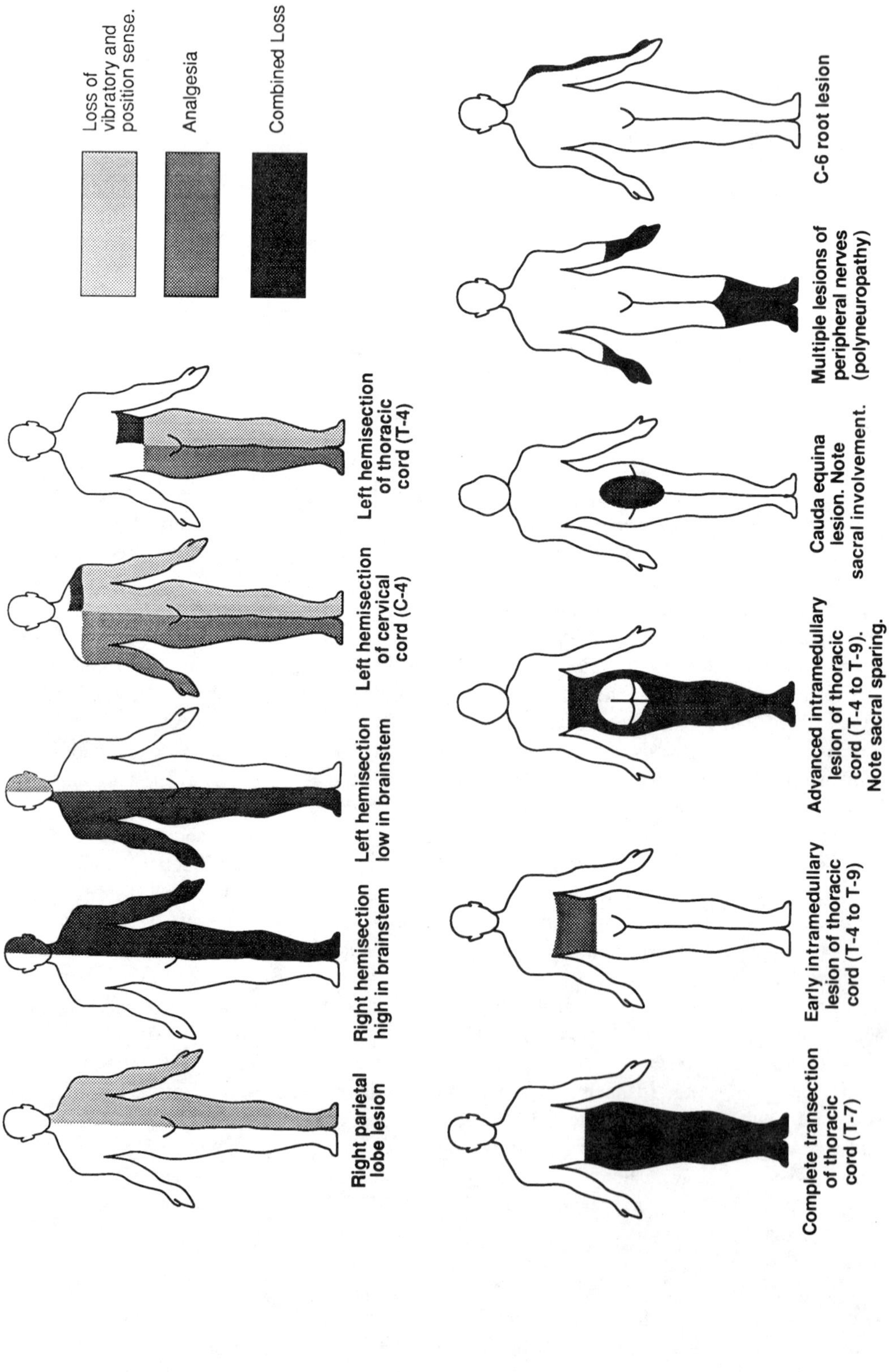

Figure 5-1 Sensory disturbances and location of lesions.

but also makes it difficult for the patient to see the procedure being performed. The history should include questions regarding sensation, so that the examiner is aware of patient-reported sensory aberrations, though many sensory abnormalities will be uncovered by the examination for the first time. The type (sharp, dull, etc.) and quality (e.g., perversions) of any sensory disturbance, as well as the quantity or degree and location of involvement, must be noted. It is often useful to draw the area of sensory loss on the patient with a skin-marking pencil, for later comparison to various charts. Also of import is the observation of any injuries that may have gone unnoticed by the patient (a sign of analgesia) or of trophic skin changes, which are often related to sensory problems. Side-to-side differences, as well as grimacing, withdrawal of the part, pupil dilation, pulse acceleration, and perspiration, should also be noted. Testing should be performed several times in succession if a sensory abnormality is unveiled, and repeated testing on follow-up examination is important as well. This will verify a finding as well as document improvement or progression. The findings of the examination can be documented quite easily by coding them on a figure in your progress notes similar to the one shown in Figure 5-2.

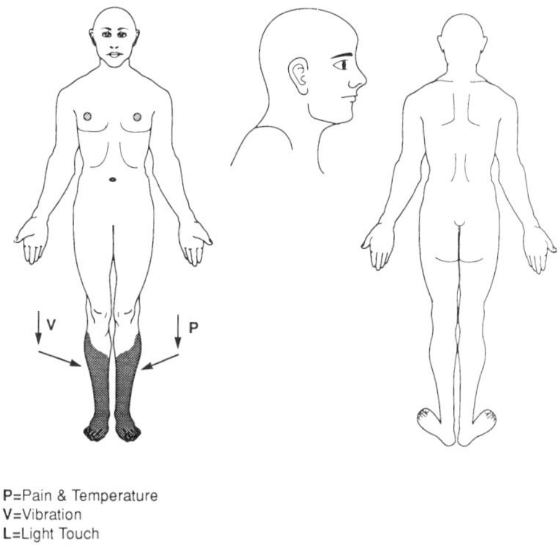

Figure 5-2 Sample form for recording the findings of the somatic sensory exam. The left-hand figure shows one method of recording findings.

As with most parts of an examination, but especially true for sensory testing, a complete explanation of the procedure should be undertaken prior to examination performance. Increased patient understanding will aid him or her in compliance and decrease apprehension, especially about tests performed with a pin, or with the patient's eyes closed.

Sherrington's[2] list of sensations: exteroceptive, proprioceptive, and interoceptive, is a very usable breakdown in clinical neurology, but describing sensation as either superficial, deep, or multimodal is even simpler and more suited to understanding examination procedures. A review of deep and superficial sensory pathways within the peripheral and central nervous systems is of paramount importance when attempting to understand the rationale behind sensory examination procedure performance. Therefore, each division of this chapter will be prefaced by a review of the anatomical pathways of each sensation discussed.

BASIC CONCEPTS OF SENSORINEURAL INNERVATION: THE THREE-NEURON PATHWAY

Recent studies of neurocircuitry have successfully challenged many pre-existing concepts. We would be well advised to use these anatomical discussions as clinically relevant guidelines and not as absolutes. Indeed, the nervous system is far too complex to be imagined as some kind of switchboard. Instead, it must be thought of in more holographic terms. Plasticity or changeability of the nervous system is well documented, and neural areas and pathways in general are better thought of as areas with higher concentrations of neurons contributing to specific function(s) rather than as areas of specific functions. From a strictly clinical standpoint, however, the following pathways are quite valid, and their understanding is still required in order to be a competent clinician.

Generally speaking, specific end organs (see Figure 5-3) are attached to nerve cells whose cell bodies lie in the dorsal root ganglia. Relatively specific stimuli excite these nerve end organs; if threshold is reached in any one of them, an impulse travels along its attached peripheral nerve (neuron 1) back to the nerve root from which the nerve arises.

There the impulse is ultimately shunted to the dorsal root of neuron 1, either as lateral (superficial) or medial (deep) division information. Neuron 1 then enters the spinal cord and synapses with neuron 2, which crosses the midline and ascends a central nervous system tract (lemniscus), carrying the impulse to the nucleus ventralis posterolateralis and nucleus ventralis posteromedialis of the thalamus. The impulse finally is transferred to neuron 3 (also termed a thalamocortical radiation) at these thalamic nuclei; the thalamocortical radiations travel to the somesthetic cortex, located on the postcentral gyrus of the parietal lobe, where body part reorganization and localization of stimuli probably occur (see Figure 5-4). (Information from the lower part of the body [sacral, lumbar, lower thoracic] always ascends medially within the cord whereas information from higher parts of the body [upper thoracic and cervical] travels more laterally [i.e., superficially] within the cord.)

THE SENSATIONS AND THEIR CLINICAL ASSESSMENT

The sensations can, as has been noted, be divided into two types, superficial and deep. The superficial sensations, also classified as exteroceptive or cutaneous sensations, are pain, temperature, and touch. The receptors for these sensations lie in the skin and mucous membranes and are responsible not only for these sensations in themselves but also for the sensory leg of the so-called superficial reflexes (Chapter 6). Testable entities in the office include superficial pain, temperature, and superficial (light, nondiscriminative) touch. These are carried in the anterolateral district of the cord. The deep sensations also encompass pain and touch, as well as proprioception. Deep pain is a poorly localized, slower, deep, and "achy" variety of pain. Deep sensations are carried in the posterior district of the spinal cord. The highest level of sensation is the multimodal or association cortex sensations. These sensations require intact superficial and deep systems and are responsible for perception of things such as weight and texture.

Pain

Pain is the primary reason an individual seeks the services of a physician. In most instances pain is a reliable indicator of underlying pathophysiology. In other cases it can be confusing and misleading in regard to the pain's origin.

What is of utmost importance to the clinical investigator is an appreciation of the relationship between pain and nociception. Pain is a completely subjective experience. It is a final perception based upon the interpretation of some stimulus as unpleasant. It is very difficult to measure to any significant degree, due to wide variations between individuals. It has been intensively investigated, but psychological, genetic, congenital, familial, physical, and sociological factors continue to confound its study in the human. In the office we can only evaluate the patient's sensibility to a painful stimulus elicited by exciting either the superficial or the deep pain receptors. That is, we can never truly tell whether or not a patient is perceiving something as unpleasant. Of course, you may establish a personal opinion as to whether or not an individual is or is not having a perception of discomfort. Keep in mind, however, that while this opinion is based upon experience, and perhaps the judicious use of certain tests used to detect malingering or to objectify pain, it is merely an educated opinion.

Nociception is the transmission and modulation of potentially or frankly noxious stimuli. Free nerve endings are responsible for a range of non-nociceptive sensations, but their increasing stimulation will usually result in nociception. The density of nociceptive fibers is in direct proportion to the sensitivity of specific tissues,

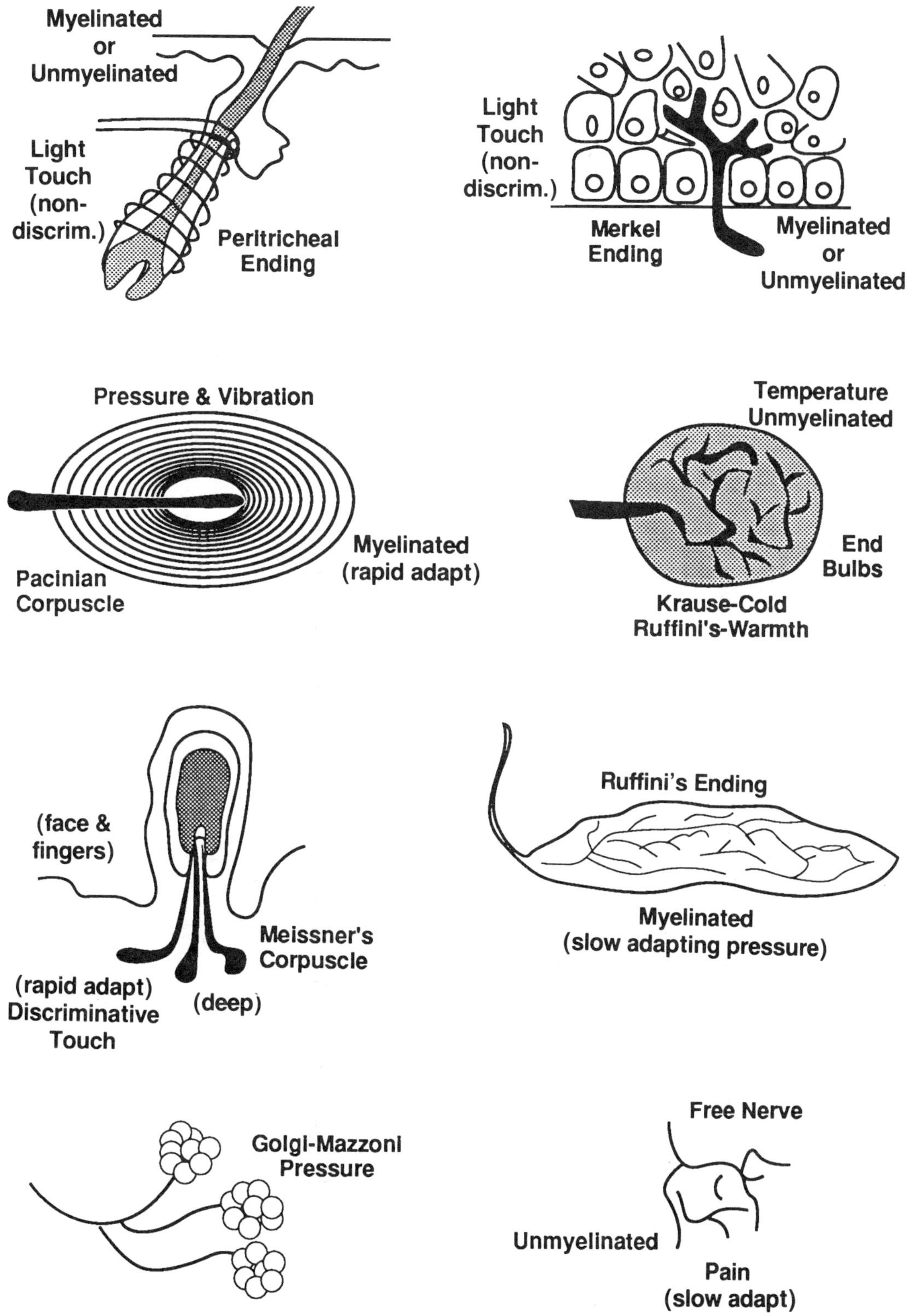

Figure 5-3 Sensory receptors.

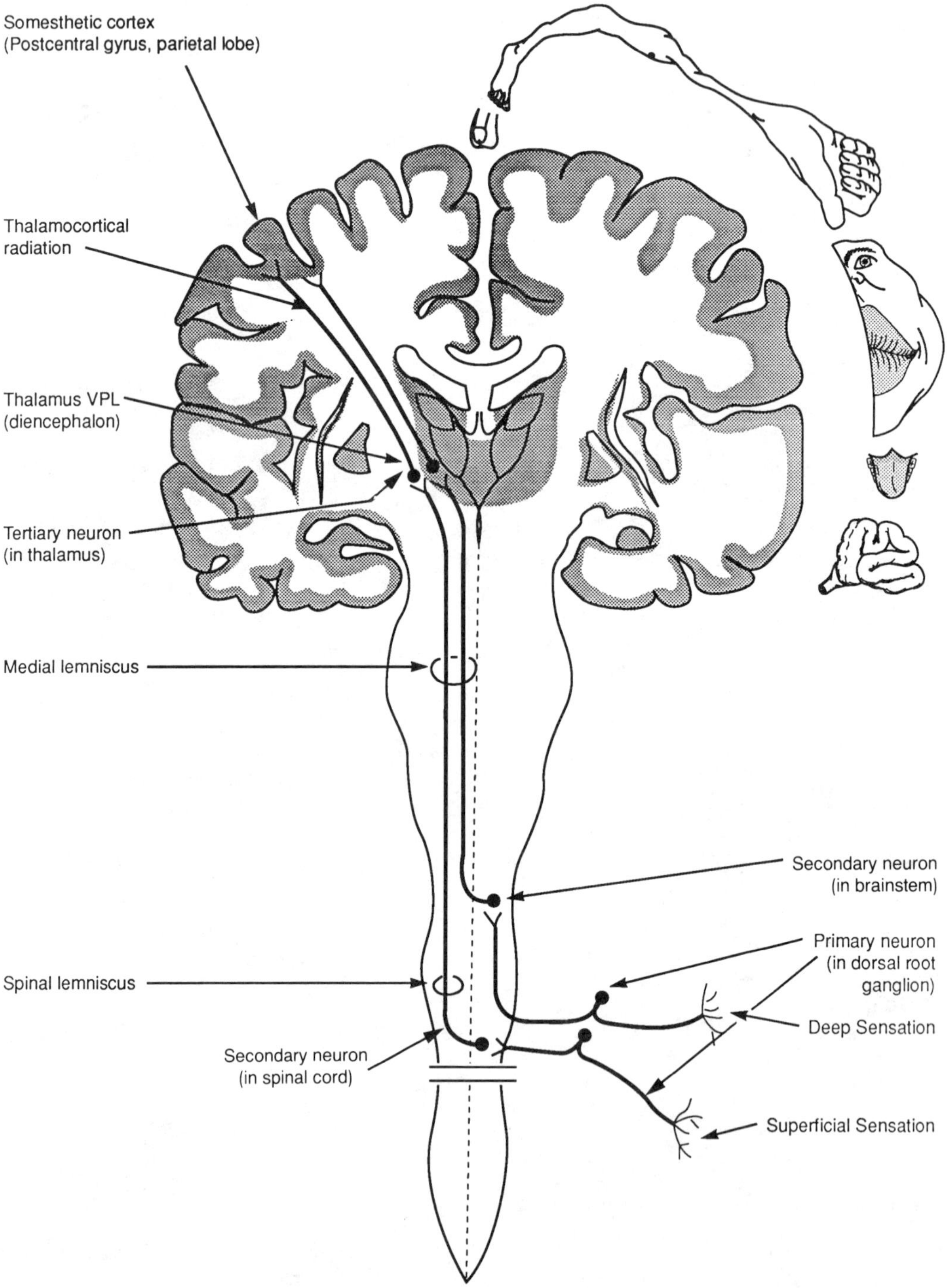

Figure 5-4 The three-neuron pathway. VPL indicates ventralis posterolateralis.

with the spinal joints receiving more than their fair share. Certain joint tissues are devoid of nociceptors: articular cartilage, the inner annulus and nucleus of intervertebral discs, and synovial membranes.

Since the nociceptive system is inactive in the normal joint, to activate these fibers you must first have noxious stimuli, which may be mechanical, thermal, or chemical. Noxious mechanical stimuli may be caused by acute trauma or associated with repetitive microtrauma. The subluxation syndrome might also be considered a mechanical stimulant of nociception. Noxious thermal stimuli may be due to exposure to excessive heat or coldness. Chemical causes of noxious stimuli are traditionally overlooked by most primary care physicians. Many substances have been shown to excite nociceptors, for example, potassium, histamine, serotonin, plasma kinins, prostaglandins, and substance P, which may be released directly from damaged tissues or from contiguous undamaged tissues.

Nociceptive impulses travel, for the most part, along the slightly myelinated A delta fibers and along the unmyelinated C fibers. Fibers as large as A beta may be involved in modulating nociception at extremely fast speeds. These fibers project, via the dorsal root, to the dorsolateral fasciculus (Lissauer's tract; see Figure 5-5) where they may ascend or descend several cord levels, or they may synapse at the same segment where they enter. The synapse may be made in the outer laminae (I and II), or it may occur deeper in the dorsal horn. Lamina I contains a population of second-order afferents (neuron 2 of the three-neuron path) that travel directly to the nucleus ventralis posterolateralis of the thalamus as the anterolateral spinothalamic tract, where they synapse with third-order afferents (neuron 3 of the three-neuron pathway), the cortical radiations, and ascend to the primary somesthetic cortex (see Figure 5-6). Anterior and lateral spinothalamic tracts appear to carry similar overall information. About 45% of the information carried by the spinothalamic

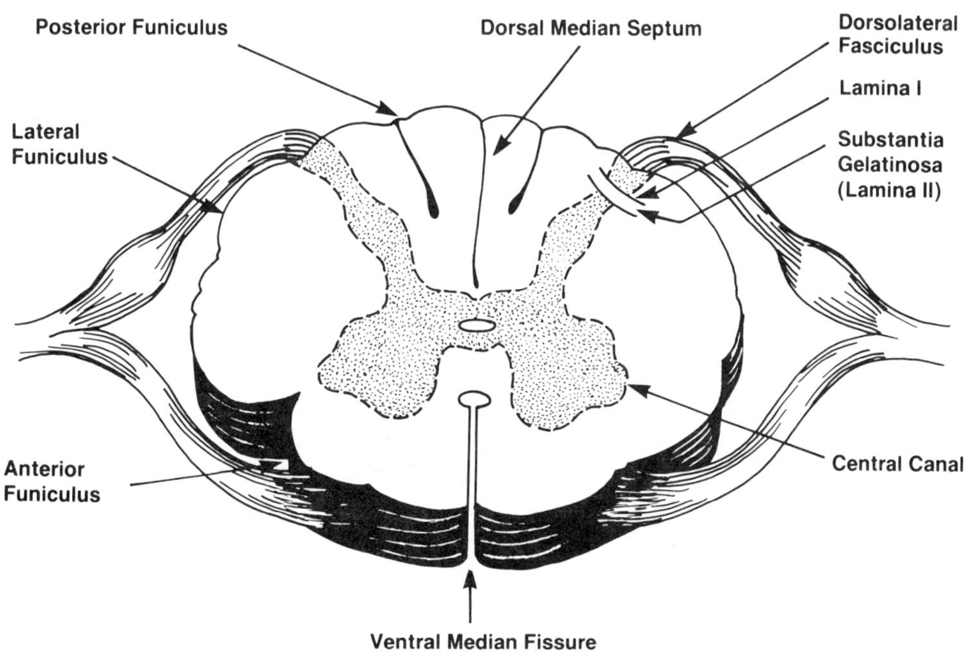

Figure 5-5 Anatomy of the spinal cord.

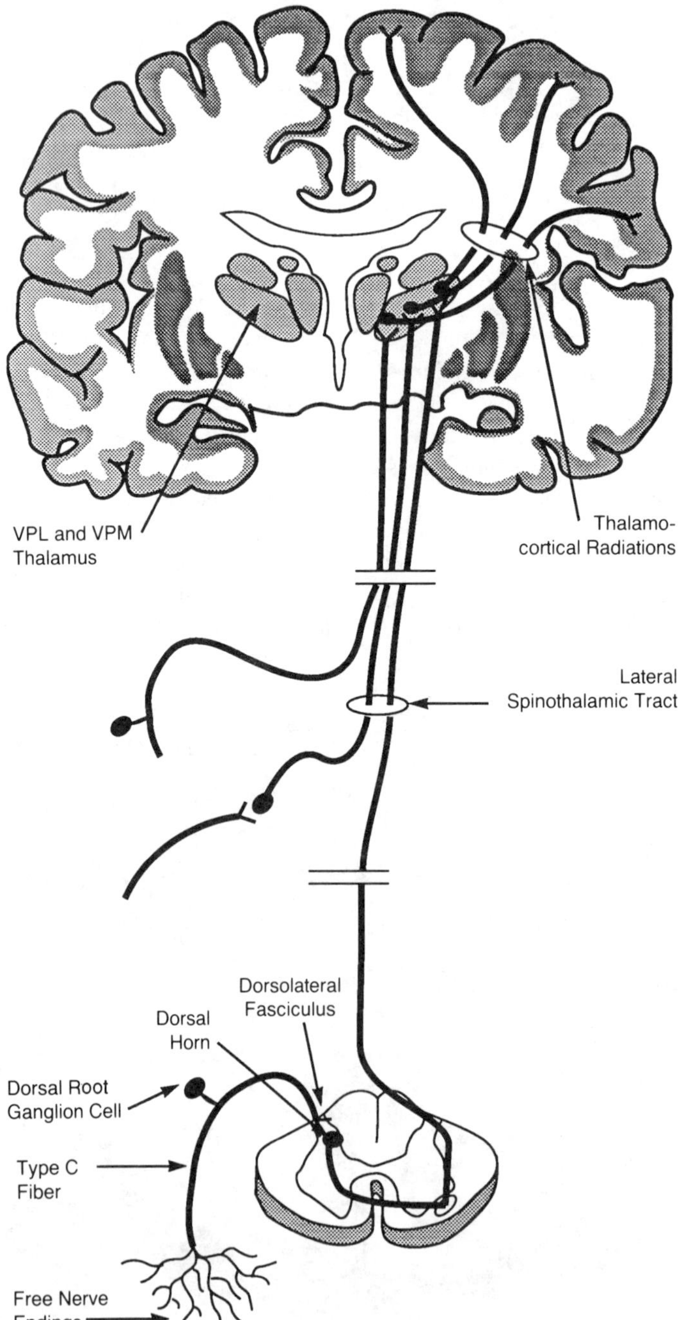

Figure 5-6 The fundamental pain pathway. VPL indicates ventralis posterolateralis; VPM, ventralis posteromedialis.

tracts is nonspecific, 35% is nociceptive, and 20% is non-nociceptive. It appears that information that strictly retains its somatotopical organization (ascending in lamina I) would be used more in relation to localization of pain and not to the painful experience itself.

Lamina II (the substantia gelatinosa) contains a population of interneurons (short neurons interposed between neuron 1 and neuron 2) that synapse with deeper dorsal horn cell groups. These cells use enkephalin neurotransmitters and may actually inhibit the further centripetal movement of nociceptive signals. Deeper laminae appear to contain cell groups that project to medial thalamic centers and appear to be involved with more of the nondiscriminating phenomena associated with the pain response. These projections make connections with the reticular formation (for an autonomic pain component), the periaqueductal gray matter (for possible pain suppression), and the hypothalamus (for endocrine-limbic system and emotional responses). Spinocervical and propriospinal connections are also present.

Descending inhibition places a second feedback-type level of pain modulation. Nociception, as well as cortical input, seems to stimulate activity in the cells of the periaqueductal gray matter. These cells, via enkephalin neurotransmitters, stimulate cells in the nucleus raphe magnus. Cells in this nucleus inhibit, via serotonergic synapses, the second-order dorsal horn cells from centripetal transmission of nociception. A similar descending system of inhibition may be achieved through the nucleus reticularis paragigantocellularis, and others, whose cells employ the neurotransmitters serotonin, noradrenaline, and endogenous opioids to exert an inhibitory effect on incoming nociceptive stimuli.

Clinical Examination

It should be apparent that a complaint of pain involves complicated neurocircuitry. In the clinical setting we may test the most fundamental pain pathways, but we must be cautious about using expected patient responses and known neurological distributions as absolutes. One can appreciate how pain thresholds and levels of inhibition may cloud the clinical picture.

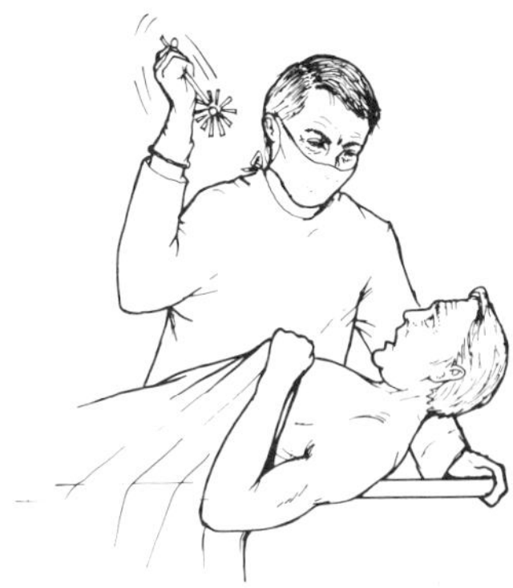

Figure 5-7 Approach testing of superficial pain perception in a manner that minimizes patient fears.

Superficial pain is the most commonly tested sensory modality. It is tested routinely with a pin or pinwheel.

The patient should be supine and comfortable. The instructions must be clear: "After you close your eyes, I am going to gently touch you with the sharp or dull side of this pin(wheel) in several places. Please tell me whether it feels sharp or dull." While offering these simple instructions, be sure to demonstrate what you intend to do on yourself. This will help eliminate the apprehension associated with being stuck with a pin while the eyes are closed (see Figure 5-7). Be sure to hold the pinwheel at its marked balance point, so only a minimal amount of pressure is applied to the patient's skin (see Figure 5-8). Should the patient move suddenly, the points should easily bounce away.

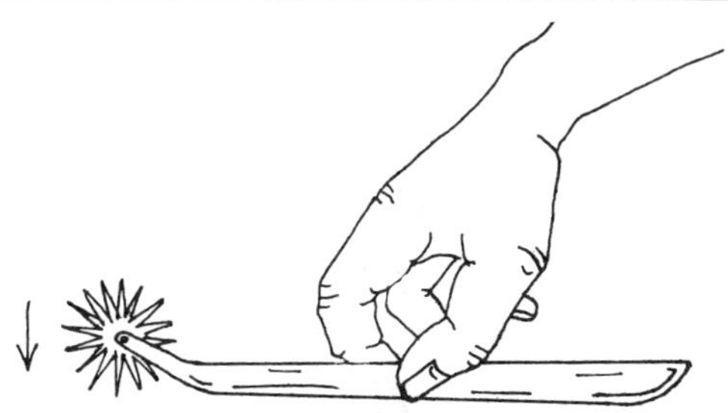

Figure 5-8 Hold pinwheel gently at the balance point.

You are actually testing only for sharp sensation, but an occasional dull stimulus should be used as a reliability check. This is useful for the patient who actually cannot feel the sharp stimulus but does sense the touch or pressure of the stimulus and responds "sharp." This patient would respond "sharp" to even a dull stimulus. Be sure to stagger the time sequence between stimuli, as a patient's response of sharp may become an automatic one as opposed to an accurate one. Be sure to offer a sharp stimulus in every area where a dull stimulus is offered. Obviously, a dull stimulus would only be testing touch or pressure and not achieve the goal of testing for pain.

If an abnormality is found, always test from areas of decreased sensation to areas of greater sensation. If a hypalgesia is noted, begin in the area of greatest loss and instruct the patient to tell you when he or she feels the sharp stimulus. Mark that point with a skin-marking pencil and then begin again in a different direction until a map of the hypalgesia or analgesia is obtained. If an area of hyperalgesia is noted, move from the normal area to the hypersensitive one and again make a map. This procedure, when painstakingly performed, will yield the highest degree of accuracy.

Nerve roots receive stimuli in a dermatomal pattern (see Figure 5-9), and peripheral nerves receive stimuli in a peripheral nerve pattern. In a screening examination it is usually sufficient to simply run the pinwheel down each side of the patient's paraspinal area and across several suspect dermatomes or peripheral sensory areas. Marked differences between dermatomes, or between right and left sides of the same dermatome, may warrant further investigation.

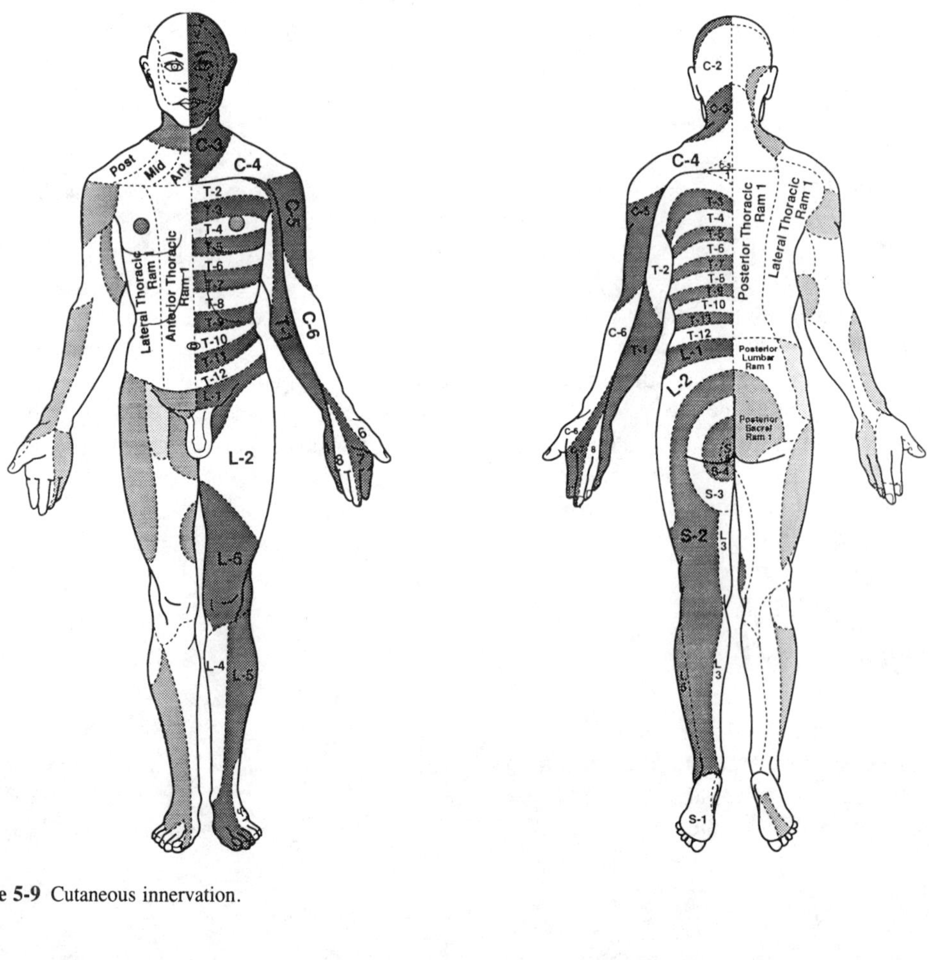

Figure 5-9 Cutaneous innervation.

An additional clinical application for the pain-sensory exam, which I have found to possess surprising clinical value, is that areas of increased sensitivity to pinprick (hyperalgesia) are often related to areas of spinal subluxation. During the sensory evaluation of the typical chiropractic patient, it is uncommon to find areas of frank sensory loss. It is far more common to have the patient wince or retract the body part being tested due to increased sensitivity (see Figure 5-10). The particular dermatomal or paraspinal level of this patient reaction will often correlate well with the area of primary spinal subluxation. This is probably due to the facilitative or irritative effect that spinal subluxation may have on the nervous sytem at a specific segmental level.

Temperature

Specialized receptors for cold and hot exist (the end bulbs of Krause and Ruffini), though intense stimulation by an extreme of either temperature (especially heat) will stimulate free nerve endings and therefore cause pain. The pathway for temperature sensation seems to be identical to that for pain, and it is therefore unnecessary to routinely perform a test of temperature since testing for pain sensation will effectively test temperature sensation as well. Furthermore, the equipment needed to test for pain sensation is much simpler than that needed to test temperature sensation, i.e., hot and cold test tubes. However, it is believed that temperature testing is superior for specific localization of a deficit, so it may be performed after a sensory abnormality is unveiled using a pin or pinwheel.

Clinical Examination

Again, patient instructions must be clear: "Please respond to my touching you with these objects, while your eyes are closed, by saying whether you feel hot or cold." Cold stimuli should be between 41° to 50°F, and hot between 104° and 113°F. These ranges must be adhered to to avoid free nerve ending stimulation.

Touch

Specialized receptors, known as the tactile discs of Merkle, present in the skin and mucous membranes and in peritricheal endings around the hair follicles, are sensitive to light or non-discriminating touch. The neural pathway for light touch is basically the same as for pain, using mostly slightly myelinated fibers that ascend in the anterolateral columns of the cord to the thalamus. Deep touch, or discriminatory (well-localized) touch, is thought to be initiated by receptors in the hairless portions of the skin known as the corpuscles of Meissner. This sen-

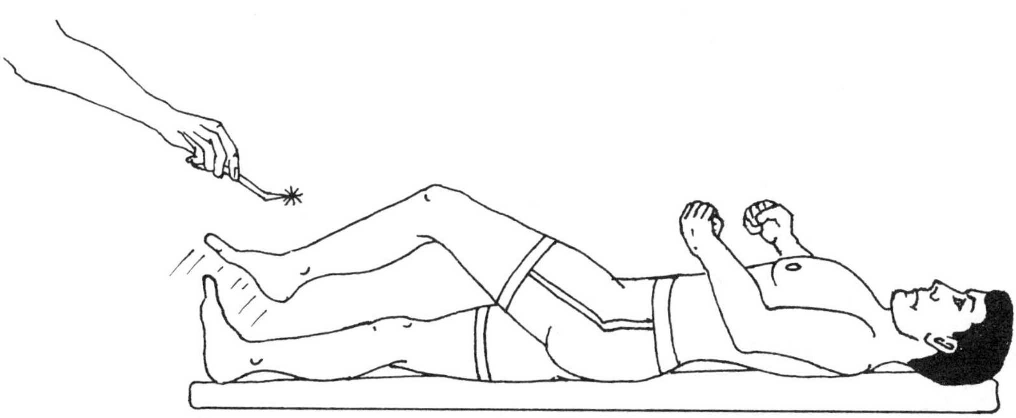

Figure 5-10 Exaggerated response to skin pricking. Cutaneous hyperalgesia noted in spinal subluxation syndrome.

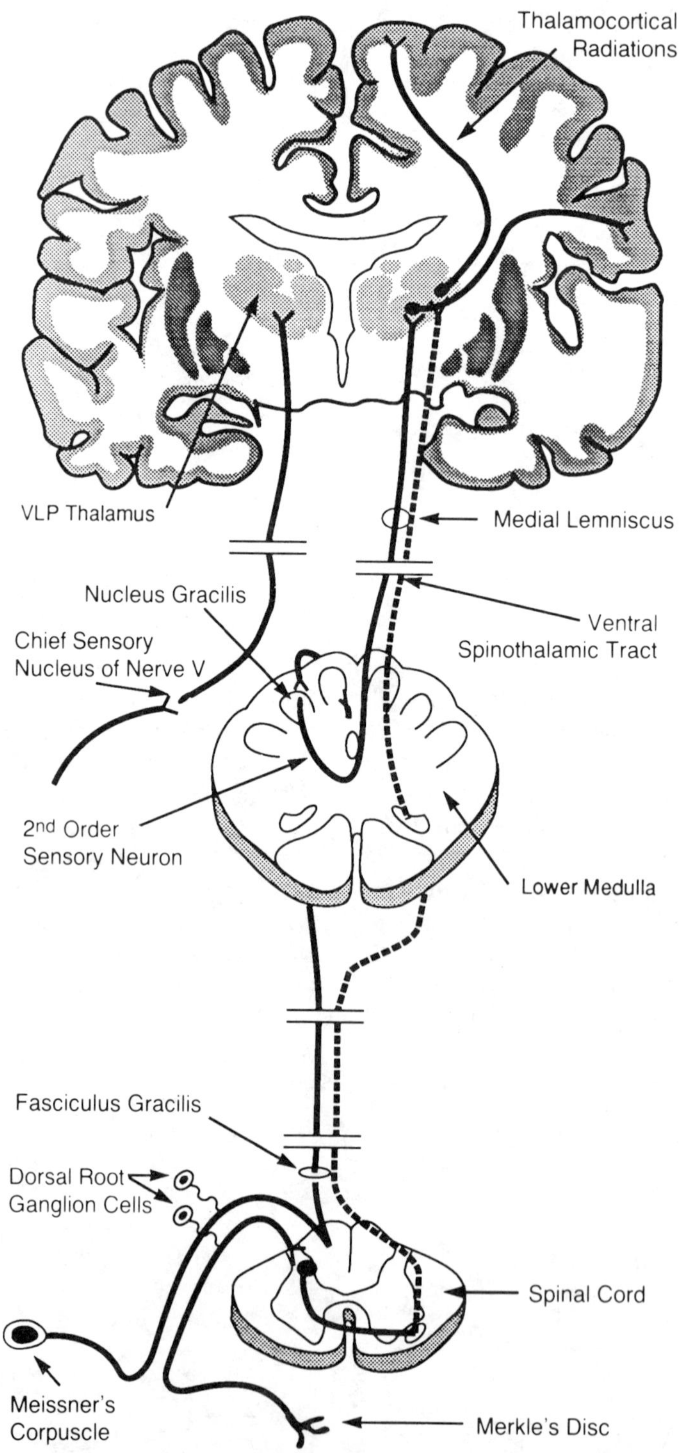

Figure 5-11 The afferent pathways for superficial and deep touch. VLP indicates ventralis posterolateralis.

sation is apparently carried primarily by large-diameter, heavily myelinated fibers through the posterior spinal cord district. Figure 5-11 shows the afferent pathway for both types of touch. There are, therefore, two separate and highly different pathways mediating the sensation of touch.

Due to overlap and duplication of function, touch is considered the least desirable sensation to use for evaluation and localizing of neurological lesions.

Clinical Examination

The clinical examination of light touch is performed quite simply by touching a wisp of cotton, a piece of tissue, or a soft brush to the patient's face, upper and lower extremities, and trunk; gentle fingertip touch may also be employed (see Figure 5-12). The patient's eyes should be closed, and he or she should be instructed to say when a stimulus is felt, as well as point to where it was felt and comment on side-to-side differences. I have found that doing both sides of the body simultaneously is the most useful method. It allows the patient to compare side to side immediately and is therefore far more sensitive to subtle differences. Expect thick-skinned and calloused areas of the body to be proportionally less sensitive.

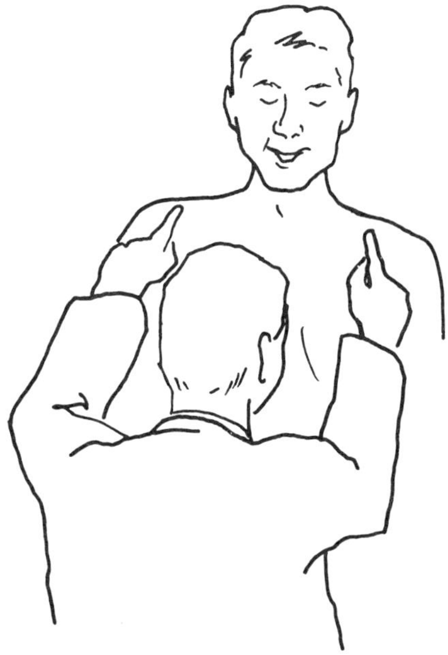

Figure 5-12 Testing the sense of light touch bilaterally.

Proprioception

Proprioception, or knowledge of oneself, arises from information about movement and position obtained from receptors in the joints, bones, muscles, tendons, and ligaments. Much of this information does not reach the level of consciousness (unconscious proprioception) but is involved in movement, balance, and coordination reflexes. Clinically testable proprioceptive functions include motion, position, vibration, pressure, and deep pain.

The pathway for proprioceptive sensations is different from that of exteroceptive or superficial sensation, in that the stimulus is carried by a first-order sensory neuron that ascends the spinal cord ipsilaterally in the posterior columns before its first synapse in the lower brainstem. The principal receptors for proprioception are the neuromuscular and neurotendinous spindles, the Golgi tendon organs, and four varieties of joint mechanoreceptors. Information regarding position, movement, and deep pain causes stimulation or sedation of these receptors. Impulses are carried by large-diameter, heavily myelinated fibers (type A), which traverse the medial division of the spinal nerve root to ascend ipsilaterally in the posterior spinal cord columns of the fasciculus cuneatus (fasciculus of Burdach) and the fasciculus gracilis (fasciculus of Goll). The first synapse occurs in the corresponding medullary nuclei, the nucleus cuneatus or the nucleus gracilis, depending upon whether the information originated in the upper or the lower half of the body, respectively (see Figure 5-13).

A synapse occurs at these medullary nuclei with second-order sensory neurons, known as the internal arcuate fibers, which cross (the great sensory decussation) at the level of the lower medulla to ascend in the medial lemniscus, pri-

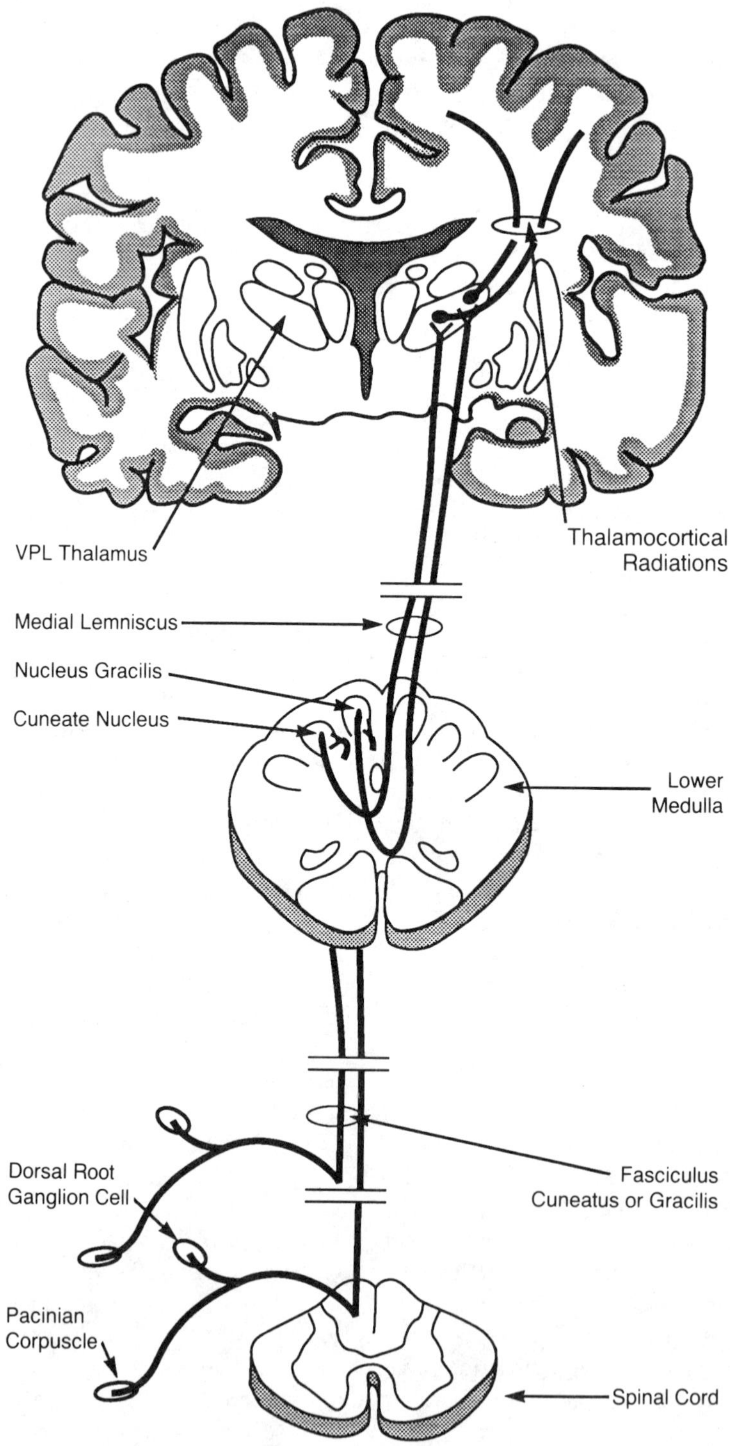

Figure 5-13 The deep pathway. VPL indicates ventralis posterolateralis.

marily to the nucleus ventralis posterolateralis of the thalamus. As with all other sensory pathways discussed, the third-order sensory neurons with which the arcuate fibers synapse are thalamocortical projections to the somesthetic cortex on the postcentral gyrus of the parietal lobe.

Clinical Examination

It should be emphasized that since specific modalities of sensation (e.g., as position sense, vibration pressure, texture movement, localization of touch, two-point discrimination, weight, and ability to decipher letters or numbers written on the skin) are carried in the posterior columns of the cord, lesions that affect these sensations while sparing sensations associated with anterolateral (spinothalamic) cord function (pain, temperature, light touch) are likely of spinal cord origin. This splitting of sensory modalities may be of diagnostic value.

Vibration. Vibration is best tested by using a 128- or 256-Hz tuning fork. I much prefer the lower-frequency fork, as it is barely audible and the vibration is sustained for a longer period of time than is the case for the higher-frequency fork. It is generally believed, however, that the higher-frequency fork may be slightly more sensitive to subtle vibratory sense losses. The fork should be held at its node, or point of least movement, where the two branches of the fork come together. This will minimize damping of the vibration by your hand.

Since the synapse is in the brainstem, the primary neuron runs the length of the extremity, as well as the length of the spinal cord above the level of entry. Due to this fact, it is only necessary to test for vibration sense at the most distal points, such as the medial or lateral malleolus, and perhaps at the fingertips, in a routine screening procedure. Any diseased point along the peripheral nerve proximal to the area tested, as well as any lesion affecting the posterior columns, should be picked up using this method. If a deficit is noted, then testing can be done at any bony area of the body—classically, at the tibia, anterior superior iliac spine, sacrum, spinous process of a vertebra, sternum, clavicle, and styloid processes of the radius and ulna.

Tell the patient, "I am going to take this tuning fork and place it against your ankles while you close your eyes. Tell me if you feel a buzzing or vibration, and then tell me when you can't feel it anymore." Strike the tuning fork against your leg, hand, or any convenient structure, and wait to press it against the bony prominence until you can no longer hear it vibrating in the air. Be careful to palpate the area before application of the tuning fork, so as to place it over the boniest point. When the patient indicates that he or she can feel the vibrations, stop the fork from vibrating with your other hand and wait for the patient to tell you that he or she can no longer feel it. This serves both as verification that the patient understands the instructions and as a reliability check for a patient who can feel the coldness or touch of the fork but not the buzzing. Compare each side to your own ability to feel the vibration, as well as check side-to-side differences for the patient. The patient's sense of both the intensity and the duration of the vibratory stimulus is important, but usually it is the duration—specifically, a shortened duration of sensation—that alerts you to disease. Should the patient report what appears to be a decreased duration of sensation from one side to the other, I have developed a useful way of objectifying the difference. Retest the side that appears to be abnormal, or the side on which the patient felt the vibration for the shorter amount of time. When the patient reports that he or she can no longer feel the vibration, quickly place the fork on the opposite side of the body without restriking the fork. Ask the patient again if he or she can feel any vibrations. If the reply is yes, the patient's sensitivity is obviously diminished on the side tested first. Keep in mind that vibration should be stronger proximately, and that the upper extremities are usually more sensitive than are the lower extremities. Older patients are quite a bit less sensitive generally, and this is especially notable with the tuning fork test. Testing with the tuning fork is probably the most sensitive way to check for posterior spinal cord disease. Because larger diameter fibers carry vibratory sensations and these fibers are affected by compression, peripheral compression neuropathies may be demonstrated by tuning fork testing.

Joint Position. Joint position sensibility is not commonly tested in clinical practice unless Romberg (see below) or vibratory sensation testing reveals abnormalities. The results are more highly variable between patients, and the testing is more fatiguing, more difficult to interpret, and therefore far less practical as a screening tool than is vibration sense testing. However, in cases of obvious neurological disease, such as post-stroke patients, testing for sense of joint position is valuable.

A crude but quick and fairly reliable way to screen for abnormalities of this sense is the Romberg test. This test is performed having the patient stand with a narrow base and comparing his or her balance with eyes open and with eyes closed. Ability to stand followed by significant swaying or falling with the eyes closed is considered a positive Romberg and is often an early sign of posterior column disease (see Figure 5-14).

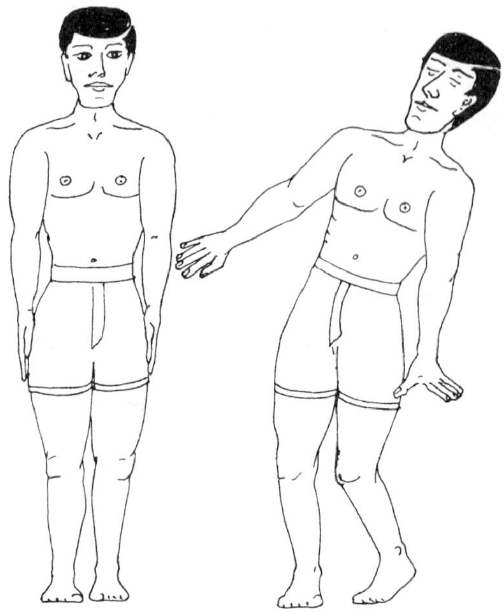

Figure 5-14 The Romberg test.

It is within normal limits for a patient to exhibit slight swaying with the eyes closed. This is especially true for older patients. The hysterical or malingering patient might fall against a convenient support. Involvement of the peripheral vestibular system may also cause the patient to sway more with eyes closed, though the presenting features of this disorder, such as nausea, vertigo, vomiting, etc., will usually clarify the test interpretation. Classically, the most severe response will always be associated with posterior column disease.

Many a doctor and student have confused the Romberg test with a test of cerebellar function. It is easy to see how this would occur, as the first part of the test, standing with a narrow base, will be difficult or impossible for the patient with cerebellar disease, who will act as though he or she is being flung from the midline by some force. The differentiation is clear when one understands that a positive Romberg occurs when the swaying or falling occurs dramatically upon closing the eyes, as the test is designed to compare station sense with eyes open versus eyes closed.

Both joint position and joint movement should be tested together. Early proprioceptive disease may be noted only in the distal extremities; later it will involve the larger, more proximal joints.

Usually one first tests a digit of the hands or feet. This digit should be isolated from the surrounding digits by physical separation with your hand. This will void the patient's receiving additional information about where the digit is by being able to feel it against a neighboring digit. Further, the digit should be grabbed by its sides, not by its top and bottom, so that pressure from below will not tell the patient that the joint is moving upward (see Figure 5-15).

Tell the patient, "I am going to move your second toe either up or down while you close your eyes. Respond by saying 'up' or 'down.'" The test must be repeated at least five or six times, as the patient has a 50% chance of guessing correctly the first time; the percentage of correct guesses diminishes rapidly with repetition. If poor results occur, compare side to side and move to larger, more proximal joints. Even a young, healthy person may have some difficulty with submaximal movements of the third and fourth digits, a tribute to the sensitivity of the test.

Alternatively, one of the patient's hands may be put in a position with the patient's eyes closed. He or she is then asked to describe the

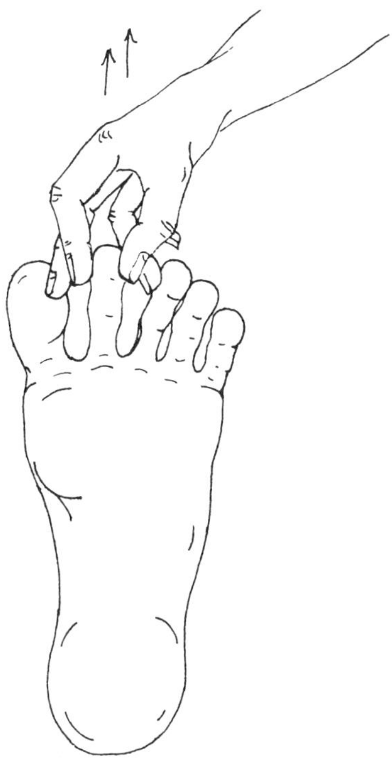

Figure 5-15 Testing for joint proprioception.

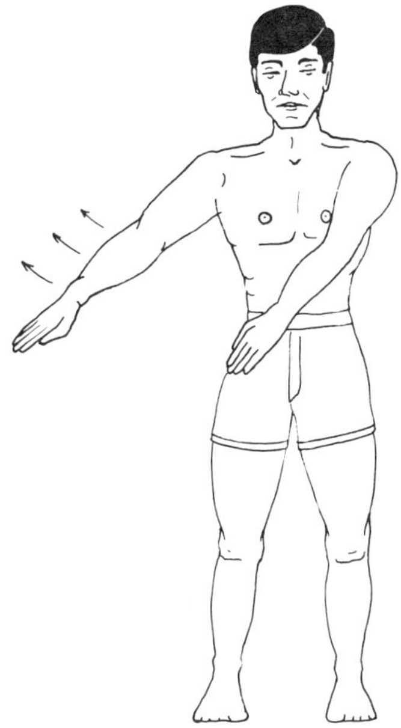

Figure 5-16 Testing for arm drifts.

position or imitate it with the other hand. Another commonly used procedure is to have the patient steadily hold both arms out in front with the eyes closed. Notable drift of one extremity is suggestive of joint sense difficulty, hemiparesis, or cerebellar disease (see Figure 5-16).

A good follow-up test for these procedures would be to hold one of the patient's extremities out in front of the body at a certain height and have the patient then move the other extremity to the same position at the same height while the eyes are closed.

Other methods of testing position and movement sense are exactly the same as methods of testing coordination, only they are performed with the eyes closed. Ability to perform coordinated movements may be greatly diminished by removing visual clues (closing the eyes). This is always a strong indicator of proprioceptive disease.

Deep Pain and Pressure Sensation. Deep pain and pressure sensations are more diffuse and less well localized than superficial pain. It is mediated by the dorsal columns of the spinal cord and is generally tested by pressing on deep structures that do not have much overlying tissue containing superficial pain receptors. Delay or loss of pain sensation in tissues such as the Achilles tendon (Abadie's sign) (see Figure 5-17), testicles (Pitres' sign), ulnar nerve

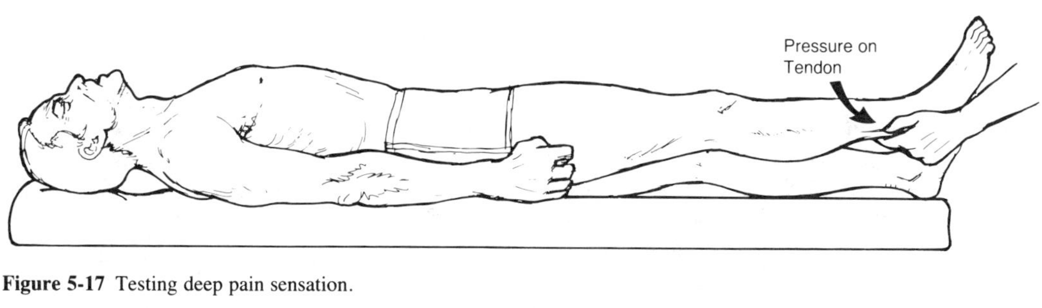

Figure 5-17 Testing deep pain sensation.

(Biernacki's sign), and eyeballs is usually indicative of dorsal column disease with tabes dorsalis as the classic example. Increased deep pain responses are seen in some peripheral neuropathies and myopathies. Tinel's sign is a distal tingling or feeling of an electrical shock brought about by direct palpation of a nerve. It is thought to be related to nerve regeneration.

Multimodal Sensations

Multimodal or combined sensations are combinations of both superficial and deep sensations, which are then subject to integration with higher cortical functions and memory; examples are stereognosis, barognosis, topognosis, graphognosis, two-point discrimination, somatognosis, and nosognosis. The final product is an overall perception and not merely the presence or lack of a specific stimulus. These are also referred to as the gnostic sensations ("gnosis,'' knowledge). Primarily, the association area of the parietal cortex, posterior to the primary sensory cortex, is involved in these functions. It then follows that disease of this area leads to the agnosias.

In addition to agnosias, testing may also uncover the pathological finding of sensory extinction, which is usually caused by a right-sided parieto-occipital lesion. Extinction is a term used for the peculiar loss of one's ability to observe two stimuli simultaneously. Instead, the sensation contralateral to the lesion site is ignored. The presence of sensory extinction, or inattention, is tested for by performing simultaneous bilateral stimulation. The stimulus applied is usually tactile or visual, but light touch or pinprick may be used.

Stereognosis

Stereognosis may be assessed by placing a common object (pen cap, key, button, paper clip—no pinwheels please) in the patient's hand with the patient's eyes closed. He or she may manipulate it around in the hand but should not, of course, be allowed to transfer the object to the other hand or look at it. Within only a few seconds the patient should accurately be able to name the object.

Barognosis

This is tested by having the patient assess the relative weights of special objects of similar size and shape but of different weights.

Topognosis

This is tested by touching the patient somewhere on the integument and having him or her point to the area just touched.

Graphognosis

This is tested by writing letters or numbers on the patient's chest, back, or palm of the hand. The alphanumerics used must be large, right-side-up, and exaggerated by the examiner in order to be decipherable by the patient.

Two-Point Discrimination

This is tested by stimulating two points at a known distance apart simultaneously on various body areas with a paper clip or special instrumentation, to determine the minimum amount of distance between two discriminable points, for a given patient. Tell the patient, "I am going to touch you with either one point or two points, and I want you to respond each time I touch you by saying 'one' or 'two.'" The examiner must intermittently use only one point as a reliability check. The examiner should start with the points far apart and gradually move them closer together until the patient makes consistent errors. Since certain areas, such as the fingertips, have nerve endings capable of detecting at a distance of 2 to 4 mm (in the healthy adult) and other areas, such as the dorsum of the hand, might have a 20 to 30 mm minimum threshold, it is essential that this test be done painstakingly and with a two-point discrimination chart nearby. In light of all of the other ways to test both posterior column and multimodal sensations, it is not usually necessary to perform this time-consuming test, and, in fact, it is not often used in clinical practice.

Somatognosis

This is knowledge of the body parts as being one's own. You may test for this by placing your arm next to the patient's arm and saying, "Touch your arm with your finger." If there is a disorder of somatognosis, the patient may touch your arm. Several repetitions may be necessary to ensure a valid response. This is not a screening test, however, and to use it as such may cause the patient to lose confidence in you.

Nosognosis

This refers to the knowledge of one's being ill. Interestingly enough, some patients, even in the light of obvious, overwhelming evidence of neurological disease, such as hemiplegia, will deny that there is a problem. This is usually tested in the judgment portion of the mental status examination.

REFERENCES

1. Ferezy JS. The somatic sensory system. *MCA Journal*. 1988;

2. Sherrington CS. *The Integrative Action of the Nervous System*. New York, NY: Charles Scribner's Sons; 1906.

SUGGESTED READING

Arnold LA. *Chiropractic Procedural Examination*. 2nd ed. Seminole, Fla: Seminole Printing, Inc; 1979:40, 52–53.

Chusid JG. *Correlative Neuroanatomy & Functional Neurology*. 17th ed. Norwalk, Conn: Lange Medical Publications; 1982:195–210.

DeJong RN. *The Neurologic Examination*. 4th ed. New York, NY: Harper & Row; 1979:39–78.

Fields HL. *Anatomy and Physiology of Pain*. American Medical Association video clinic notes.

Haldeman S. *The Neurophysiology of Spinal Pain Syndromes: Modern Developments in the Principles and Practice of Chiropractic*. Norwalk, Conn: Lange Medical Publications; 1979:119–141.

Van Allen MW. *Pictorial Manual of Neurologic Tests*. 2nd ed. Chicago, Ill: Year Book Medical Publishers, Inc; 1981:65–83.

Watson T. Pain and nociception—mechanisms and modulation. In: Grieve GP, ed. *Modern Manual Therapy*. Edinburgh: Churchill Livingstone; 1981:206–232.

Appendix 5-A

Terms Descriptive of Sensory Examination Findings

abarognosis: Loss of ability to differentiate weights.

allesthesia (synesthesia): Experience of a sensation at a site remote from the point of stimulation.

allochiria: Referral of sensation to the opposite side of the body.

analgesia: Absence of sensitivity to pain.

anesthesia: Absent sensation.

anosognosia: Ignorance of the existence of a neurological deficit.

arthresthesia: Perception of joint movement and position.

astereognosis: Inability to recognize objects through the sense of touch.

autotopagnosia (somatotopagnosia): Inability to identify or orient the body in relation to its individual parts.

baresthesia: Pressure or weight sensation.

bathyesthesia: Deep sensibility (muscles and joints).

dysesthesia: Unpleasant abnormal sensation.

extinction (suppression): Mechanism whereby a normally perceived stimulus is not perceived when the opposite side is simultaneously stimulated.

graphanesthesia: Inability to recognize letters or numbers written on the skin.

hypalgesia: Diminished sensitivity to pain.

hyperalgesia: Increased sensitivity to pain.

hyperesthesia: Increased sensation.

hyperpathia: Extremely disagreeable unilateral perception associated with only mild sensory stimuli, usually occuring after thalamic damage (e.g., with cerebrovascular accidents).

hypesthesia: Diminished sensation.

kinesthesia: Sense of muscular motion, weight, and position.

myalgia: Muscle pain.

myesthesia: Muscle sensation.

pallanesthesia: Loss of vibratory sensation.

pallesthesia: Vibratory sensation.

paresthesia: Abnormal sensation.

phantom: A spontaneous sensation referred to an insensitive area.

piesesthesia: Pressure sensation.

statognosis: Awareness of posture.

topoanesthesia (topagnosia): Inability to localize a cutaneous stimulus.

Appendix 5-B

Sensory Innervation of the Spinal Joint and Effects of Manipulation

INNERVATION AND EFFECT OF MANIPULATION ON SPINAL JOINTS

Cervical spinal joints are categorized as planar synovial joints. The synovial joint is the most common variety of joint in the human being. It has three basic characteristics consisting of separate bones held together by a fibrous cuff (capsule) that is lined by a synovial membrane; the articular surfaces are covered by hyaline cartilage. Essential to the understanding or appreciation of the effects of spinal manipulation is a working knowledge of spinal joint innervation. This knowledge enables one to more clearly recognize the relationship between symptoms, such as dizziness or ataxia, and the cervical spine. The purpose of this appendix is the requisite discussion of joint innervation, as well as the effects of spinal adjustments on these nerves.

Spinal joints have a tremendous amount of innervation, with cervical joints being the most heavily innervated of all of the spinal joints. In addition to sympathetic nerve fibers, spinal joints receive the input of three of four varieties of specialized joint neuroreceptors known as mechanoreceptors. Many different types of fibers serve as the parent neurons of these receptors, ranging from the smallest variety, the unmyelinated C fibers, to the largest, the heavily myelinated A alpha fibers. These fibers travel through the dorsal rami, as well as the recurrent and ventral rami of the segmental spinal nerves. Proprioceptive and pain information gathered from these receptors is dispersed among many segmental levels due to the ascending and descending nature of these primary afferent nerves.

Type I Mechanoreceptors

Type I mechanoreceptors are located in the outer layers of the spinal joint capsule. When stimulated, they fire at a frequency proportional to the degree of any active or passive joint movement or traction. The firing rate is inhibited by joint end approximation. They have a low threshold and are therefore very sensitive to movement. They are termed dynamic receptors because they only fire with movement. Some will continuously fire at 10 to 15 Hz even with no joint movement; these are known as static receptors. Type I receptors are slow adapting, so movement effects on them are longer lasting.

Their functions include

- perception of posture and movement
- reflex modulation of postural background and movement through constant monitoring of outer joint tension
- inhibition of centripetal flow from pain receptors via an enkephalinergic synaptic interneuron
- tonic effects on lower motor neuron pools involved in neck, limb, jaw, and eye muscles

This relationship between cervical joint innervation and musculature in the limbs, jaw, and eye helps us better understand how chiropractic adjustive therapy achieves results with complaints such as shoulder and temporomandibular joint pain and diplopia. Additionally, contributions of joint mechanoreceptors to pain perception, posture, and movement, as well as to reflex actions related to the above, would clarify the role of chiropractic adjustments in treating pain, dystaxia (gait disorders), and postural conditions such as primary kyphosis, scoliosis, thoracic outlet syndrome, etc.

Type II Mechanoreceptors

Type II mechanoreceptors are found within the deeper layers of the joint capsule. They also have a low threshold (dynamic), sensing even minor changes in inner joint tension. But unlike type I mechanoreceptors, they are very rapidly adapting (accelerator); firing may cease within 0.5 second of joint movement. Type II mechanoreceptors are completely inactive in immobilized joints. Functions of type II mechanoreceptors appear to include

- monitoring of joint movement for reflex actions and perhaps perceptual sensations
- inhibition of centripetal flow from pain receptors via an enkephalinergic synaptic interneuron
- phasic effects on lower motor neuron pools involved in neck, limbs, jaw, and eye movement

Type III Mechanoreceptors

These mechanoreceptors are, interestingly enough, completely absent from all spinal joints. They are slow adaptors with a very high threshold and appear to be the joint version of golgi tendon organs, which have an inhibitory effect on motoneurons.

Type IV Receptors for Nociception

Type IV receptors are the free nerve endings associated with pain perception. They possess an intimate physical relationship with the type I and II mechanoreceptors and are omnipresent throughout the fibrous portion of the joint capsule and the ligaments of the spine but are absent from articular cartilage. They are very high threshold receptors and are, of course, completely inactive in the physiologically normal joint. Joint capsule pressure, narrowing of the intervertebral disc, fracture of the vertebral body, dislocation of the apophyseal joints, chemical irritation, and interstitial edema associated with acute and/or chronic inflammation may all activate the nociceptive system. The basic functions of these spinal nociceptors include

- evocation of pain
- tonic effects on neck, limb, jaw, and eye muscles
- provision of central reflex connections for pain inhibition
- provision of central reflex connections for myriad autonomic effects

EFFECTS OF MANIPULATION ON SPINAL JOINT RECEPTORS

The events that take place during and after a spinal adjustment or manipulation point to the probability that there is a sudden change in joint tension, followed by a proportional increase in type I static and dynamic mechanoreceptor activity, and a burst of type II activity. A simultaneous reduction or abolition of static type I activity may occur in the destretched or approximated portion of the joint capsule.

The type I discharge might then be described as signaling the direction, amplitude, and velocity of the adjustment. This breakdown of information seems to lend credence to the development of techniques that describe different clinical effects from similar chiropractic applications using different degrees of thrusting force. The type II receptors only would appear to send information regarding movement.

The cervical articular mechanoreceptor system seems to hold special importance as it appears that with the adaptation of the human to the biped posture came a shifting of the level of importance from vestibular system proprioception to the cervical articular system proprioception. Degenerative, inflammatory, and/or traumatic disorders of the cervical spine may cause a loss of input from the mechanoreceptor system, but not from the nociceptive system. This may account for the characteristic changes in posture which become apparent in most elderly humans in addition to the increased complaint of minor joint pains and stiffness in the elderly.

The addition of nociceptive input from the spinal joints severely distorts normal cord reflex patterns and may therefore severely affect normal perceptual, postural, and kinesthetic functions. Clinical effects of joint manipulation on articular receptors may be artificially divided into three categories: reflexogenic effects, perceptual effects, and pain suppression effects.

Reflexogenic effects on muscle tone include facilitation and inhibition of gamma motor neurons via polysynaptic projections. The gamma motor neurons modulate activity of the muscle spindles at many levels due to ascending and descending input. As the spinal joints receive heavy sensory innervation, it follows that a chiropractic spinal subluxation may be sufficient to provide that irritation. Remove the irritation via normalization of articular biomechanics, and you may allow the reflexes to function optimally, thereby allowing the body to function in homeostasis.

Though most of these neurological reflexes do not lend themselves to direct in-office testing, the results of abnormal sensory input are clearly visible and often manifest in conditions such as pain, paraspinal muscle spasm, dizziness, ataxia, vertigo, light-headedness, and diplopia.

Perceptual effects are realized through the sizable contribution of type I receptors to consciousness of posture and movement. Obviously, the perception of pain would fall into this category as well.

Pain suppression is effected via enkephalinergic interneuronal inhibition of nociceptive afferents.

SUGGESTED READING

Dvorak J. Neurological and biomechanical aspects of back pain. In: Buerger AA, Greenman PE, eds. *Empirical Approaches to the Validation of Spinal Manipulation*. Springfield, Ill: Charles C Thomas, Publisher; 1985:241–266.

Hamilton WJ. *Textbook of Human Anatomy*. St Louis, MO: CV Mosby Co; 1986.

Korr IM. *Neurobiologic Mechanisms in Manipulative Therapy*. New York, NY: Plenum Press;

Wyke BD. Neurology of the cervical spine. *Physiotherapy*. 1979;65:72.

chapter 6

The Reflex Examination

A reflex may be defined as an involuntary response to some stimulus. It is essential that you note that a stimulus and a response are necessary. The reflection of light on the cornea observed during the corneal reflection test (see Chapter 3) is not a reflex. Yet many a student will erroneously refer to this test as the corneal light reflex. Poor use of terminology only breeds confusion, misinterpretation, and misunderstanding. The human body is complex enough without added difficulties.

The reflex must always consist of an applied stimulus (usually by the examiner), a stimulus receptor, a sensory arc neuron (or several), a synapse (or several), a motor arc neuron (or several), and an effector organ. After applying the stimulus, we observe the effect. We can determine a tremendous amount of information from observing a normal reflex—that is, that the receptor is functioning, the sensory arc is intact, the synapse is working, and the motor nerve and effector organs are responding. However, when we apply a stimulus and the desired effect does not occur, we must use other methods of examination to determine (if possible) at what level the failure occurred.

To aid in learning, the reflexes may then be looked at as being deep, superficial, visceral, or pathological.

DEEP REFLEXES

The deep reflexes are basically the muscle stretch reflexes (MSRs). They are also termed tendon reflexes, deep tendon reflexes (DTRs), and myotatic reflexes. Muscle stretch reflexes may well be the single most important test performed during the neurological examination. The MSRs yield volumes of information when they are intact, as well as when they are abnormal. I much prefer referring to them as the muscle stretch reflexes instead of the deep tendon reflexes, because these reflexes have receptors that are not particularly deep, nor are they located solely in the tendons! In fact, they are only termed "deep" because their receptors are located deeper than those of the superficial reflexes, which are found in the skin and mucous membranes.

Anatomy

In order to understand the muscle stretch reflexes, one should appreciate the basic anatomy of the nerve-muscle relationship. Muscle spindles (see Figure 6-1), also known as intrafusal muscle fibers, run in parallel, or side by

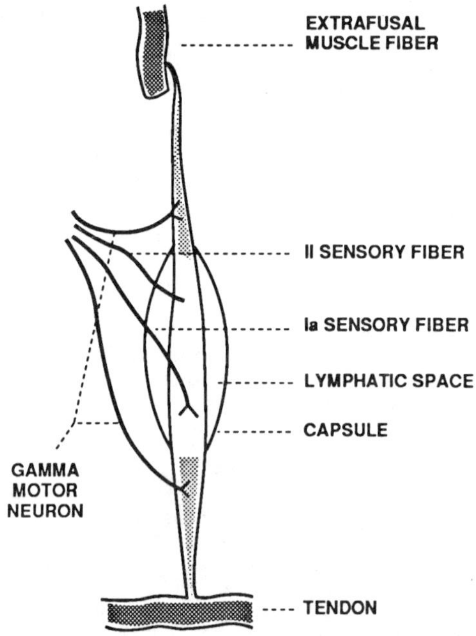

Figure 6-1 Anatomy of the muscle spindle.

side, with the skeletal muscle fibers, or extrafusal fibers. They occur in greatest concentration in the musculotendinous junction of all skeletal muscles. These intrafusal fibers are the receptors for the muscle stretch reflex.

Each intrafusal fiber has both a central, noncontractile portion and terminal portions that have motor innervation via the gamma (fusimotor) neurons. Although these fibers do contract, they do not aid in the muscle contractions we see and feel in skeletal muscles but act instead as modulators of muscle tone.

Muscle spindles are both static and dynamic receptors, like type 1 joint receptors; they constantly relay information about position (based upon degree of stretch) to the central nervous system. When stretched, either by active or passive movement, muscle spindles are excited and initiate neural impulses that travel afferently along type IA and type II neurons to synapse on alpha motor neurons in the spinal cord, monosynaptically. The alpha motor neurons (lower motor neurons) then cause skeletal muscle contraction via extrafusal muscle fibers, thereby altering the muscle tone. When the spindles are destretched or approximated, the pattern of firing is slowed; this diminution of the rate of incoming impulses provides useful information about position to the central nervous system.

Gamma motor neurons modulate this reflex by causing the terminal contractile portions of the intrafusal fibers to contract, thereby stretching the central noncontractile portion. The change in the tension of the central portion changes the firing pattern along the type IA nerve fibers, invoking the muscle stretch reflex again, and leading to altered muscle tone (see Figure 6-2).

Generally speaking, with a slow movement, the change in the length of the spindles is slow, and the type IA and type II afferents send an asynchronous volley of information to the spinal cord centers. This slight stimulus may not be sufficient to cause a visible or palpable reflex muscle contraction. With a more instantaneous

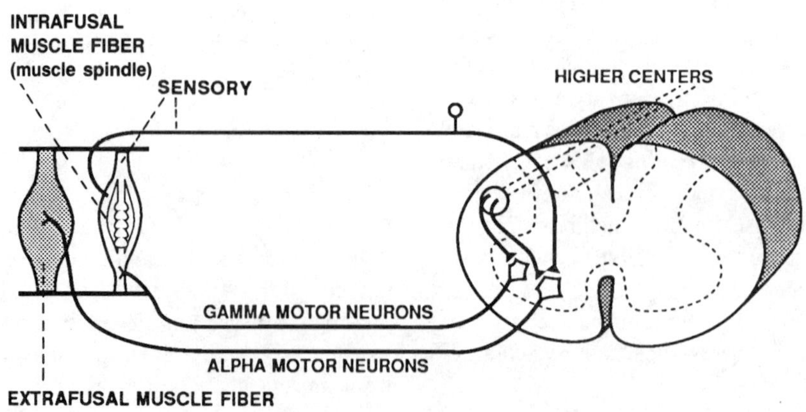

Figure 6-2 Diagram of the muscle spindle reflex.

stretch, a large, synchronous volley of afferent information causes a larger stimulus, sufficient to yield a visible or palpable contraction, or a muscle stretch reflex. Due to the speed of this reflex contraction, muscle spindle tension in the involved muscles suddenly decreases, causing the spindles to abruptly stop firing. The muscle stretch reflex then ends abruptly.

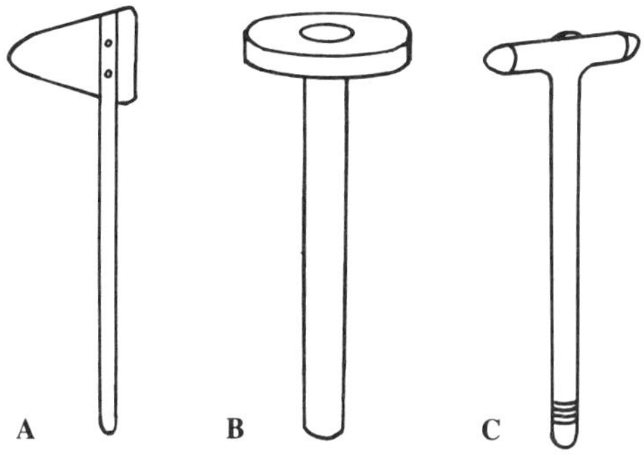

Figure 6-3 **A,** The tomahawk hammer; **B,** the Babinski hammer; **C,** the mallet hammer.

Technique of Muscle Stretch Reflex Testing

The muscle stretch reflex is tested by causing sudden stretch of a tendon, leading to sudden, sharp, involuntary contraction of the tendon's attached skeletal muscle. This is accomplished by striking the tendon with a hammer. The three most popular types of hammers to use are the tomahawk, Babinski, and mallet hammers, shown in Figure 6-3. For most purposes the tomahawk hammer is quite sufficient, though many prefer the Babinski or tire-style hammer. The mallet type is generally inferior and discouraged, even though many are sold with clever attachments. Regardless of which hammer you choose, proper technique is absolutely essential in order to yield valid, reproducible results.

The hammer should be held loosely, though it should not fly across the room! The wrist should be limp. By allowing the hammer to pivot between your fingers, and by allowing your wrist to move freely, a double whiplash effect is generated, thereby moving the hammer head with considerable velocity (see Figure 6-4). As stated above, it is absolutely essential to briskly stretch the muscle being tested. If this is not done, then an insufficient intensity of spindle stimulation occurs, and no reflex contraction of muscle will take place. Indeed, this is by far the most common difficulty experienced by the student in eliciting muscle stretch reflexes.

The patient's position is also quite important. He or she must be comfortable and relaxed and not using the muscle to be tested for any postural support. The muscle must be relaxed, which may be particularly difficult for the patient to achieve. Just saying relax while standing there with a hammer in your hand may not work. It is a good idea to passively move the joint around for a few seconds, in an erratic fashion, to facilitate relaxation or simultaneously assess muscle tone. The muscle being tested must also be disrobed, as it must be inspected for contraction.

The muscle being stretched by the hammer should also be in a state of partial contraction. A muscle that is either fully stretched or fully contracted will not yield an adequate muscle stretch reflex. The joint the muscle acts across should be in an intermediate position between flexion and extension.

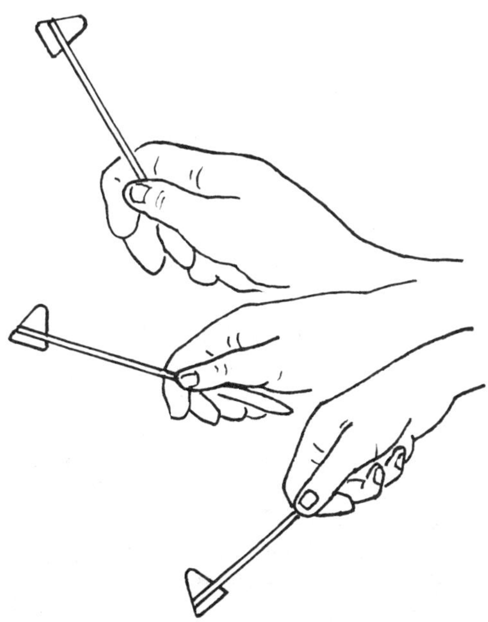

Figure 6-4 Proper technique in wielding the hammer.

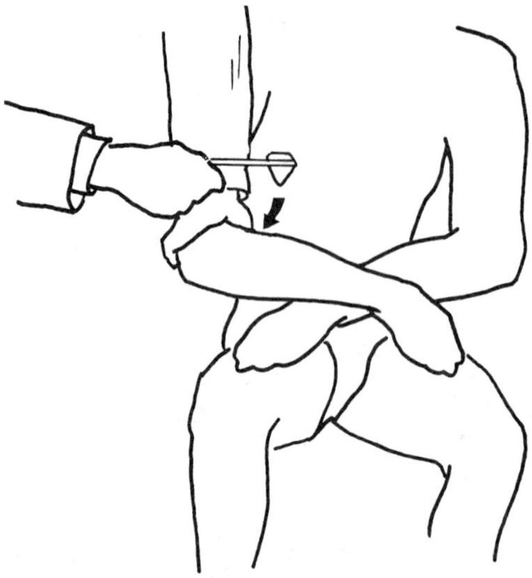

Figure 6-5 Testing the biceps reflex.

Figure 6-6 Testing the triceps reflex.

While every skeletal muscle in the human body should theoretically respond to stretch by contracting, only a few have tendons readily available for this purpose. While dozens of different muscle reflexes are described, such as the jaw (or maxillary) jerk response and the wrist and pectoralis reflexes, the following are without question the most useful and common ones to test since many of the other muscle stretch reflexes may only be elicited when the reflex is hyperactive.

1. Biceps reflex (C5-6 musculocutaneous nerve): Causes flexion at the elbow when the bicipital tendon is struck (see Figure 6-5).
2. Triceps reflex (C6-7 radial nerve): Causes extension at the elbow when the triceps tendon is struck (see Figure 6-6).
3. Brachioradialis reflex (or periosteoradial reflex; C6-8, radial nerve): Causes flexion and supination of the forearm when an area about 1 inch superior to the radial styloid process is struck (see Figure 6-7).
4. Quadriceps (or knee jerk or patellar reflex; L2-4, femoral nerve): Causes extension of the leg when the patellar tendon is struck (see Figure 6-8). Absence of this reflex is known as Westphal's sign. (I often refer to the quadriceps reflex as the laugh reflex. While I cannot cite the specific pathway, some neuron must run directly from the knee to the laugh center of the brain, because patients always laugh after one

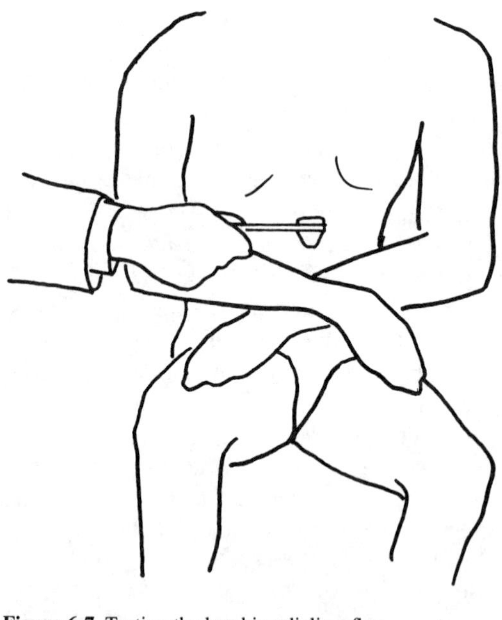

Figure 6-7 Testing the brachioradialis reflex.

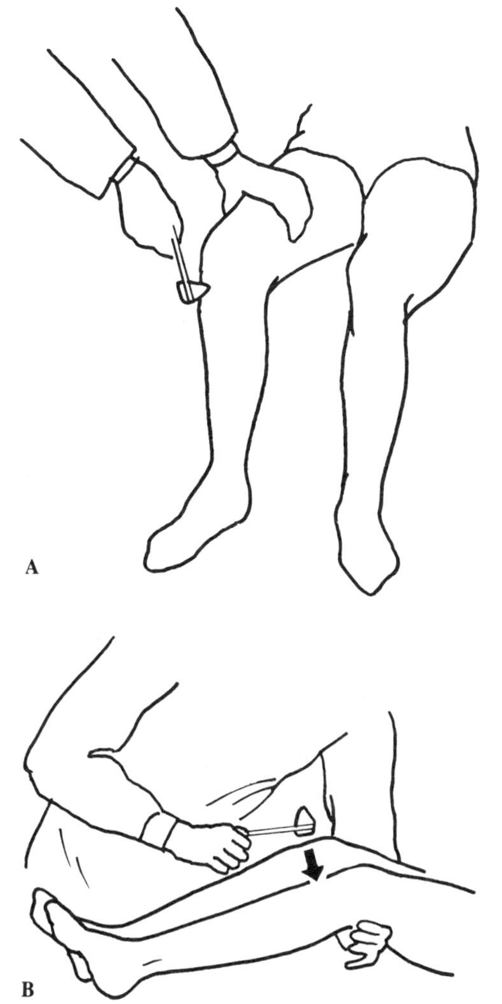

Figure 6-8 Testing the quadriceps reflex (**A**). Alternate method (**B**) of testing the quadriceps reflex in the recumbent patient.

successfully elicits the knee jerk response.)

5. Achilles reflex (ankle jerk reflex; S1-2 tibial nerve): Causes plantar flexion when the Achilles tendon is struck (see Figure 6-9).

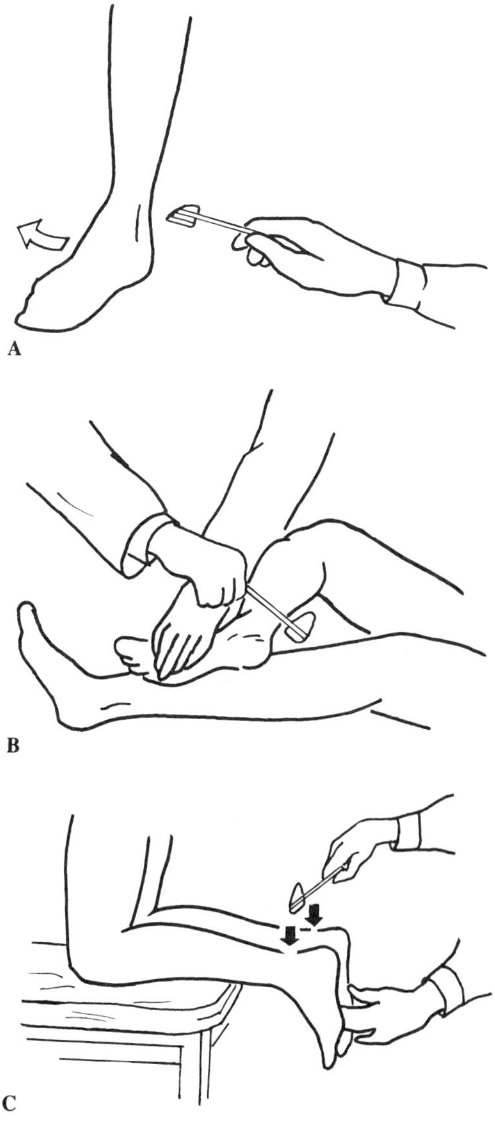

Figure 6-9 Testing the Achilles tendon reflex (**A**). Two alternate methods are shown (**B** and **C**).

Many variables can affect proper evaluation of the muscle stretch response. The degree of muscle contraction obtained in testing a muscle stretch reflex is completely dependent on the stimulus for the reflex (i.e., the hammer blow) and the state of the muscle at the time the stimulus is introduced. This can confound one's ability to reproduce the same degree of response in the same patient during different tests, not to mention the variability of responses obtained by different examiners. Was the patient completely relaxed? Did you evenly strike the tendon on the same position? Did you exert the same amount of force with each test? These are all important questions.

One method of reducing the variability is simply by averaging. That is, repeat the testing 5 to 15 times. You may even retest an area at two separate times during the examination, though this may be overkill. When dealing with the quadriceps reflex, you may rapidly strike and restrike the quadriceps tendon, eventually causing a tonic contraction of the quadriceps muscles resulting in the patient's leg remaining partially extended until the barrage of stimuli from the hammer blows ceases. This yields a very reproducible effect, helping one judge the extent of the response.

If you have difficulty eliciting a muscle stretch reflex, it may not mean that it is not present. First, make your blow crisper. Be sure that you are delivering a blow directly to the tendon (palpate the tendon first), and redouble your efforts to hit it with great velocity (though not great force). If redirecting the location and velocity of the blow fails to get a response, do it again. As stated above, deliver 5 to 15 blows before trying the next steps.

If you are still having difficulty, try changing the length of the muscle by repositioning the joint slightly, while encouraging better relaxation on the part of the patient. Should you still be unable to elicit a reflex, methods of reinforcement should be used.

Reinforcement

One simple method of reinforcing a reflex is to distract the patient. Many times the patient is anticipating the hammer blow and unconsciously making the reflex harder to elicit. You may simply distract the patient with conversation, but I have developed an even better method: Give the patient reinforcement instructions to follow, then tell him or her to wait until you say "now" before executing the instructions. Be sure that the patient understands that he or she is not to do anything until you say "now." Then, without saying "now," retry the reflex. Almost 100% of the time a reaction will be noted. This is a true reaction and not necessarily noted as a reinforced reflex. If no reaction is elicited after several tries, proceed to the methods of reinforcement discussed below.

The most common method of reinforcement is known as the Jendrassik method. While the method is usually assumed to involve testing the quadriceps reflex, it also works rather well in testing the Achilles reflex. The exact mechanism by which this maneuver makes the reflex easier to elicit is not known, but it goes beyond simple distraction of the patient. The patient is asked to voluntarily contract a group of muscles distant from the ones involved in the reflex, *just prior* to eliciting the reflex. If upper extremity reflexes are being tested, have the patient squeeze his or her knees together, grasp his or her thigh (see Figure 6-10), or clench his or her teeth. If a lower extremity reflex is being tested, have the patient clasp his or her hands together and try to pull them apart, without actually doing so (see Figure 6-11). Instruct the patient by saying "now" or "pull" just before the tendon is struck. The signal to the patient might be given right at the instant the hammer is brought into motion. In fact, it is also useful to swing the hammer one more time without saying "now." Often, the patient's attention is diverted to the procedure of reinforcement, and the reflex is suddenly readily available.

A final method of reinforcement may be termed counterpressure. Counterpressure is obtained by asking the patient to slightly contract the *same* muscle being tested. Patients have some degree of difficulty with this on some mus-

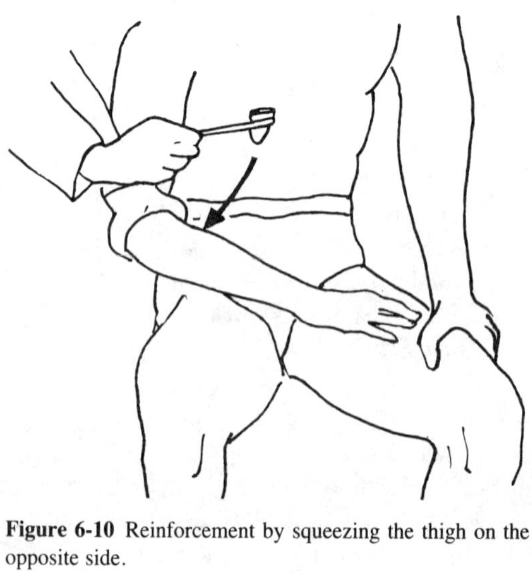

Figure 6-10 Reinforcement by squeezing the thigh on the opposite side.

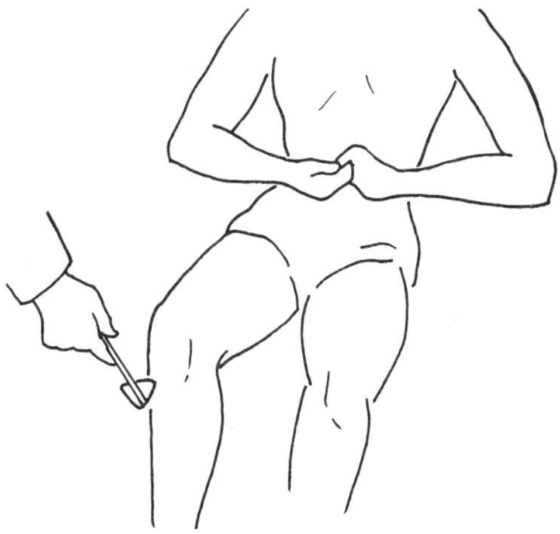

Figure 6-11 The Jendrassik method for the quadriceps reflex.

cles, and counterpressure is therefore used less frequently than the methods described above.

Grading Reflex Responses

Muscle stretch reflexes have been graded using many different methods. Most widely accepted is a grading scale of 0, +, ++, +++, and ++++. The plus (+) sign should be used so that confusion with the numerical grading of muscle strength (0 to 5; see Chapter 4) is avoided. If reinforcement is used, be sure to note that by placing "(R)" after the notation. It is common to see a number replace the multiple plus signs: 0, 1+, 2+, 3+, 4+. It is a common mistake for the student to see the number, and the +, and to then reason that 3−, 3, and 3+ would signify varying grades of reflex activity. It does not. This system of grading would cause the categories to be clinically indistinguishable from one another.

A grade of 0 is usually considered to denote pathological reflex hypoactivity. A grade of 4+ is usually considered to denote pathological reflex hyperactivity. The most common question and cause of confusion to the student is how to grade responses somewhere between these two extremes (i.e., is the right quadriceps reflex increased at 3+, or the left reduced at 1+). First, grades 1+, 2+, and 3+ are not by definition normal or pathological as they may represent low, middle, and high average responses. Biological variability in muscle stretch reflexes is great, and therefore a person with all 1+ reflexes is no more or less normal than a person with all 3+ reflexes.

The creation of a different grading system does not serve as an answer to this problem, as variability between testing technique on different visits and by different examiners is great, and refining the scale would merely amplify minor differences, creating confusion.

The proper approach is to note side-to-side variability. Side-to-side differences are the most essential findings indicative of pathology in regard to muscle stretch reflexes. Of course, a situation like the above-referenced example in which a right quadriceps reflex was graded as 3+ and the left at 1+ would still pose difficulty—which side is abnormal? The answer to this question can, almost always, be obtained from the balance of the exam, including the history, general physical exam findings, and results of other neurological tests.

Areflexia (no reflex) is virtually *always* pathological. Only very rare individuals, as well as infants and children whose tendons are not well defined, may not possess an elicitable muscle stretch reflex.

Interpreting the Results of Muscle Reflex Testing

Abnormal findings of muscle stretch reflex testing indicate that some portion of the reflex arc is not functioning. One must think of the reflex arc as a circuit loop; a malfunction in any of the arc segments causes a diminution or loss of reflex function. By thinking through all of the components of the reflex arc, one may recognize all of the places in which the loop may be broken.

First, since there is no known disease specific to muscle spindles, that portion of the reflex apparatus may be ignored. Loss of function along the afferent or sensory limb would indicate sensory nerve disease which should be manifested in a loss of cutaneous sensation of the related dermatome. Nerve root encroachment; entrapment neuropathy; or primary sensory disorders such as tabes dorsalis, diabetic neuropathy, and others may be responsible.

Disease of the synapse in the spinal cord does not seem to be a clinical problem, so the next area of concern would be the body of the lower motor neuron (efferent limb). As you would suspect, lower motor neuron disease sufficient to cause a muscle stretch reflex deficit would probably manifest other findings typical of lower motor neuron disease, such as paresis, paralysis, muscle atrophy, fasciculations, and hypotonia. The same symptoms are produced regardless of the site of disease on the lower motor neuron. Examples of lower motor neuron body disease include anterior poliomyelitis and amyotrophic lateral sclerosis. Examples of lower motor neuron axon disease include damage due to neuron cuts or compression and the motor neuropathy of lead poisoning.

Nerve root lesions and peripheral motor nerve lesions usually display signs of both motor and sensory involvement (sensorimotor neuropathy), which is also useful in diagnosis. Arsenic poisoning is another sensorimotor neuropathy.

More rarely, disease of the myoneural junction is responsible for decreased or (very rarely) absent muscle stretch reflexes; the usual cause is myasthenia gravis.

Finally, the muscle itself (end organ) may be responsible for the decreased or absent reflex. Primary muscular disease (myopathy) is considerably rarer than the other above-mentioned causes. Noted myopathies include muscular dystrophy, myositis, and myopathic atrophy.

There is only one cause of true hyper-reflexia: upper motor neuron disease. The decrease or absence of cortical inhibition of the muscle stretch reflex results in a facilitation (release) of that reflex. Hyper-reflexia may occur following interruption of the upper motor neuron pathway at any point between the cerebral cortex and the lower motor neuron (see Figure 6-12).

Hyper-reflexia following upper motor neuron disease is part of a diagnostic pattern or syndrome. It is seen in the chronic stage of such a lesion (as you recall, only deficit phenomena will be present in the acute stage—see Chapter 4). This syndrome consists of paresis or paralysis of unilateral, independent movements; hyper-reflexia; clonus; spasticity; and the presence of pathological reflexes (discussed below).

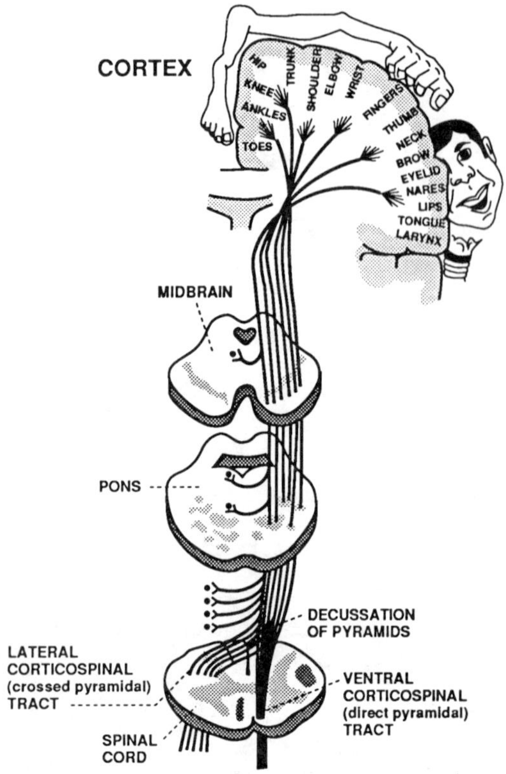

Figure 6-12 Lesions at any point along the pathway will cause an upper motor neuron syndrome.

SUPERFICIAL REFLEXES

Superficial reflexes differ from deep reflexes in that here the receptor is located superficially, usually in the skin or mucous membranes. Additionally, this is not a monosynaptic but a polysynaptic reflex (see Figure 6-13).

Superficial reflexes are generally interpreted by the clinical neurologist in one of two ways: They are present, or they are absent. Like deep reflexes, the presence of superficial reflexes tells a great deal about the segmental pathway involved. Often, all superficial reflexes become

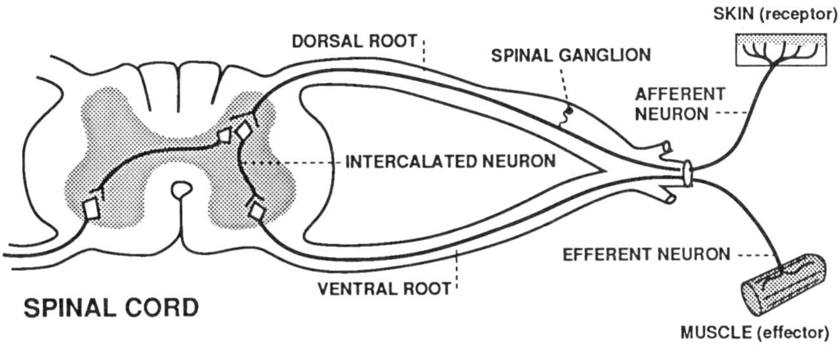

Figure 6-13 Diagram of the superficial reflex arc.

absent in the acute and subacute stages of an upper motor neuron lesion. Superficial reflexes tend to return in the chronic stages of upper motor neuron disease and may become hyperactive, though this is not diagnostic.

Corneal Reflex

The operative afferent is cranial nerve V; the operative efferent, cranial nerve VII. A piece of cotton is gently touched to the cornea of a patient as he or she looks away. Care is taken both that the patient looks away (so visual clues won't give away when to blink) and that no contact is made to the eyelid, eyelashes, or conjunctiva (see Figure 6-14). Visual and tactile clues must be avoided. Upon touching the cornea a brisk bilateral, unmistakable blink, associated with head turning and pain, is observed. This reflex may be absent in long-term wearers of contact lenses.

Pathological causes of absence of this reflex may be diseases of cranial nerve V (loss of this reflex occurs at early stages, making its assessment a useful tool in early diagnosis), the brainstem, or cranial nerve VII (usually also associated with eyelid ptosis). Corneal ulcers may be present due to a lack of this protective mechanism. If volitional blinking of the eye is well performed but the reflex is not present, suspect cranial nerve V disease.

Figure 6-14 Testing the corneal reflex.

Mucous Membrane Reflexes

Pharyngeal (Gag) Reflex

The operative nerves are cranial nerves IX and X, via the medulla. The physiology and testing of this reflex are described in Chapter 3. Lesions of cranial nerve IX or X or their medullary connections may cause a disturbance of this reflex. Sword swallowers and individuals who regularly stick other things deep into their throats may also be devoid of this protective reflex.

Uvular (Palatal) Reflex

The operative nerves are cranial nerves IX and X, via the medulla. The physiology and testing of this reflex are described in Chapter 3. Asymmetrical palatal elevation is usually due to biological variability, scarring from a tonsillectomy, or a cranial nerve IX or X lesion. Since presence of the gag reflex is evidence of intactness of cranial nerves IX and X and their medullary connections, presence of palatal elevation during a gag reflex with absence of palatal elevation on voluntary request (while saying "Ahhh") is evidence of a cortical or corticobulbar lesion.

Skin Reflexes

Superficial Abdominal Reflex

The operative nerves are the thoracic nerve (T7-10 root level) (above umbilicus) and T10-12, for the lower abdomen (below umbilicus). This reflex may be elicited by gently stroking the abdomen, divided into quadrants intersecting at the umbilicus, toward the umbilicus. The normal response is a brick contraction of the abdominal musculature on the side of stimulation, causing a jerking of the umbilicus toward the stimulus (see Figure 6-15). This reflex is usually absent in women who have given birth, and in obese patients as well. Additionally, it is not present in many normal individuals, making this test only selectively useful. An instance where it may be useful is in helping determine the level and extent of a thoracic spinal cord lesion.

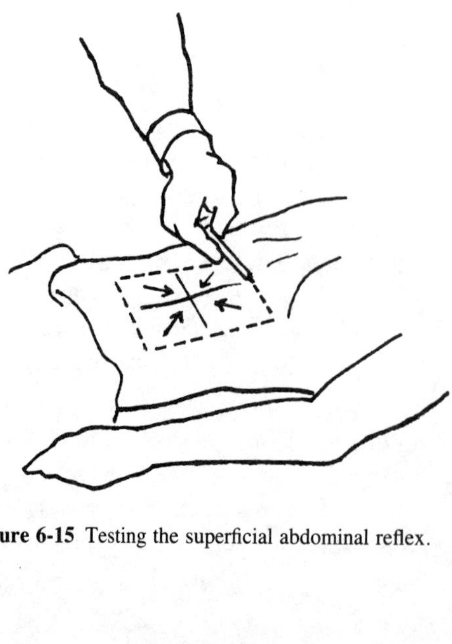

Figure 6-15 Testing the superficial abdominal reflex.

Cremasteric Reflex

The operative nerve is the femoral-genitofemoral nerve (L1 root level). An upward stroking of the inner thigh causes ascent of the ipsilateral testicle. It is also referred to as the "high bush" or "hurdler's" reflex. Testing it is useful in suspected upper lumbar root lesions or in suspected upper motor neuron disease, when it would be expected to be absent. Unlike the unreliable superficial abdominal reflex, it is rarely absent in the healthy male. For reasons of patient embarrassment, it is not routinely tested.

Gluteal Reflex

Irritation of the skin over the buttocks causes a bilateral contraction of the gluteal muscles. For reasons of patient embarrassment, it is not routinely tested.

Plantar Reflex

The operative nerve is the tibial nerve (S1-2 root level). Curling of the toes and plantar flexion of the foot are seen when the lateral portion of the sole of the foot is stroked. This reflex is commonly performed during the neurological examination. Replacement of the normal reflex with the Babinski sign, described in the next section of the chapter, signifies pathology.

Anal Reflex

The operative nerve is the pudendal nerve (S4-5 root level). Contraction of the sphincter ani occurs upon stimulation of the perianal area, or upon insertion of a gloved finger into the anus. For reasons of patient embarrassment and discomfort, it is not routinely tested. This reflex is invaluable, however, in the assessment of very low spinal cord or nerve root (S4-5) disease; there is no other substitute reflex for these levels.

Therefore, it must be used when disease of these levels, such as might occur in a cauda equina syndrome, is suspected.

VISCERAL (ORGANIC) REFLEXES

Testing this group of reflexes may be quite useful in the neurological examination. These are reflexes that, when abnormal, are absolutely unequivocal signs of neurological disease

Pupillary Reflexes

Light Reflex

The operative nerves are cranial nerve II, for the sensory portion of the arc, and cranial nerve III, for the motor portion. The physiology and testing of this reflex are discussed in Chapter 3.

Accommodation Reflex

The operative nerve is cranial nerve III. This reflex and its testing are discussed in Chapter 3. An alternate way to test this reflex, and one that has an exaggerating effect upon it, is to ask the patient to focus ahead in the distance and then place your finger about 3 inches from the patient's nose and say, "Now look at my finger." As the patient focuses upon the near finger, observe for pupillodilation.

Ciliospinal Reflex

The operative nerves are the cervical nerves (sensory arc) and sympathetics (motor arc). Firmly pinching the skin over your patient's neck causes brisk, bilateral dilation of the pupils. This is an uncomfortable test and may cause your patient to seek the services of a less thorough doctor. This reflex is lost in Horner's syndrome and other disorders of sympathetic function as well as with cervical sensory nerve disease.

Oculocardiac Reflex

The operative nerves are cranial nerves V (sensory arc) and X (motor arc). Pressure over the eyeballs (through the closed eyelids) causes a slowing of the heart rate. Some have suggested this as a treatment for tachycardia, but this is not prudent or recommended.

Carotid Sinus Reflex

The operative nerves are cranial nerves IX and X (carry both sensory and motor arcs). Pressure over one of the carotid arteries causes slowing of the heart and a drop in the blood pressure. Lesions of cranial nerves IX and X may abolish this reflex, and hypersensitivity of this reflex may lead to fainting (carotid sinus syncope). Carotid sinus syncope should be considered when syncopal episodes accompany head movements, especially when a tight collar is worn.

Bulbocavernosus Reflex

Operative nerves are pudendal S4-5 root level. Pinching, pricking, or stroking the glans penis causes a contraction of the bulbocavernosus muscle, palpated in the perineal area. This tests sacral nerve integrity in suspected cases of cauda equina syndrome.

PATHOLOGICAL REFLEXES

Pathological reflexes are actually just superficial or deep reflexes gone wrong. Most of the time you are observing the loss of cortical inhibition or control over a reflex, and that release phenomenon is called a pathological reflex. Many pathological reflexes have been described in the literature, and rather than give an exhaustive list, this text will focus on the more common and useful ones. Pathological reflexes are part of the upper motor neuron syndrome, signifying discontinuity of the motor cortex or pyramidal (corticobulbar/corticospinal) tracts.

Lower Extremity Pathological Reflexes

Babinski's sign (or extensor toe sign) is defined as extension of the large toe with fanning of the small toes upon stimulation of the plantar surface of the foot. Extension of the great toe is really the event of importance; fanning of the other digits is not important or particularly diagnostic of anything. In fact, flexion of the second through fifth toes often accompanies both normal and pathological responses and confuses the examiner. Flexion of the other toes may cause the appearance of extension of the great toe. Therefore, it is recommended that you observe not only the toe, but the hallucis extensor tendon. Prominence of this tendon during the test is clear evidence of an extensor toe sign. Actually, some authors recommend forcibly flexing the second to fifth toes while eliciting Babinski's response.

The path you should take in stroking the sole of the foot is shown in Figure 6-16. Be sure to securely hold the extremity down, because movement of the foot, which inevitably follows the stimulation, will void that particular attempt. It is important to use a very consistent stimulus in eliciting this reflex. Remember, it is the nociceptors that are stimulated in this reflex; therefore, the sensation will be uncomfortable to many. It is important that you forewarn the patient of this, such as by saying, "I am going to scratch up the side of your foot. It may be uncomfortable or it may tickle, but bear with me as best you can—it only takes a few seconds."

Due to patient discomfort and ticklishness, this reflex may be difficult to interpret. In those cases it should be repeated several times. A true extensor toe sign does not vary much from attempt to attempt.

If you are still uncertain as to whether the toe went up or down, list the reflex as "equivocal." Note that the Babinski sign is not positive or negative. Use of that type of terminology is confusing, because a negative Babinski might then be a positive plantar response (see "Plantar Reflex," above). Would a negative plantar response be a positive Babinski? Therefore, an extensor toe sign is either present, absent, or equivocal. The preferred method of describing the response is to say either "The toe went up" or "The toe went down."

The following test procedures offer good alternatives to stroking the lateral foot. If the response to plantar stimulation is equivocal, the patient is overly sensitive or ticklish on the bottom of the foot, or you suspect pathology, some of these other areas may be stimulated. Generally they do not give as satisfactory results as plantar stimulation, but they do provide excellent backups and validation procedures.

1. Chaddock's toe sign: An extensor toe sign is elicited by stroking the area around the lateral malleolus (see Figure 6-17).

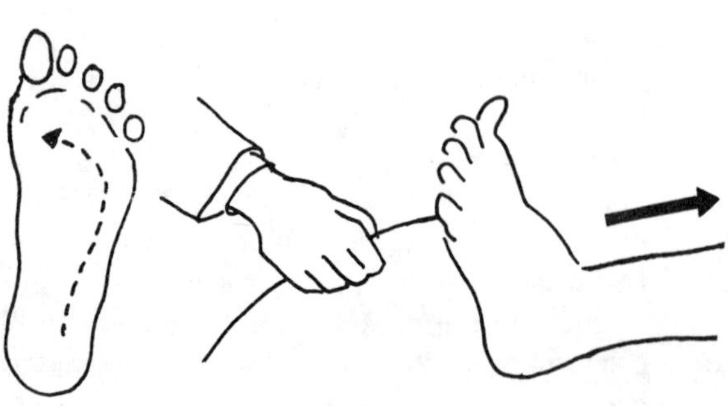

Figure 6-16 Testing for the extensor toe sign.

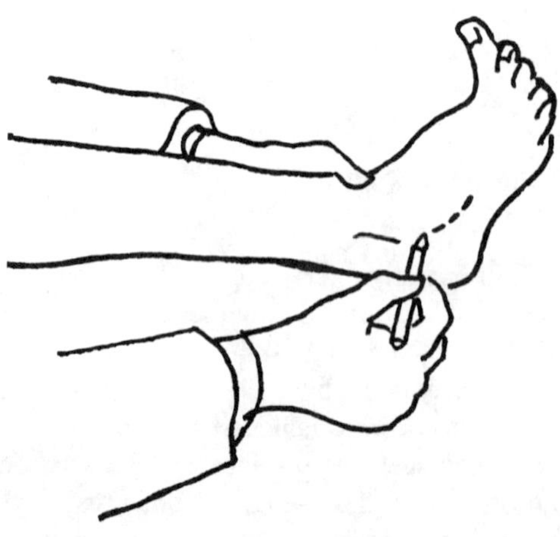

Figure 6-17 Testing for Chaddock's toe sign.

2. Gordon's leg sign: An extensor toe sign is elicited by squeezing the calf muscle (see Figure 6-18).
3. Oppenheim's sign: An extensor toe sign is elicited by firm downward stroking of the tibia and tibialis anterior muscle (see Figure 6-19).
4. Gonda reflex: An extensor toe sign is elicited by pressing one of the other toes downward and releasing it sharply.
5. Schaefer's sign: An extensor toe sign is elicited by squeezing the Achilles tendon (see Figure 6-20).
6. Huntington's sign: The patient is supine with legs hanging over the edge of the examination table. Coughing and straining cause flexion at the hip, extension at the knee, and elevation of the affected weak lower extremity.
7. Marie-Foix retraction sign: Upon forcing the toes of a paretic limb downward, the knee and hip are drawn into flexion.

Upper Extremity Pathological Reflexes

Disease involving the corticospinal tract between the cortex and the cervical spine may cause some or all of the following reflexes:

1. Gordon's finger sign: Extension of the flexed fingers or the thumb and index finger is elicited by applying pressure over the pisiform bone.
2. Chaddock's wrist sign: Flexion of the wrist with extension and fanning of the fingers is elicited by stroking the ulnar side of the forearm, near the wrist.
3. Babinski's pronation sign: The patient's hands are placed in approximation with the palms upward, and they are then jarred several times by the examiner's own hands from below. The affected hand will fall into pronation; the sound hand will remain supinated.

Figure 6-18 Testing for Gordon's leg sign.

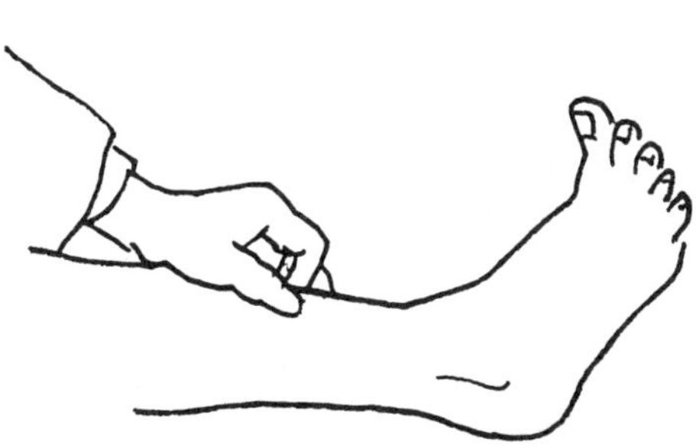

Figure 6-19 Testing for Oppenheim's sign.

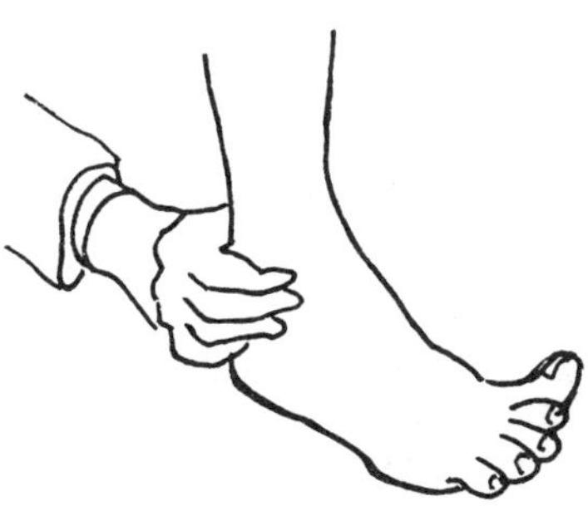

Figure 6-20 Testing for Schaefer's sign.

4. Klippel-Feil thumb sign: When the flexed fingers of the patient are quickly extended by the examiner, flexion and adduction of the patient's thumb ensues.
5. Leri's sign: Forceful passive flexion of the wrist and fingers fails to produce normal flexion of the elbow.
6. Strümpell's pronation sign: Upon flexing the forearm, the dorsum of the hand instead of the palmar surface approaches the shoulder.
7. Grasping sign: Firm radial stroking by the examiner's fingers across the subject's palm causes a grasp reaction of the hand.

Head Reflexes

Pathological reflexes may also be present and elicited in the head with UMN disease.

1. Babinski's platysma sign: If resistance is offered to flexion of the chin against the chest or to opening the mouth, the platysma on the sound side will contract, whereas that on the affected side will be reduced or absent.
2. McCarthy's sign (glabella reflex): Percussion of the supraorbital ridge results in reflex contraction of the orbicularis oculi muscle bilaterally.
3. Snout reflex: Sharp tapping of the middle of the upper lip induces exaggerated reflex contraction of the lips.
4. Head retraction reflex: Sharp downward percussion upon the upper lip with the head bent slightly forward produces head bending followed by brisk head retraction.

Reflexes Attributable to Increased Muscle Stretch Reflex Activity

Some of the pathological reflexes, including clonus, are due to increased muscle stretch reflex activity. Some of these reflexes are, therefore, elicitable in the patient with muscle stretch reflexes at the upper end of normal, and therefore they must be interpreted carefully and in the presence of many other findings.

Clonus

Pathological or sustained clonus is a to-and-fro oscillation of a joint under sustained resistance. It is due to rapid-fire elicitation of muscle stretch reflexes. Its presence may be assessed at the wrist, knee, and ankle. At the knee, sharp pressure is exerted down on the patella with the knee extended. The examiner forcibly extends the muscle being tested, eliciting a muscle stretch reflex resulting in a palpable contraction. The continued examiner's pressure restretches the muscle, and another cycle of stretch-reflex contraction begins. Because activation of stretch receptors is necessary for elicitation of this reflex, the movement must be brisk. It is common for patients with muscle stretch reflexes at the upper end of normal to have one, two, or even three or more beats of clonus, but then it disappears. This is referred to as abortive clonus and is completely physiological. Sustained or pathological clonus will cause repeated stretch-reflex contract cycles as long as the resistance is applied by the examiner (see Figure 6-21).

Ankle Clonus. A continued involuntary rapid flexion and extension of the foot is obtained by forcibly and quickly dorsiflexing the foot while the leg is held up by the examiner's other hand placed under the popliteal space. Often it is possible to elicit clonus by offering resistance to plantarflexion of the foot while testing the Achilles tendon muscle stretch reflex. The hammer strike activates the muscle stretch reflex, and the pressure into plantar dorsiflexion offered the examiner allows it to continue.

Patellar Clonus (Trepidation Sign). A rapid up-and-down movement of the patella is noted when it is forcibly depressed with a quick move-

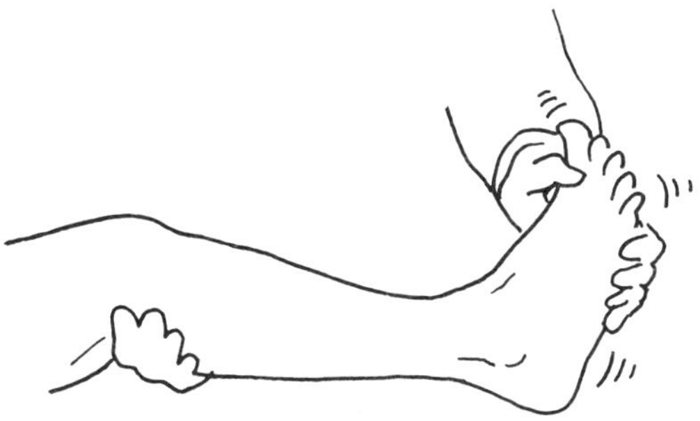

Figure 6-21 The appearance of ankle clonus.

Figure 6-22 Testing for Hoffmann's finger flexion reflex.

ment while the leg is in extension. The pathological mechanism is the same as for ankle clonus.

Wrist Clonus. Forcible extension of the wrist causes wrist flexor contraction. As pressure is applied to keep the wrist in dorsiflexion, the cycle begins again, and continued oscillations are felt. The pathological mechanism is the same as for ankle clonus, above.

Miscellaneous Other Reflexes

Some degree of these reflexes may be present in those at the upper end of completely normal reflexes.

Rossolimo's Sign. Sharply flicking the toes upward causes brisk stretch of the flexor muscles of the toes, which, when hyperactive, cause prompt flexion of the toes.

Hoffmann's Sign. Flicking the distal phalanx of the index finger produces a so-called "clawing" movement of the fingers, which is actually just exaggerated contraction of the flexor muscles of the fingers (see Figure 6-22).

Finger Flexion Reflex (Trömner's Sign). An exaggerated contraction of the flexor muscles of the fingers (as Hoffmann's) is present. It is tested the same as Rossolimo's sign except involving the fingers (see Figure 6-23).

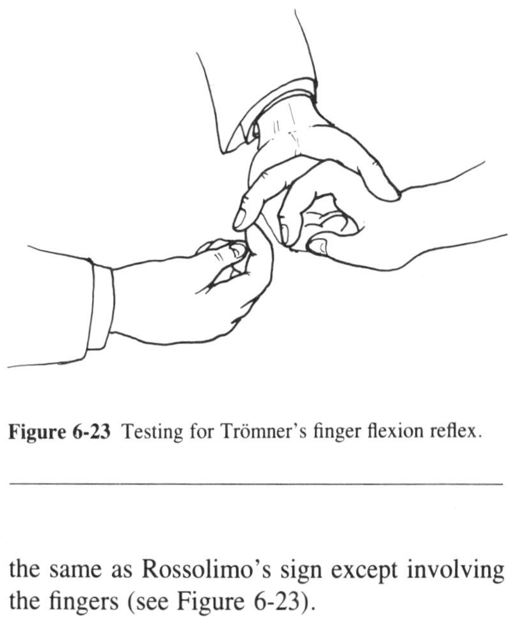

Figure 6-23 Testing for Trömner's finger flexion reflex.

SUGGESTED READING

Arnold LA. *Chiropractic Procedural Examination*. 2nd ed. Seminole, Fla: Seminole Printing, Inc; 1979:40, 52–53.

Chusid JG. *Correlative Neuroanatomy & Functional Neurology*. 17th ed. Norwalk, Conn: Lange Medical Publications; 1982:195–210.

DeJong RN. *The Neurologic Examination*. 4th ed. New York, NY: Harper & Row; 1979:39–78.

Van Allen MW. *Pictorial Manual of Neurologic Tests*. 2nd ed. Chicago, Ill: Year Book Medical Publishers, Inc; 1981:65–83.

chapter **7**

The Examination of Movement and Coordination

The evaluation of movement actually involves assessment of many facets of the neurological system, all working together.

Coordinated, voluntary movement is an action that requires an integration of all aspects of the neurological examination. Disorders of any system (motor, sensory, cerebellar, or extrapyramidal) will affect movement in a characteristic way. It is therefore necessary that the clinician test movement as a part of the routine neurological assessment. Even though the testing of movement is a sensitive screening tool, it may also be a crude one. Diagnostic confusion can easily exist unless more definitive tests are performed to isolate which system is primarily at fault.

The relation of the extrapyramidal system to movement is most easily understood by observing a person affected by extrapyramidal function disease. There is a profound slowing of movement. The patient must think through each movement as though the ability to initiate the movement is present, but the ability to carry out the movement is not. Only primary movements are affected; reflex and emotionally related movements are retained. Emotional movements may be exaggerated (emotional incontinence).

Gait observation is an important aspect of screening patient movement. Gait should be smooth and rhythmic. Arm swing should be symmetrical and natural. The patient's base should be narrow and foot placement specific, with the heel striking first, followed by controlled placement of the foot and finally the big toe. Extrapyramidal gait is very slow and shuffling with a stooped posture. Hemiparesis causes a gait that is asymmetrical. The patient circumducts ("swinging out'' of the involved extremity) the paretic lower extremity to avoid dragging the big toe due to weakness of the distal lower extremity musculature. There is also a loss of arm swing on the affected side with a flexion posture of the upper extremity.

The cerebellar system coordinates all willfully directed muscular contractions. Since the cerebellar system is the primary system that is examined when there is a discussion of voluntary movement, it will be discussed in some detail in this chapter.

CEREBELLAR ANATOMY

In the posterior fossa of skull, straddling the pons and medulla, lies the cerebellum. An outgrowth of the vestibular nuclei, its surface is composed of sulci and gyri. Grossly, the cerebellum has two lateral masses or hemispheres and a median structure, the vermis.

The developmentally oldest part of the cerebellum is known as the flocculonodular lobe, or archicerebellum. This is the reptile-like portion of the cerebellum; it is primarily associated with coordination of the head and trunk. It is closely related to the vestibular system and is sometimes referred to as the vestibulocerebellum.

The anterior lobe, or paleocerebellum, is mostly concerned with lower limb coordination and therefore receives most of its input from ascending spinocerebellar tracts.

The posterior lobe, or neocerebellum, helps coordinate voluntary movement of the ipsilateral body side. As you might have guessed, most of the input comes from the cerebral motor cortex, giving rise to the corticopontocerebellar tracts. This is the largest and most developed portion of the cerebellum and is generally the portion one tests in the office, when using specific tests for coordination.

The cerebellum is connected to the balance of the nervous system by three pairs of cerebellar peduncles. Information enters the cerebellum, is processed and modulated, and then exits the cerebellum. The cerebellum, then, acts as a refinement center. The superior peduncle (brachium conjunctivum) is responsible primarily for carrying already modulated information back up to the motor cortex. Most of its fibers are therefore exiting the cerebellum. The middle peduncle (brachium pontis) is the one through which fibers originating along the motor cortex and synapsing in the pons enter the cerebellum (corticopontine fibers). The inferior peduncle (restiform body) carries primarily vestibular and spinocerebellar communications, though the anterior spinocerebellar tract may ascend to the superior peduncle prior to entering the cerebellum.

Generally, cerebellar hemisphere circuitry follows this pathway: Impulses from the motor cortex travel to the pontine nuclei and synapse. The pontocerebellar neurons decussate and arrive via white matter to synapse on Purkinje fibers of the cerebellar cortex. The Purkinje fibers travel in white matter to the dentate nucleus of the cerebellum. Impulses then travel from the cerebellum and decussate just prior to their distribution to the red nucleus of the midbrain (extrapyramidal communication) and the thalamus and then back to the motor cortex, influencing corticospinal pathways. This is the so-called corticopontocerebellorubrothalamocorticospinal pathway (see Figure 7-1).

It is important to remember that the two decussations result in the cerebellum's modulating the opposite cerebral hemisphere and, therefore, the ipsilateral side of the body.

CLINICAL SIGNS OF CEREBELLAR DYSFUNCTION AND THEIR ASSESSMENT

General Weakness and Fatigue

This is often very prominent in cerebellar disease. It may be observed during the general patient assessment.

Swaying When Standing with a Narrow Base

Prior to performing a Romberg test, ask the patient to stand with feet together (i.e., heels and big toes touching). Inability to do this with the eyes open may well indicate cerebellar dysfunction.

Ataxia/Dystaxia

Ataxia/dystaxia (unsteady walking) is a cardinal sign of cerebellar dysfunction but may well be the result of disturbances of proprioception or other sensory modality, disturbances of the motor system, or joint disease. Always observe the patient's gait. An abnormal gait associated with cerebellar disease is the broad-based gait (the "long time in the saddle" gait): Instead of swinging toward the midline with each forward step, the lower extremities appear to swing away

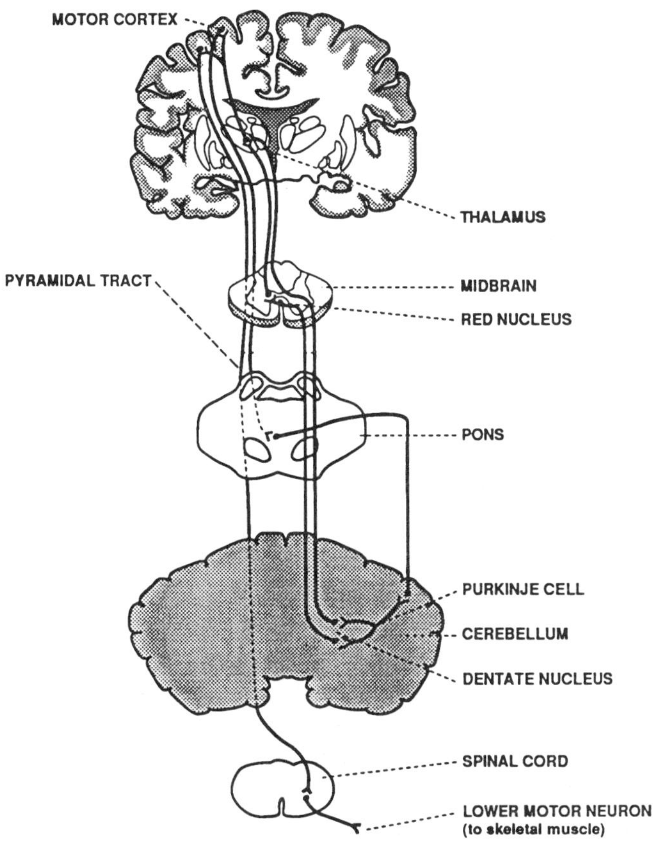

Figure 7-1 The corticopontorubrothalamocorticospinal pathway.

from the midline (see Figure 7-2). This is a sensitive and useful observation.

Dysarthria

Listen for dysarthria, or slurring of speech, that is of recent onset. To verify its presence, ask the patient to clearly repeat "Whosoever, whatsoever, or perfect pleasures" or any tongue twister, such as "I smart fellow, I fellow smart."

Nystagmus

Observe for nystagmus during the cranial nerve test.

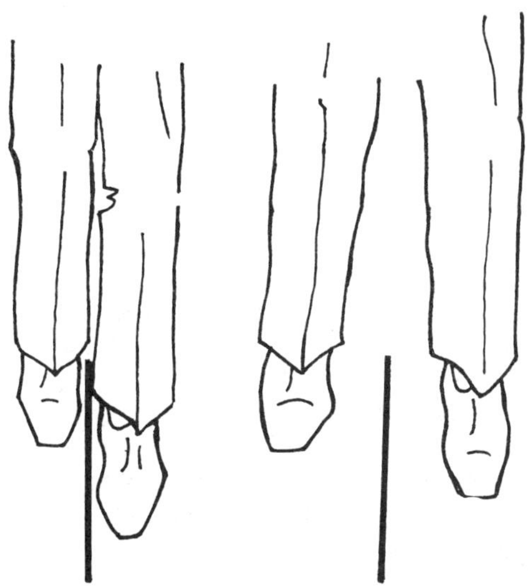

A B

Figure 7-2 A, A normal gait. **B**, A broad-based gait.

Hypotonia

Hypotonia often accompanies cerebellar disease. Observe for a ''rag doll'' posture and gait.

Decomposition of Movement

Due to decreased refinement of movements, coordination between movements is lost. Watch the patient for an appearance of ''movement by the numbers'' or choppiness.

Dysdiadochokinesia

This condition is marked by an inability to perform rapidly alternating movements. It can be tested by asking the patient to extend both arms and rapidly supinate and pronate the hands in the air (see Figure 7-3A). Observe for the ability to perform these movements, as well as their symmetry. A superior method of testing for this condition is the thigh slap variation. Here the patient is asked to slap the thighs with the hands, first with the fronts and then with the backs of the hands (see Figure 7-3B). With this test the doctor can see and hear any difficulties. To test for dysdiadochokinesia with the lower extremity, have the patient place a heel on the floor and tap that foot rapidly (see Figure 7-3C); be sure to test both feet.

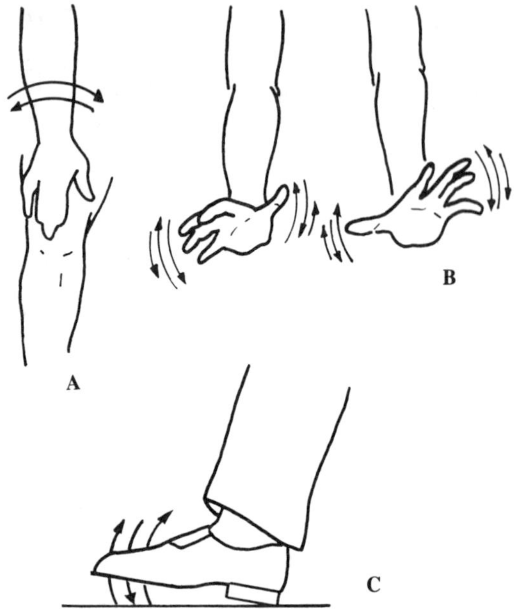

Figure 7-3 Three methods of testing for dysdiadochokinesia.

Pendular Reflex

Due to the hypotonicity associated with cerebellar disease, the knee jerk reflex tends to cause the lower leg to swing back and forth more times than usual, giving the appearance of a pendulum (see Figure 7-4). In some instances the hyperactive reflexes associated with upper motor neuron lesions have been described as pendular, but this is inappropriate and confusing. The term should be reserved for freely swinging knee-jerk reflex responses associated with cerebellar disturbances.

Overshooting/Undershooting

Patients with cerebellar disease experience difficulty in measuring distances and therefore will overestimate or underestimate the distance to a particular point. It is important to note that when cerebellar tests for overshooting and

Figure 7-4 A pendular reflex.

undershooting are performed with the eyes closed, the patient is actually relying more on proprioceptive information than on visual information. Therefore, markedly worse performance on cerebellar function tests with the eyes closed is often actually revealing proprioceptive losses. A classic example of this marked worsening in test performance is seen with the tandem gait (walking a straight line with a narrow base) and Romberg tests. As stated above, a patient with cerebellar disease may not be able to stand with a narrow base, even with his or her eyes open. When a patient does relatively well standing with a narrow base but quickly loses balance when asked to close his or her eyes, a defect of proprioceptive, not cerebellar, function is thought to be responsible.

There are many methods for testing for overshooting or undershooting, but it is usually best tested using the finger-to-nose test. The patient is asked to touch the very tip of the nose with the very tip of the finger and then to come back and touch the very tip of your finger. This movement should be repeated several times. Each time the patient breaks contact with your finger and heads toward his or her nose, move your finger slightly. This way, the return trip to your finger has not been "memorized" by proprioceptive pathways but requires the patient to make course adjustments, which helps isolate cerebellar function. Be careful not to move your finger while the patient's finger is headed toward it, as this will cause the patient to be chasing your finger around, and not test anything. Observe for tremor during the test, as well as general ability to accomplish the task. Remember, cerebellar dysfunction usually results in a tremor that gets worse with fine or detailed movements and may be completely absent at rest (intention tremor). Intention tremor may be more easily observed if the patient is asked to bring his or her finger back to, but not quite touching, the nose.

This is a quick and easy test to perform, and most normal individuals have little difficulty performing it. Truly abnormal test results speak volumes about cerebellar dysfunction. The test does have some drawbacks, though, the most important of which is that most patients know (or quickly figure out) that an abnormal response is signified by missing the target. Therefore, a hysterical or malingering patient may be more difficult to identify with this test.

An excellent and more objective method of testing for overshooting or undershooting is the wrist slap test. Here, the patient holds both upper extremities out to the front with the palms down. The patient is instructed, "Hold your arms out there, and don't let me move them." At that time gently slap the dorsum of one wrist, displacing it slightly downward. The patient will be surprised, thinking that you were going to push against his or her resistance, as in a muscle strength test. Since the patient knows not to let the hands drop down, he or she will respond by raising or pushing the upper extremities upward. The normal individual will check the upward travel of the extremities, but patients with cerebellar dysfunction have remarkably unchecked upward travel, such that the involved side well overshoots the uninvolved side (see Figure 7-5).

For testing in the lower extremity, the heel-to-shin test is often used. This is accomplished by asking the seated or supine patient to place the heel of one foot squarely on the upper shin of

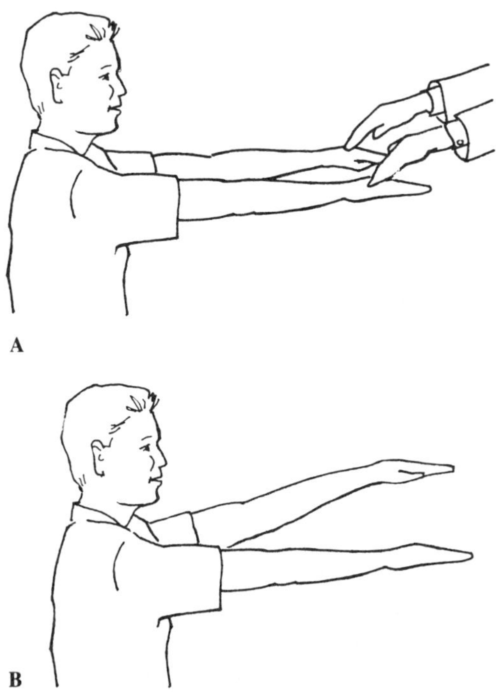

A

B

Figure 7-5 The wrist slap test. **A**, The starting position. **B**, Overshooting of the left arm.

the other leg and run the heel down the front of the shin and foot and off the big toe, without breaking contact between the heel and the shin. Observe wavering, difficulty, or loss of contact between heel and shin. The test is actually more difficult for the patient to perform than it sounds, but most normal individuals will perform it adequately. Tests for stationary or tandem stance (feet together) and gait (narrow based) are probably easier to interpret and therefore more reliable.

The rebound sign test is another variation of overshooting/undershooting tests, but it adds little or nothing to the above methods. The rebound sign is observed when the strength of the patient's biceps is challenged and the resistance is then suddenly removed. The patient will be unable to check the travel of his arm and would strike himself or herself if allowed to do so.

SYNDROMES OF CEREBELLAR DISEASE

A cerebellar syndrome is recognized for each of the anatomical areas. While each cerebellar area has unique characteristic findings, disequilibrium of stance and gait, as well as nystagmus, are shared by all of the syndromes described below.

Rostral Vermis or Anterior Lobe Syndrome

Primarily spinocerebellar pathology causes decreased coordination of the lower extremities and trunk. This syndrome is most commonly associated with alcoholism and nutritional deficiencies.

Caudal Vermis or Flocculonodular Lobe Syndrome

Pathological involvement of the vestibulocerebellum produces mostly stance and gait impairment (trunk or axial disequilibrium). This syndrome is often associated with a neoplasm of the cerebellopontine angle.

Hemisphere or Posterior Lobe Syndrome

Disease of the cerebellar hemispheres affects coordinated motor function of the ipsilateral side of the body. If seen in a child, a neoplasm or brain abscess should be suspected.

Pancerebellar Syndrome

Hereditary or toxic-metabolic disease is the usual cause of this syndrome. All cerebellar components are affected, resulting in movement disturbances involving the whole body.

SUGGESTED READING

Arnold LA. *Chiropractic Procedural Examination*. 2nd ed. Seminole, Fla: Seminole Printing, Inc; 1979:40, 52–53.

Chusid JG. *Correlative Neuroanatomy & Functional Neurology*. 17th ed. Norwalk, Conn: Lange Medical Publications; 1982:195–210.

DeJong RN. *The Neurologic Examination*. 4th ed. New York, NY: Harper & Row; 1979:39–78.

Van Allen MW. *Pictorial Manual of Neurologic Tests*. 2nd ed. Chicago, Ill: Year Book Medical Publishers, Inc; 1981:65–83.

chapter 8

The Chiropractic Spinal Examination

Thomas F. Bergmann

The doctor of chiropractic sees the human being as a dynamic, integrated, and complex being having an innate intelligence that provides a marked capacity for self-healing. As a primary health care provider, the doctor of chiropractic must utilize findings derived from the case history, physical examination, clinical laboratory, and special testing procedures to assess the patient's state of health and determine the nature and cause of any ailments. Though the examination considers all aspects, it especially emphasizes the assessment of the spinal column and the nervous system and employs all reliable evaluative procedures in order to identify musculoskeletal derangements that may be impairing the normal function of the nervous system. It is the chiropractic spinal examination that sets apart chiropractic from other areas of the healing arts.

Since the most specialized and significant therapy employed by the chiropractor involves the adjustment of the articulations of the spinal joints, the spinal examination becomes the focal point of the patient evaluation. In order to conduct a thorough examination, it is absolutely essential to have knowledge of the anatomy, physiology, biomechanics, and kinesiology of the spine and extremities.

The approach to treatment of joint problems that are mechanical in nature should have a biomechanical basis. Therefore, knowledge of normal biomechanics and kinematics, the ability to detect changes in joint mechanics, and the ability to restore normal component movement to a joint are necessary in the successful management of joint problems that are of a mechanical etiology or in which mechanical dysfunction is a prime factor. A thorough evaluation is necessary to clarify the nature and extent of the lesion.

It has long been a basic premise of chiropractic that a relationship exists between dysfunction of the nervous system and disease. It is also fundamental that some aberration within the spinal column produces the nerve dysfunction, or more specifically, that a malpositioned vertebra is at fault. It must be clearly understood, however, that the nerve dysfunction results from more than misalignment. A complex clinical entity that produces physiological changes that in turn lead to pathophysiological changes is responsible for the dysfunctional process. Chiropractors call these complex clinical entities subluxations. To bring about a subluxation, a force of either severe nature or prolonged duration must be applied upon a vertebra or its supporting structures. It is hypothesized that correction of a subluxation via the chiropractic adjustive thrust will restore normal physiological processes.

If it is accepted that this complex clinical entity called subluxation exists, a procedure to locate it is necessary. It is the role of the chiropractic spinal examination to accurately and objectively detect and monitor spinal dysfunction by noninvasive procedures. Just as most of the reliability studies have been done on single evaluative tools, there is the suggestion that single evaluative tools are employed in clinical practice. Knowing how complex the human body is, and specifically the neuromusculoskeletal system, it is appropriate to employ a system that uses a combination of numerous clinical indicators to locate those joints in greatest need of intervention. No one evaluative tool should be used or relied upon to make clinical decisions. Multiple evaluative approaches to spinal assessment have been suggested.[1]

However, chiropractors as well as other practitioners of manipulative therapy have not come to consensus on the most valid, objective, and efficient means of detecting the maniputable/adjustable spinal lesion. Although chiropractic and other physicians have shown increased attention in recent years to quantitative evaluation of the reliability of spinal examination procedures, this area of investigation is still embryonic.[2] Reliability studies have been done on the assessment of visual observation;[3] static (misalignment) palpation[4,5]; assessment of osseous and soft tissue pain[6–8]; motion, movement, and percussive palpation[4,6,7,9–16]; instrument measurements[8,17,18]; assessment of soft tissue texture changes[6,15]; assessment of static and stress radiographic changes[19,20]; and leg length evaluation.[18,21]

Structural evaluation of the spinal column will, then, be viewed in terms of a multidimensional index of segmental abnormality. Furthermore, the examination of the musculoskeletal system should never be done in isolation but should be done within the context of the history and physical examination of the patient. If the examination is inadequate, failing to reveal the source of the problem or its extent, treatment cannot be maximally effective. Moreover, the use of spinal assessment procedures should be a part of a critical, continual assessment of the patient to monitor the effects of care. Knowing when to stop is as important as knowing when to start and when to continue. The better the assessment, the fewer the treatment sessions. Practice makes perfect—there are no shortcuts.[22]

PRINCIPLES OF SPINAL EXAMINATION

The methods utilized in spinal examination are the same as those utilized in other aspects of evaluation, that is, observation, palpation, percussion, and auscultation. Using the modified acronym PARTS, the five diagnostic criteria for spinal dysfunction are as follows:[23]

1. *Pain/Tenderness*: The perception of pain and tenderness may be evaluated in terms of location, quality, and intensity. Most primary musculoskeletal disorders manifest primarily by a painful response. The patient's description of the pain and its location should be obtained. Furthermore, the location and intensity of tenderness produced by palpation of osseous and soft tissues should be noted. Pain and tenderness findings will be identified through the procedures of observation, percussion, and palpation.
2. *Asymmetry*: Asymmetrical qualities on a sectional or segmental level should be noted. This would include observation of posture and gait, as well as palpation for misalignment of vertebral segments. Findings of asymmetry will be identified through observation (posture and gait analysis), static palpation, and static radiography.
3. *Range of Motion Abnormality*: Changes in active, passive, and accessory joint motions should be noted. These changes may either be an increase or a decrease in mobility. It is thought that a decrease in motion is a common component of joint dysfunction. Range of motion abnormalities will be identified through the procedures of motion palpation and stress radiography.
4. *Tissue Texture/Temperature Abnormality*: Changes in the characteristics of contiguous and associated soft tissues, including skin, fascia, muscle, and ligaments, should be noted. Tissue texture/temperature changes will be identified through the procedures of observation, palpation,

and instrumentation and tests for length and strength.

5. *Special Tests*: Those testing procedures that are peculiar or specific to a technique system.

Specific Procedures

While many approaches may be taken to the evaluation of the spine, the most important one is the use of a systematized routine. This will help to avoid the possibility of omitting procedures or tests, which may prevent accurate interpretation. The following chiropractic exam outline is offered only as a suggested systematized routine. It is done positionally and therefore does not require the patient to move much. The accuracy and efficiency of the spinal examination will increase with the examiner's increased ability to instruct and position the patient. The goals of the examination procedure are to minimize patient discomfort and maximize the doctor's comfort, thereby allowing the doctor to concentrate on observations rather than on his or her own aching back.

While a number of skills are necessary for a thorough and competent spinal evaluation, palpation is by far the most important assessment skill used in the art of chiropractic. Surface measurement of temperature should be performed before other procedures. The dorsum of the fingers may be used as well as any of the temperature-detecting instruments available. Patient position and draping would be as recommended by the specific instrument procedure.

Prone Position

With the patient in the prone position, the examination begins with the examiner placing double thumbs over the patient's spinous processes and applying a posterior-to-anterior percussive-type pressure. The patient is instructed to respond if the pressure is painful; the doctor should feel resilience (a springing sensation) if there is a normal relationship of the tested segment with its neighboring segments above and below. Abnormal findings include the patient's response to pain production. It is characteristic of joint dysfunction for the doctor to perceive a loss of that springy quality, which may be indicative of a chronic problem, or a soft or "mushy" quality, which may be indicative of a more acute inflammatory process.

Palpation of the contiguous soft tissues is performed next. It is felt that suppleness and flexibility of muscle and connective tissue are of prime importance to the normal functioning of the spinal functional units. Comparisons are done side to side to evaluate changes in tone, texture, and tenderness. Paraspinal muscle hypertonicity may occur as reflex muscle spasm secondary to nociceptor irritation in joints and associated structures, or it can occur with direct involvement of the muscle itself from trauma and inflammation. Palpable textural changes in the musculature have been described as lumpiness, thickness, stringiness, ropiness, bogginess, and slipperiness. These palpable changes have been described as characteristic of myriad problems, including fibrositis, interstitial myofibrositis, muscle callus, muscle gelling or myogelosis, muscle hardening, muscular rheumatism, nonarticular rheumatism, soft-part rheumatism, myofascial pain syndrome, myofascitis, trigger points, and myalgic spots. There is still considerable controversy as to just what is the pathogenesis of these texture changes found within the soft tissues. Nevertheless, there is apparent agreement that they represent some form of less than desirable change in the supporting and stabilizing soft tissues of the spinal functional units.

A pinwheel can then be run paraspinally, covering a couple of spinal segments at a time. The patient is asked to identify any increase or decrease in sensation from side to side and level to level. A change in sensation may indicate involvement of the posterior primary division.

Osseous palpation of the bony landmarks (spinous processes—articular processes in the cervical spine, transverse processes in the thoracic spine, and mammillary processes in the lumbar spine) is done to locate misalignments of spinal segments and spinal sections (see Figure 8-1).

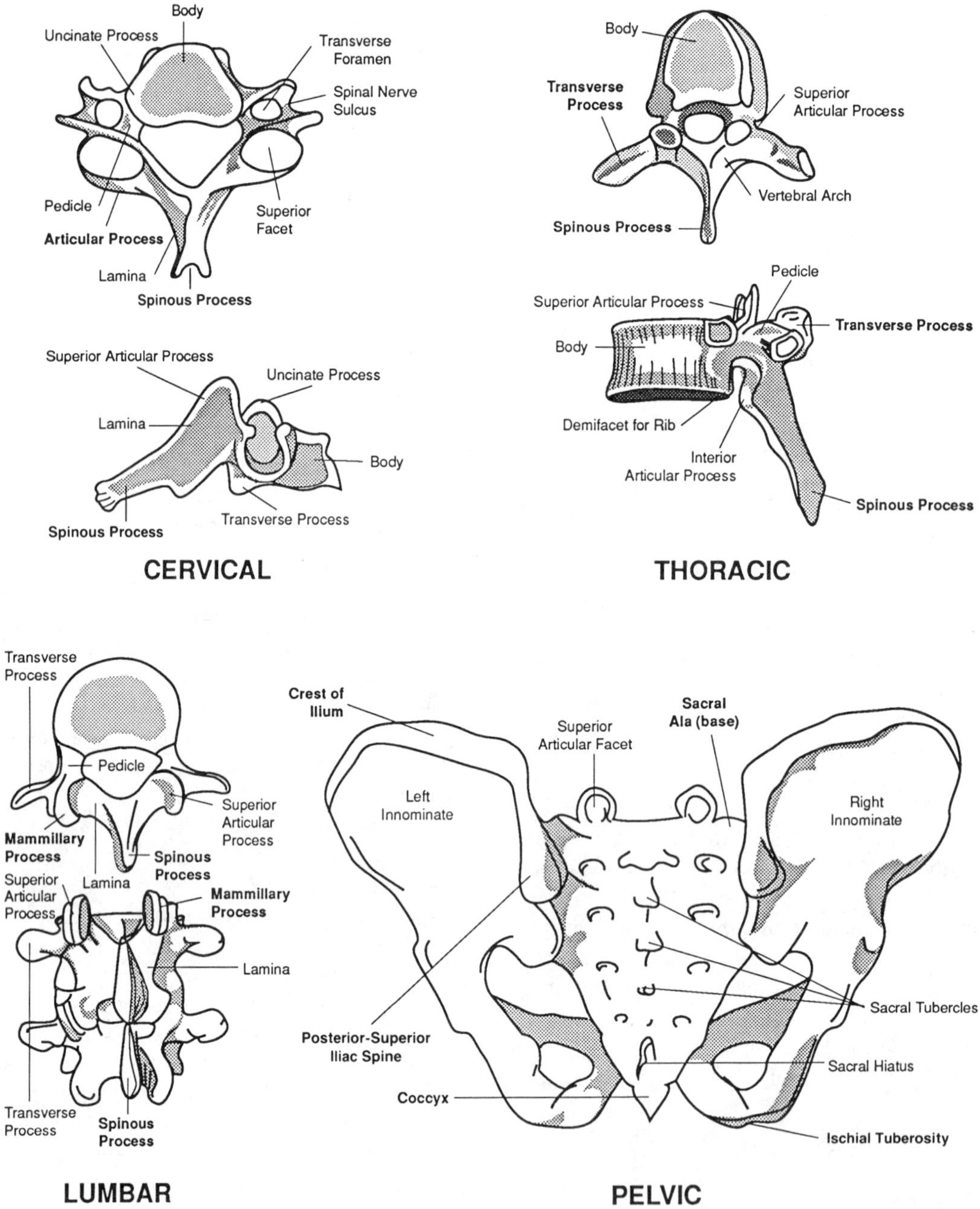

Figure 8-1 Bony landmarks of the spine and pelvis, with palpable structures in bold.

Interspinous spaces are palpated for flexion and extension positional changes. An increased interspinous space indicates flexion, while a decreased interspinous space indicates extension (see Figure 8-2). Also of note is that when the interspinous space increases (flexion), a stretch is placed on the intraspinous and supraspinous ligaments, which will likely be painful on palpation. The lateral processes (articular processes in the cervical spine, transverse processes in the

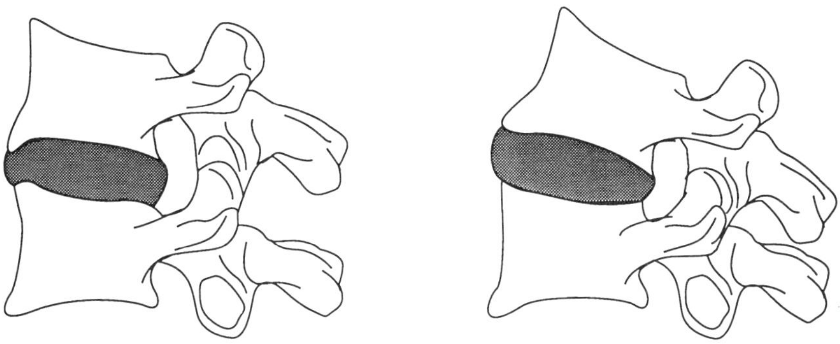

Figure 8-2 The interspinous spaces open on flexion and close on extension.

thoracic spine, and mammillary processes in the lumbar spine) are used to identify rotation and lateral flexion positional changes. The spinous process can be used also; however, it is prone to a great deal of structural variance and is not considered a reliable anatomical landmark.

Rotational misalignment can be identified when a lateral process palpates more prominently posteriorly through the overlying soft tissues (see Figure 8-3). Sometimes, especially in the lumbar spine, this is perceived only as a slight change in the density or compressibility of the overlying soft tissue. Lateral flexion misalignment is also determined by the position of the lateral processes. They are compared side to side, trying to identify whether one side is superior (cephalad) or inferior (caudad) relative to the segment above and below (see Figure 8-4).

The relative positions of the innominates with respect to the sacrum can be identified by palpating the posterior superior iliac spines (PSISs). The examiner places both thumbs on the PSISs and first determines the relationship of each PSIS. Normally they should be in the same or equal position. If one is more posterior, medial, and inferior, it indicates a posteriorly rotated side. The planes of the sacroiliac articulations are such that if the innominate moves posteriorly, it must also move medially (Figure 8-5). The examiner then rolls the thumbs off the PSISs and onto the sacral base. The tissue tension should be equal from side to side. If more tissue tension or firmness is noted on one side, it indicates the side of posterior sacral base. The sacral apex is then palpated to determine whether it is in the midline. Apex deviation is used to identify

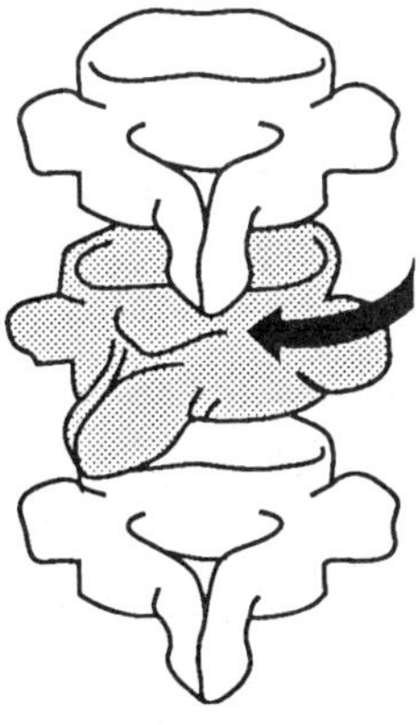

Figure 8-3 Right rotational disrelationship (misalignment).

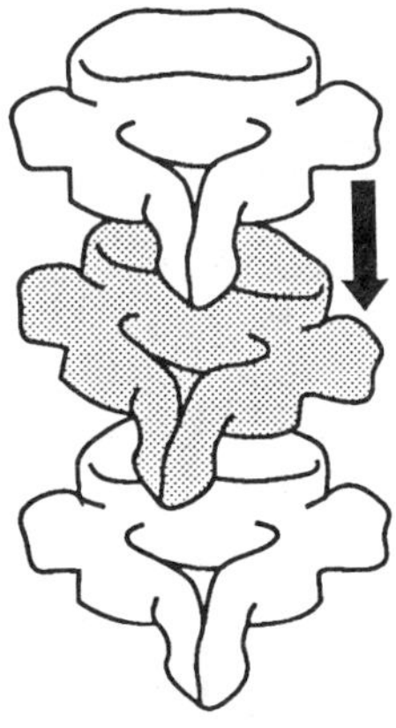

Figure 8-4 Right lateral flexion disrelationship (misalignment).

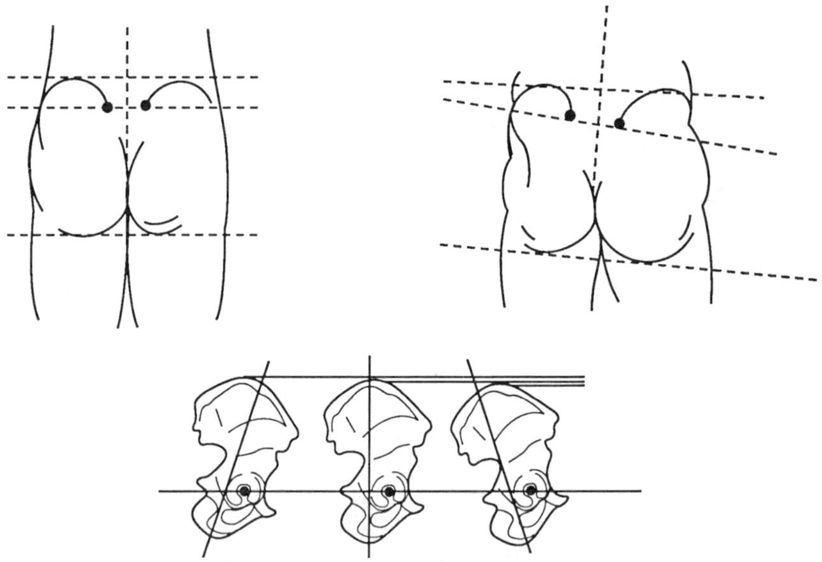

Figure 8-5 Relative position of the innominates. A posteriorly rotated innominate will have a PSIS more posterior and medial.

lateral flexion of the sacrum (see Figure 8-6). For example, if the sacral apex deviates to the left, the sacral base will be inferior on the right or in a right, laterally flexed position. Usually lateral flexion and rotation movements of the sacrum are coupled such that as the sacral base flexes laterally, it also rotates anteriorly.

A prone leg length evaluation can then be performed (see Figure 8-7). The patient's ankles are maintained in slight dorsiflexion while the relative positions of the medial malleoli are noted. A deficiency in leg length may be due to anatomical variance in the actual length of the femur and/or the tibia. When there is asymmetry in the position of the sacroiliac articulations, the posterior innominate can cause an apparent deficiency in length. The converse is also true—the anterior innominate can cause an apparent lengthening of the leg.

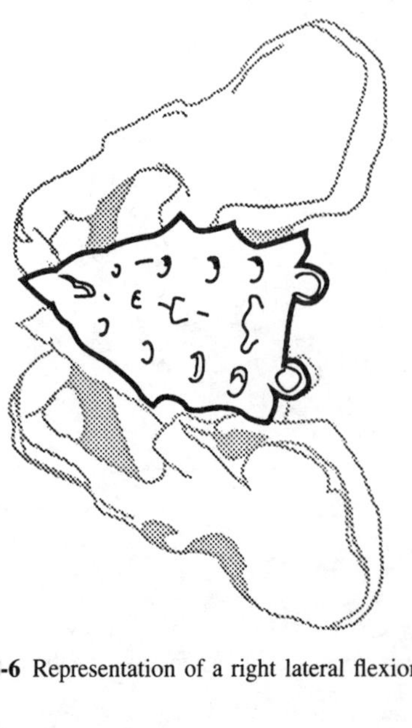

Figure 8-6 Representation of a right lateral flexion of the sacrum.

Supine Position

Positional changes in the cervical spine are more easily interpreted with the patient in the supine position. With the patient lying on his or her back, palpation of the articular processes for rotation and lateral flexion asymmetries can be accomplished. Palpation of the cervical spine soft tissues for tone, tenderness, and texture can also be performed.

A leg length evaluation can be done first with the patient supine and then sitting. A posterior innominate creates the appearance of a short leg in the supine position and a long leg when the patient sits up (see Figure 8-8). Measuring (using a tape measure) from the greater trochanter to the medial malleolus on both legs will determine actual structural leg deficiencies.

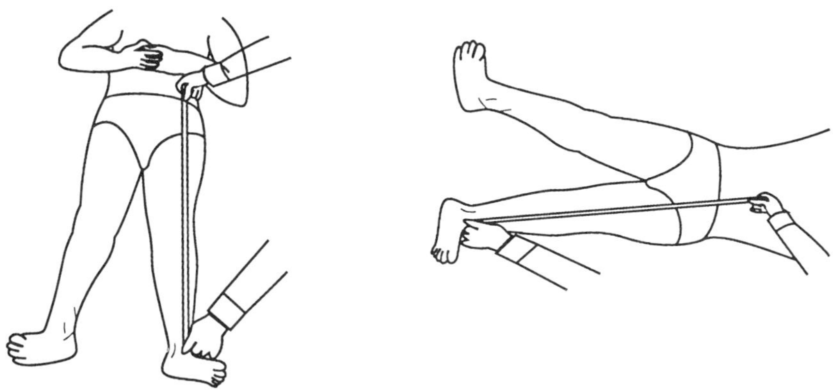

Figure 8-7 Evaluation of leg length in the supine positions. A tape measure is used to determine actual length.

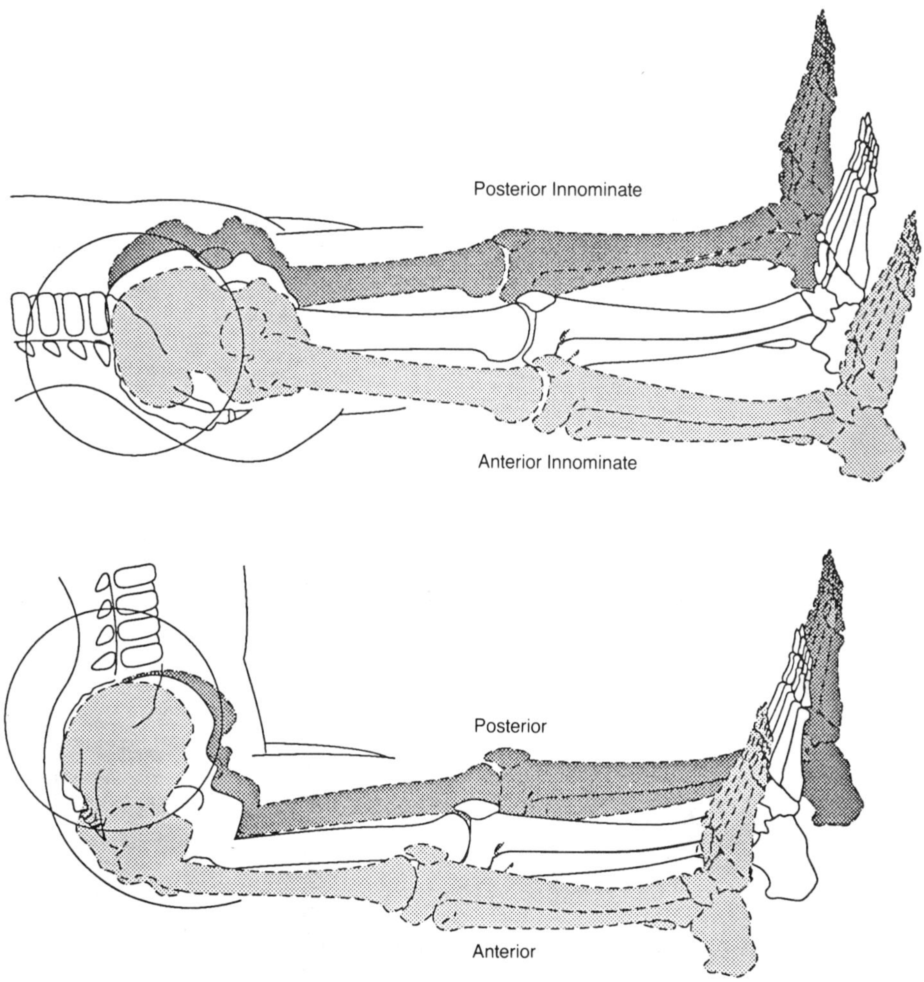

Figure 8-8 If a leg appears shorter in the supine position but longer in the sitting position, it indicates a posterior innominate on that leg's side. *Source:* Adapted from *Manual Examination and Treatment of the Spine and Extremities* (p 82) by CT Wadsworth with permission of Williams & Wilkins, © 1988.

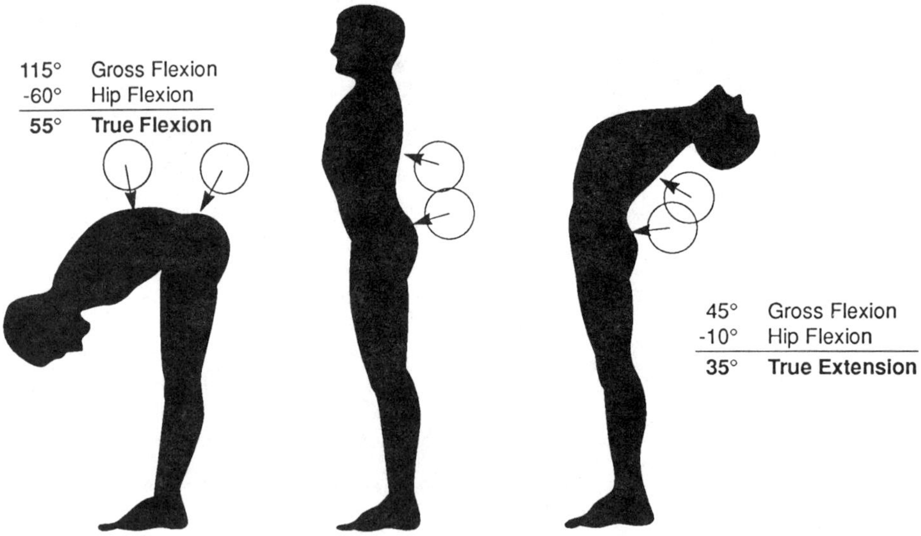

Figure 8-9 Inclinometer measurements of active ranges of motion.

Sitting Position

A spinal motion evaluation can be performed in the sitting position, with the patient either straddling the table or sitting on a palpation stool. Active ranges of motion of spinal sections can be observed and measured using an inclinometer (see Figure 8-9). Intersegmental active and accessory movements are also evaluated in this position. A passive motion screening procedure is done first. The examiner is seated closely behind the patient and with one hand introduces a forward-backward rocking motion while the other hand applies a generalized posterior-to-anterior stress on the spine from the sacrum to the occiput.

The purpose of this screening procedure is to identify and localize areas of dysfunctional movement that can then be specifically evaluated. Active segmental movements can be evaluated by contacting two spinous processes with the pads of the index and middle fingers. The patient is asked to bend forward and backward while the examiner checks whether the interspinous space opens on flexion and closes on extension (see Figure 8-10). The patient is then asked to bend sideways to the left and right while the examiner feels for equal movement and expected rotational coupling (spinous processes move toward the concavity with lateral flexion in the lumbar and lower thoracic spine and toward the convexity in the cervical and upper thoracic

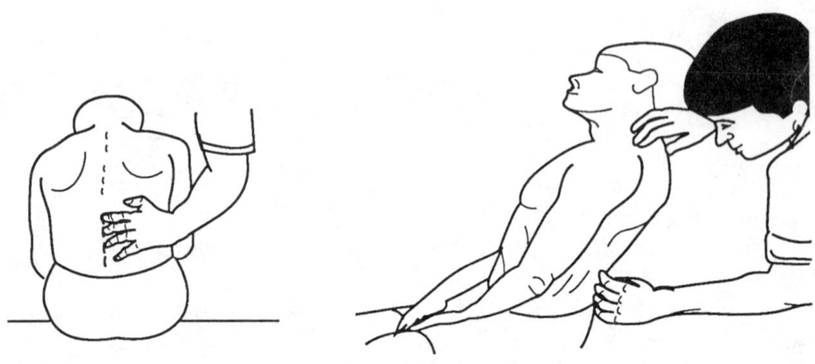

Figure 8-10 Evaluation of active segmental flexion and extension.

spine) (see Figure 8-11). Lastly, the patient is asked to turn to the right and left while the examiner feels the superior spinous process glide over the inferior spinous process (Figure 8-12).

Accessory joint movements can then be evaluated generally by applying a stress into the joint at the endpoint of movement and palpating for the presence or absence of a "springing" end feel. For flexion, the examiner places a thumb on the inferior aspect of the spinous process. The patient is then passively flexed, and the spinous process is stressed into further flexion (see Figure 8-13). Extension end feel movements are identified by placing the dorsum of the examiner's reinforced index and middle fingers over the posterior aspect of the spinous process (see Figure 8-14). The patient is passively extended, and a posterior-to-anterior stress is applied. Rotational end feel movements are elicited by placing the thumb on a lateral process (articular, thoracic, or mamillary) and turning the patient into rotation (see Figure 8-15). The lateral process is then stressed into further rotation.

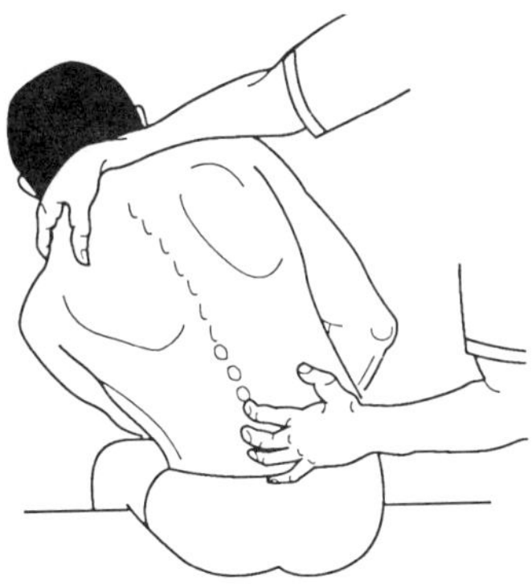

Figure 8-11 Evaluation of active segmental lateral flexion.

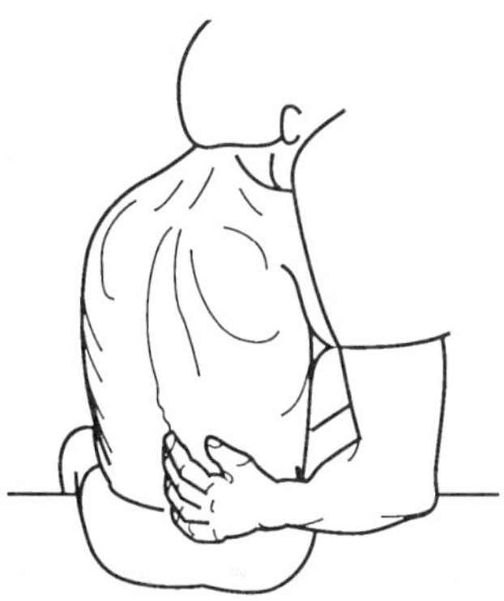

Figure 8-12 Evaluation of active segmental rotation.

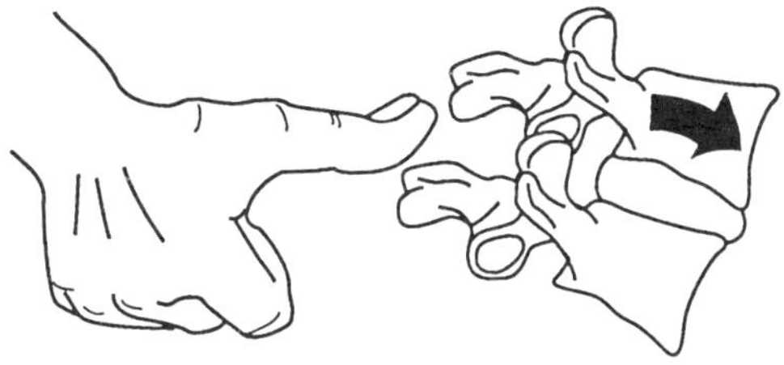

Figure 8-13 Evaluation of flexion end feel accessory movement in lumbar spinal functional unit. *Source:* Adapted from *Motion Palpation and Chiropractic Technic: Principles of Dynamic Chiropractic* by RC Schafer with permission of The Motion Palpation Institute, © 1989.

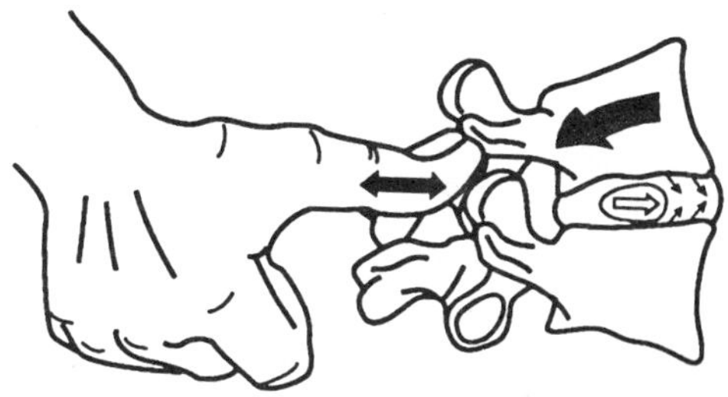

Figure 8-14 Evaluation of extension end feel accessory movement in lumbar spinal functional unit. *Source:* Adapted from *Motion Palpation and Chiropractic Technic: Principles of Dynamic Chiropractic* by RC Schafer with permission of The Motion Palpation Institute, © 1989.

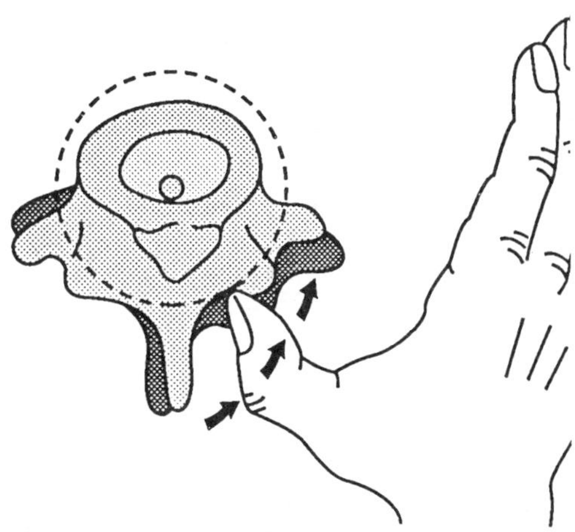

Figure 8-15 Evaluation for rotational end feel accessory movement in lumbar spinal functional unit. *Source:* Adapted from *Motion Palpation and Chiropractic Technic: Principles of Dynamic Chiropractic* by RC Schafer with permission of The Motion Palpation Institute, © 1989.

Accessory movements in lateral flexion can be assessed by contacting the side of the spinous process, laterally bending the patient to the side of contact, and stressing the spinous process from concavity to convexity (see Figure 8-16). These motions are common in the cervical, thoracic, and lumbar spine and should be evaluated in each region as indicated.

Each region also has individually unique motions that should be evaluated. In the cervical spine anterior-to-posterior rotational end feel can be identified by contacting the anterolateral aspect of the segment in question, turning the patient's head and neck toward the side of contact, and stressing the segment anterior to posterior. In the thoracic spine, the rib articulations (costotransverse, costovertebral) can be assessed for their characteristic caliper and bucket handle motions (see Figure 8-17). With the patient seated, the doctor contacts the angle of the rib just lateral to the transverse process. The patient is turned forward on that side and a posterior-to-anterior stress is applied, checking the caliper end feel. The doctor then places index and middle fingers in the intercostal spaces in the midaxillary line above and below the rib being examined. The patient is then asked to bend to each side while the examiner determines whether the intercostal spaces are opening and closing. An additional accessory joint motion that should be assessed in the lumbar spine is that of posterior-to-anterior glide at each facet. The mammillary process is the posterior aspect of the superior articulating facet, and the lumbar facet planes are primarily aligned in the sagittal plane, allowing the possibility of translational-type movement. With the patient sitting and the doctor sitting behind, the doctor places a thumb on a mammillary process. The patient is passively extended while the doctor stresses the mammillary process posterior to anterior (see Figure 8-18).

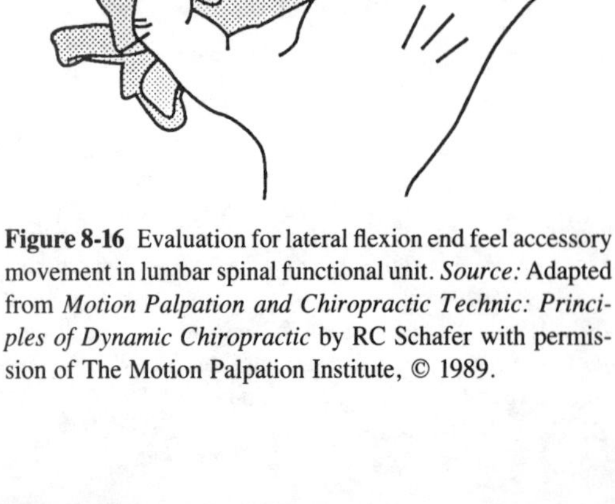

Figure 8-16 Evaluation for lateral flexion end feel accessory movement in lumbar spinal functional unit. *Source:* Adapted from *Motion Palpation and Chiropractic Technic: Principles of Dynamic Chiropractic* by RC Schafer with permission of The Motion Palpation Institute, © 1989.

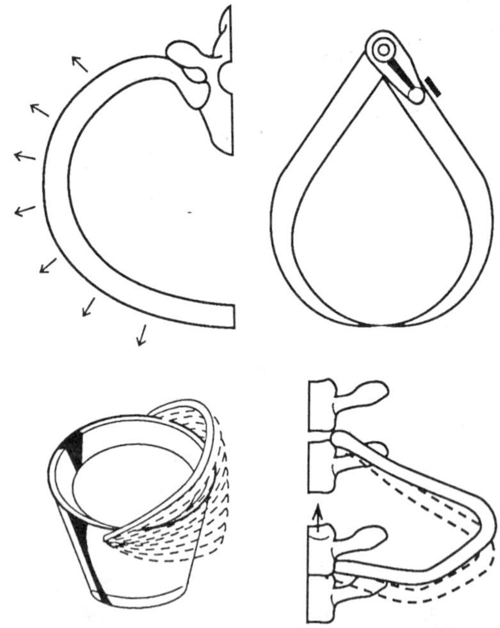

Figure 8-17 Characteristic caliper and bucket handle movements of the ribs as a part of the thoracic functional units. *Source:* Adapted from *Motion Palpation and Chiropractic Technic: Principles of Dynamic Chiropractic* by RC Schafer with permission of The Motion Palpation Institute, © 1989.

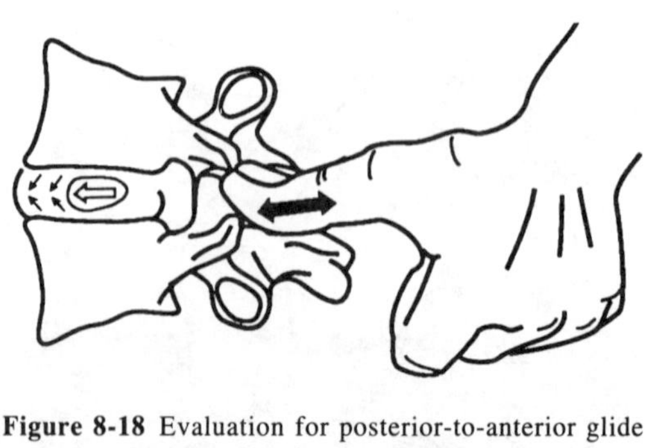

Figure 8-18 Evaluation for posterior-to-anterior glide accessory movement of the facets in a lumbar functional unit.

Standing Position

The standing position is used for evaluation of static and dynamic (gait) posture as well as specific evaluation of the sacroiliac articulations.

Static postural examination can begin with a plumb line evaluation, observing the patient from the lateral aspect. Visible surface landmarks that should coincide with the plumb line are the lobe of the ear, shoulder joint, greater trochanter, a point slightly anterior to the middle of the knee joint, and a point just anterior to the lateral malleolus (see Figure 8-19).

On posterior postural examination, the plumb line should pass through the external occipital protuberance, the spinous processes, the gluteal crease, midway between the knees, and midway between the ankles. Specific postural faults may be observed, including head tilt, head rotation, shoulder unleveling, lateral curvatures of the spine, pelvic unleveling, and pelvic rotation. Postural faults are likely to be caused by either muscular pull or laxity. Evaluation of suspected muscles for length, strength, volume, and tone is indicated.

Dynamic postural evaluation is performed by analysis of the patient's gait. This can be done by observing the patient walking at a regular pace up and down a hallway or, more conveniently, on a treadmill. Four points in the cycle of a single-step need to be assessed: heel-strike, midstance, push-off, midswing (see Figure 8-20). Each of these positions is observed for postural alignment, gross movements, fine movements, leg movements, and ankle movements. The objective of this evaluation is to identify deviations from expected norms as well as to obtain information that may help localize the cause of the deviations.

A biomechanical model for sacroiliac dynamics is important to enable clinicians to systematically evaluate and render treatment to this complex articulation. It appears that the sacroiliac joints form a three-joint complex and function similarly to the vertebral motion units. Movement in the six degrees of freedom, however slight, is evaluated with the patient in the standing position and the doctor kneeling or sitting behind. The doctor places both thumbs on the patient's PSISs and asks the patient to side bend to the left and right (see Figure 8-21). Normally, with this pelvic swaying motion the PSISs should stay relatively level. If a PSIS raises or depresses, it could be due to muscular imbalance (quadratus, psoas, abductors, and/or adductors) or sacroiliac dysfunction.

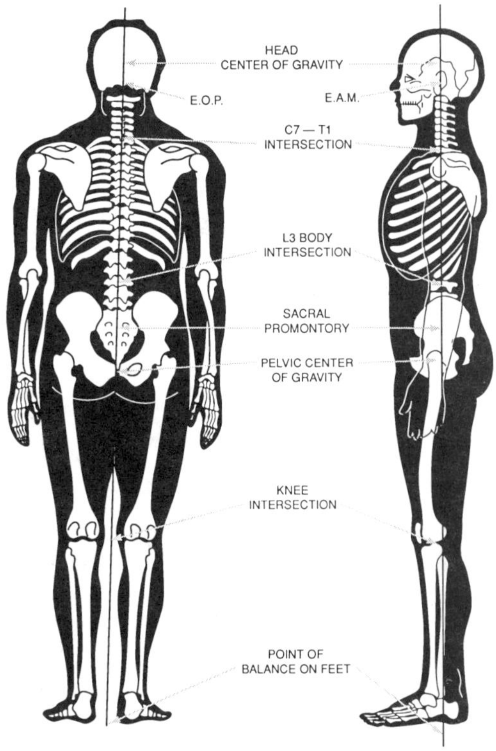

Figure 8-19 Posterior and lateral postural plumb line evaluation. EAM signifies external auditory meatus; EOP, external occipital protuberance.

The doctor places both thumbs on the apex of the sacrum and both middle fingers on each PSIS. The patient is asked to bend forward; when 60 degrees of lumbar spine flexion have been reached, the apex of the sacrum should separate from the PSISs, indicating normal movement of the sacral base posteriorly (see Figure 8-22). The patient is then asked to bend backward, and the apex should approximate the PSISs. If these movements do not occur, it indicates either abnormal flexion and extension (nutation and counternutation) of the sacrum or shortened sacrospinalis muscles.

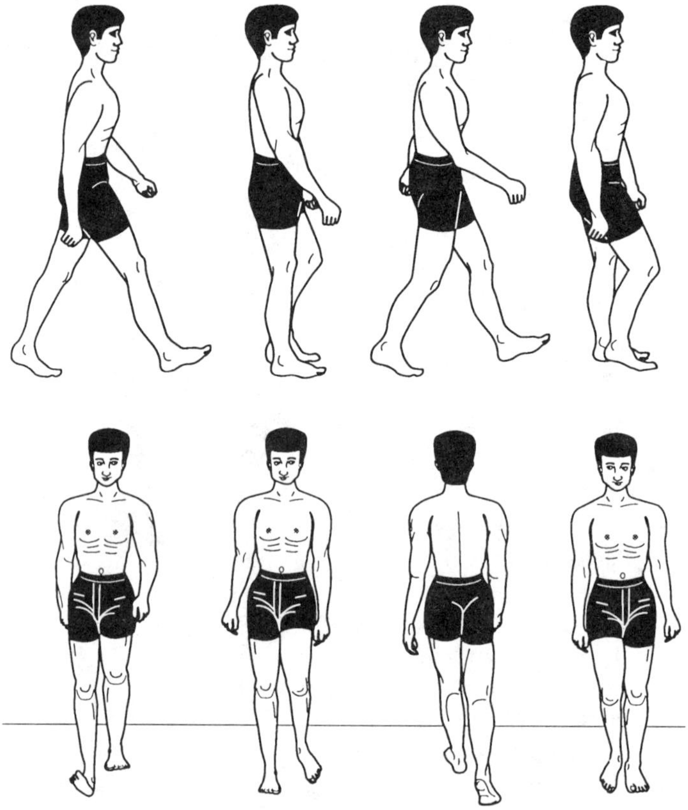

Figure 8-20 Evaluation of the four phases of gait.

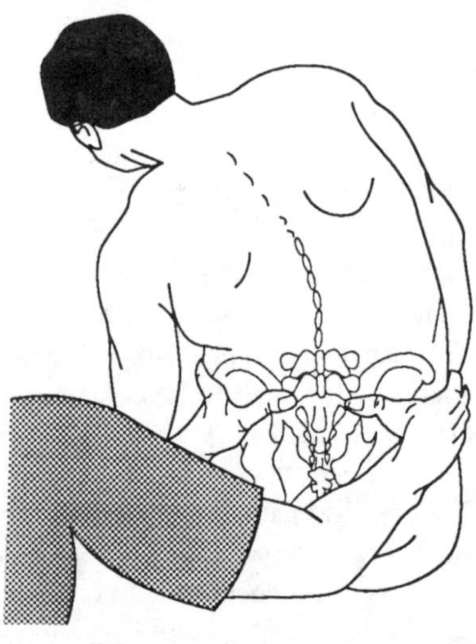

Figure 8-21 Sacroiliac functional test: side bending.

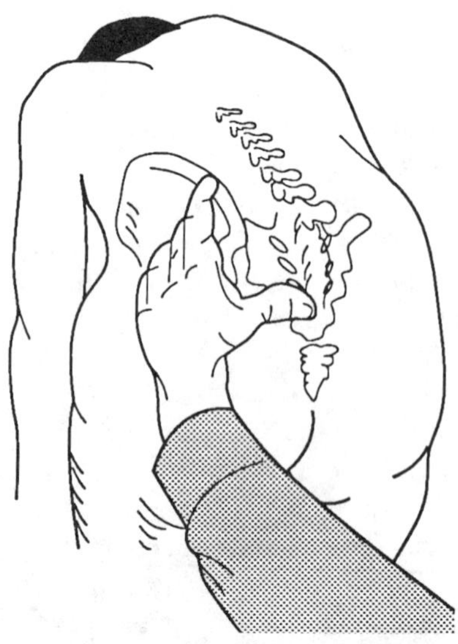

Figure 8-22 Sacroiliac functional test: flexion and extension.

The doctor then places one thumb on the homolateral PSIS and the other thumb on the first sacral tubercle. While holding on to something with one hand for balance, the patient raises the homolateral knee in a marching fashion as high as possible (see Figure 8-23). The doctor should feel the PSIS move posteriorly, inferiorly, and medially. If it does not move or in fact moves laterally, this indicates an upper ilium fixation.

With the same contacts, the patient is asked to raise the contralateral knee. The doctor should feel the first sacral tubercle move toward the PSIS. If this movement does not occur, it suggests an upper sacral fixation. This procedure is repeated on the other side.

The doctor places one thumb on the sacral apex and the other thumb in the soft tissue straight lateral to the apex contact and on a line down from the PSIS. The patient is asked to raise the homolateral knee, and the doctor should then feel the innominate soft tissue contact move anteriorly and inferiorly, in a "tucking under" fashion (see Figure 8-24). If this motion does not occur or if the movement is lateral, it indicates a lower ilium fixation.

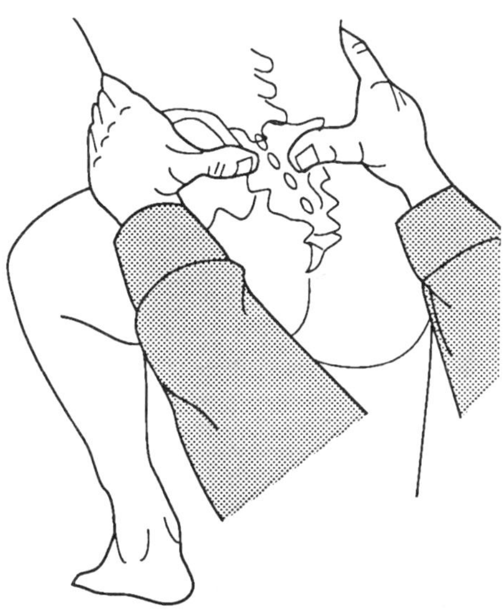

Figure 8-23 Sacroiliac functional test: left upper joint. Homolateral hip flexion is used for evaluation of innominate movement; contralateral hip flexion is used for evaluation of sacral movement.

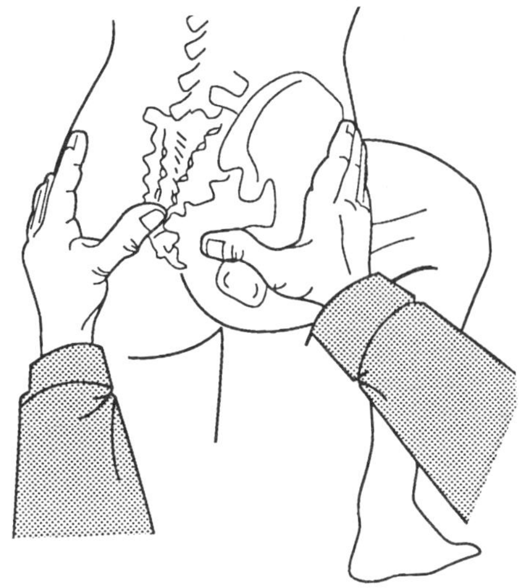

Figure 8-24 Sacroiliac functional test: right lower joint. Homolateral hip flexion is used to evaluate innominate movement; contralateral hip flexion is used to evaluate sacral movement.

With the same contacts, the patient is asked to raise the contralateral knee. The doctor should feel the sacral apex move toward the other contact as it gets covered by the gluteal mass. If this movement does not occur, it suggests a lower sacral fixation.

It should be noted that more than one fixation can occur in the sacroiliac joint. Moreover, hypermobility can occur in this joint and often manifests as a "clunking" noise with hip flexion. Sometimes encountered is a "ratcheting" sensation or fine jerking movements on leg lowering after hip flexion. This suggests lumbar paraspinal hypertonicity.

After all the data are collected, including any special tests aligned with the clinician's appropriate choice of adjustive procedure, they must be processed to determine the most clinically significant spinal dysfunction—the adjustable lesion. The failures in one chiropractor's office can be successes in another office and vice versa, because each doctor will take a different approach to the same symptom complex. Complete understanding of body mechanics and kinetics will aid in the selective approach toward spinal correction and a better understanding of the nature and extent of the treatable lesion.

REFERENCES

1. Faucret B, Mao W, Nakagawa T, Spurgin D, Tran T. Determination of bony subluxations by clinical, neurological and chiropractic procedures. *J Manipulative Physiol Ther.* 1980;3:165–176.

2. Keating JC, Bergmann TF, Jacobs GE, Finer BA, Larson K. Interexaminer reliability of eight evaluative dimensions of lumbar segmental dysfunction. *J Manipulative Physiol Ther.* 1990;13:463–470.

3. Kappler RE. A comparison of structural examination findings obtained by experienced physician examiners and student examiners on hospital patients. *J Am Osteopath Assoc.* 1980;79:468–471.

4. Aldridge J, Codieux J, Marsh D. *Motion Palpation: Static Palpation—A Comparative Study.* Toronto: Canadian Memorial Chiropractic College; 1975. Thesis.

5. Johnston WL. The role of static and motion palpation in structural diagnosis. *J Am Osteopath Assoc.* 1975; 75:421–424.

6. Boline PD, Keating JC, Brist J, Denver G. Interexaminer reliability of palpatory evaluations of the lumbar spine. *Am J Chiropractic Med.* 1988;1:5–11.

7. DeBoer KF, Harmon R, Tuttle CD, Wallace H. Reliability study of detection of somatic dysfunction in the cervical spine. *J Manipulative Physiol Ther.* 1985;8:9–16.

8. Terret ACJ, Vernon H. Manipulation and pain tolerance: a controlled study of the effect of spinal manipulation on paraspinal cutaneous pain levels. *Am J Phys Med.* 1984;63:217–225.

9. Dombrowsky N, Dunn G, Millar D. *Correlation between the Motion Palpation of Three Graduating Chiropractic Students.* Toronto: Canadian Memorial Chiropractic College; 1976. Thesis.

10. LeMoel B, Chadwick G, Goldman C, Spring J, Putnam R. *An Appraisal of the Efficacy of Movement Palpation.* Toronto: Canadian Memorial Chiropractic College; 1976. Thesis.

11. Love RM, Brodeur RR. Inter- and intra-examiner reliability of motion palpation for the thoracolumbar spine. *J Manipulative Physiol Ther.* 1987;10:1–4.

12. Mootz RD, Keating JC, Kantz HP, Milus TB, Jacobs GE. Inter- and intra-examiner reliability of passive motion palpation of the lumbar spine. *J Manipulative Physiol Ther.* 1989;12:440–445.

13. Wiles MR. Reproducibility and interexaminer correlation of motion palpation findings of the sacroiliac joints. *J Can Chiropractic Assoc.* 1980;24:59–68.

14. Gonella C, Paris S, Kutner M. Reliability in evaluating passive intervertebral motion. *Phys Ther.* 1982; 62:436–444.

15. Johnston WL, Allan BR, Hendra JL, et al. Interexaminer study of palpation in detecting location of spinal segmental dysfunction. *J Am Osteopath Assoc.* 1983;82:839–845.

16. Minor SA, King RS, McGregor M, Bernard M. Intra- and inter-examiner reliability of motion palpation of the cervical spine. *J Can Chiropractic Assoc.* 1985;19:195–198.

17. Brunarski DJ. Chiropractic biomechanical evaluations; validity in myofascial low back pain. *J Manipulative Physiol Ther.* 1982;7:243–249.

18. Addington ER. Reliability and objectivity of the anatometer, supine leg length test, Thermoscribe 11, and the Derm-term-o-graph measurements. *Upper Cervical Monogr.* 1983;3:8–11.

19. Deyo R, Tsui-Wu YJ. Observer variability in the interpretation of lumbar spine radiographs. *Arthritis Rheum.* 1985;28:1066–1070.

20. Antos JC, Robinson K, Keating JC, Jacobs GE. Interrater reliability of fluoroscopic detection of fixation in the mid-cervical spine. *Chiropractic Technique.* 1990; 2:53–55.

21. Fuhr AW, Osterbauer PJ. Interexaminer reliability of relative leg-length evaluations in the prone, extended position. *Chiropractic Technique.* 1989;1:13–18.

22. Grieve G. *Common Vertebral Joint Problems.* 2nd ed. Edinburgh: Churchill Livingstone; 1989.

23. Bourdillon JF, Day EA. *Spinal Manipulation.* 4th ed. New Haven, Conn: Lange Medical Publications; 1987.

chapter 9

Clinical Assessment of Pain and Function

A.V. Anderson, Ronald J. Berk, and David Hinz

Pain is an entity that is felt by all. It is a common companion to illness and injury, an unavoidable concomitant of the human condition. After all the miracle cures have been brought forth, pain probably will remain as the "the final frontier." Pain is not an isolated phenomenon. It is a complex perception unique to each individual. Pain is shaped by anatomy, physiology, neurology, neurochemistry, personality, environment, precipitating events, and other factors. The totality of the pain event is referred to as a "pain complex."

The sensations giving rise to pain are transmitted by the peripheral and central nervous systems. The autonomic nervous system plays a role in modulating pain, but how this works is not fully understood. The central nervous system is comprised of the brain and spinal cord. The peripheral nervous system is made up of nerves that ultimately exit from the spine. Each spinal cord segment gives rise to a pair of spinal nerves that exit the cord via plexuses in the cervical, upper thoracic, lumbar, and sacral spine regions. These plexuses reorganize into the peripheral nerves, which advance through the extremities, providing both motor power and sensory perception. The autonomic nervous system controls the somewhat misnamed involuntary functions of the body. It should be noted that all three systems—central, peripheral, autonomic—can be affected in a pain complex.

Each entity of the nervous system is an important player in the transmission, perception, and, occasionally, generation of pain stimuli. These entities include the brain, the brainstem, and the spinal cord, within which lie the spinal thalamic and reticular tracts. The postcentral gyrus of the cerebral cortex of the brain is responsible for perception; this area receives incoming stimuli via the thalamus, also found in the brain, which acts as a sort of switchboard for incoming stimuli. The brain is contiguous with the brainstem, which is contiguous with the spinal cord running down through the bony canal of the vertebral column to end at approximately T-12 to L-2. The spinal cord carries the spinal thalamic tracts that are believed to relate primarily to pain perception. The other tract related to pain is the spinoreticular tract, which probably relates to the "agony" of pain. From the reticular area, pain is transmitted through the reticulothalamic tracts to the thalamus and then from the thalamus to the postcentral gyrus. The sensory cranial nerves have pathways from the pons to the thalamus.

The peripheral nerves are the pathways conducting pain impulses to the spinal cord from the somatic areas as well as the extremities. The peripheral nerves can be irritated at various points in the body, producing a pain complex when entrapped or traumatized along their course. Thus a complete understanding of the dermatomes of the body is required to ascertain the spinal and/or peripheral nerve level of involvement when diagnosing a pain complex.

The vertebral column itself plays a significant role in producing disabling pain, since the structures therein are subject to injury. The bony structures of the vertebral column can be fractured, causing significant pain and, if compression of the spinal cord occurs, significant neurological compromise. There are numerous other structures in the vertebral column that, when injured, can cause significant pain syndromes.[1] The most obvious of these are the nerve roots that exit at the segmental levels. These are subject to compression by a herniated disc.[2] This type of pain is typically referred dermatomally along the course of the nerve to the periphery of the body. The tendons and ligaments attached to the spinal structures are capable of producing pain if injured.[2] The interspinous ligaments are subject to tearing during flexion injuries, causing significant pain.[1] The facets or epiphyseal joints of the spine are subject to stretching, causing distention of the capsular structures and injury to the joints themselves.[3] Disc injury can be a gradual event that evolves over a period of time to eventually produce a significant degenerative disc syndrome, generating pain by compressing a nerve. This pain has its origin in injury of the annular fibers, medially, with gradual deterioration of the adjacent annular fibers and dissection by the nucleus pulposus material.[2,4] Eventually this involves the more peripheral annular fibers, ultimately producing stimulation of the discal nerve supply. As this occurs there is deterioration of the disc itself, causing loss of disc height and subsequent mechanical change within the ligamentous attachments and the facet structures, a change in weight bearing on the facets, and further deterioration of the disc and facet structures. This has been described by Kirkaldy-Willis as the three-joint complex.[2]

Since all of this occurs in the vertebral column, the surrounding muscle apparatus often is overlooked in pain-producing injuries. This is especially true when a portion of the spine is projected through an atypical range of motion, causing stretching and tearing of the ligaments, muscles, and tendons.[5,6] An effort of the muscle to inhibit excessive motion in and of itself can result in additional tearing of these structures. Injury to the muscle apparatus can cause spasm and, ultimately, shortening of the muscles, which can permanently alter anatomical posture and physiological structure.[2(p25),7] This has been demonstrated in studies of the cervical physiological curve both pre- and postaccident.[8]

The various joints of the body also can be influenced by hyperextension/flexion injuries, compression injuries, etc. One joint that has been substantially overlooked in this regard is the temporomandibular joint. Significant trauma can occur even from a flexion/extension injury of the cervical spine in which this joint is stressed abnormally, causing compression as the joint is forced together and extension or tearing of the supportive structures when the joint is separated.[9–12] This can result in localized pain, dental pain, and headaches.

In pain syndromes involving accidents, particularly of the spinal column, one long-term problem that can result is injury to the muscle and ligamentous apparatus.[8] This injury frequently results in a posttraumatic strain and sprain complex, which, in turn, develops into a myofascial syndrome. It has been the experience of these authors that soft tissue problems result in a significant complexity of symptoms and alteration of lifestyle in those persons suffering posttraumatic residual pain.

It is important to consider two categories of pain: acute and chronic. Acute pain is the component that is basically protective. An example is the pain of a burn on the bottom of the foot resulting in stimulation of free nerve endings (C and A deltas), the spinal thalamic tract, and the postcentral gyrus. There is an immediate motor response mediated at the cord level known as the flexion withdrawal crossed extension reflex. There is also reflexive inspiration, which may permit the utterance of a learned exclamation, crying, or, perhaps, yelling (see Figure 9-1).

Chronic pain is defined by most authors as pain lasting more than 6 months. From the standpoint of pain as a protective mechanism, chronic pain is basically worthless.

Acute pain is a self-limited phenomenon. About 6 to 8 weeks of rest are required for

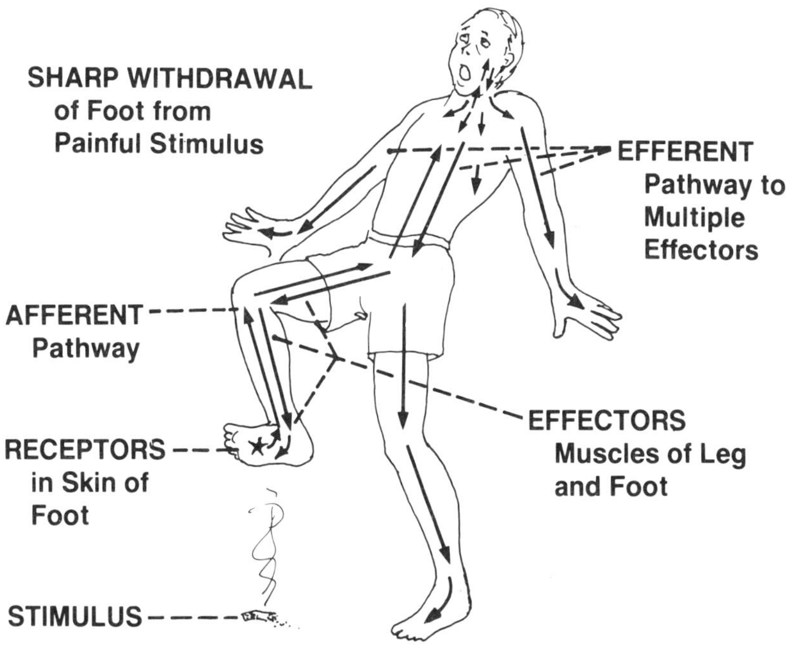

Figure 9-1 The response to the acute pain produced by burning.

healing to occur.[13] Chronic pain, on the other hand, can last indefinitely and cannot be treated in the same manner as acute pain.[13–15]

Ronald J. Dougherty, MD (Medical Director, Rehabilitation and Pain Clinic, Syracuse, New York) has stated that 1 of 10 patients will eventually develop chronic pain. Fifty percent of these patients will use between one to five pain relievers. Dr. Dougherty has also stated that these drugs are frequently prescribed by more than one physician and are not infrequently accompanied by over-the-counter medications. It is his opinion that of all chronic pain patients, 25% will become addicted and at least 50% of these will experience withdrawal with abrupt cessation of their painkiller. These authors have noted the same basic pattern of findings in over 6,000 of their own chronic pain patients.

PSYCHOPHYSIOLOGICAL PROFILE OF PAIN PATIENTS

In order to help the reader understand the complexity of chronic pain, some of the obvious traits of the patient with chronic pain should be discussed.

Various components of this profile of pain must be examined. Work effort can be defined as the amount of activity required each day. Recreational effort is usually an addendum to the work effort. These two efforts accomplished in a typical day or week serve to support another component known as endurance. Endurance is what is required by the body to function at a given level and to tolerate various levels of exertion. Recreational and work efforts help to maintain and support endurance at a given level.

Another component that must be dealt with on a daily basis is anxiety. In a well-adjusted individual this is maintained at a level that is nondetrimental. When the individual encounters significant trauma, increased anxiety will tend to occur. When this occurs in the acute phase of pain, it can be considered protective. However, if it continues into the chronic stages of pain, it can lead to a reduced or protected activity level. Recreational activity may be dropped. Endurance would then tend to drop to a level just above the work activity. This individual might eventually become "sick of feeling sick" and attempt to return to those recreational activities participated in prior to the accident. The endurance level would be exceeded by the activity demand, thereby causing increased fatigue and probably an exacerbation of the pain complex. With an increase in the pain level, the patient's anxiety level would tend to increase as well. This significant increase in pain and anxiety level may cause the patient to have significant concerns regarding the severity of the injury itself. If the patient panics, or is ill-advised by a health care practitioner or even a family member, substantial reduction in activity, including work effort, could follow. This, in turn, would cause a significant decrease in the endurance level and a further increase in the anxiety level. Any activity that the patient would then undertake would exceed the level of endurance or tolerance and increase the pain level. This would further support the idea that rest or restricted activity should be continued. This can lead even a well-adjusted individual into a chronic pain syndrome.

Pain is at the center of this syndrome. If the pain syndrome is not well understood by the practitioner and subsequently not well explained to the patient, further deterioration can occur (see Figure 9-2).

Pain will produce anger if it substantially changes the individual's ability to function. This anger, turned inward, will result in depression.[16] Fatigue is a substantial component of depression. Fatigue can further enhance the chronic pain cycle, causing an increase in anger and further depression. This results in further fatigue. Fatigue and despondence are followed by decreased activity and further deconditioning.

The patient with a significant amount of anger, depression, and fatigue frequently will try to alter this pain complex. This may result in the use of drugs or alcohol. The patient is making an effort to change the overall picture, particularly the perceived self-image, by engaging in self-medication. Under the influence of chemicals, the patient typically becomes more inactive, thereby further reducing the overall physical

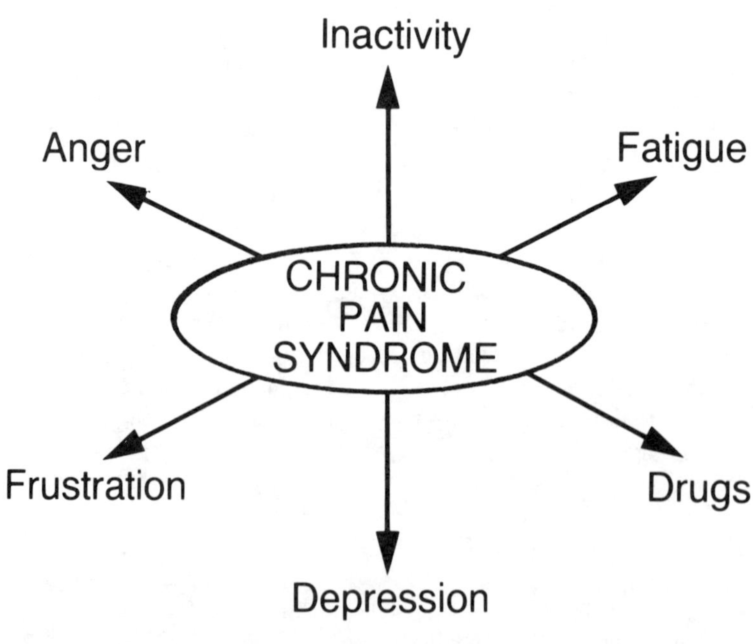

Figure 9-2 Pain is at the core of the chronic pain syndrome.

conditioning and further reinforcing the pain cycle. Sleep disorders frequently accompany depression and myofascial pain.[17] To all of this add changes in the social and family structure, fear of the unknown, interactions with third-party health care coverage providers, and lack of understanding by health care professionals. At this point the patient sinks further and further into a state of frustration. This cycle then becomes firmly entrenched and is well established as a chronic pain syndrome (see Exhibit 9-1).

One of the first and most obvious psychological symptoms to arise is the loss of self-esteem. Lacking self-esteem, the patient physically functions at a much lower level than prior to the pain-producing incident. This tends to produce aggravation of any premorbid conditions such as neurosis, shame-based behavior, self-defeating behavior, and inadequate personality. Even in a normal patient, a substantial alteration in the ability to function would bring about a loss of self-esteem.

Patient communication skills are generally blunted to the point of the patient's being unable to discuss true feelings. Those feelings tend to center about the pain complex, thereby substantially limiting the patient's ability to communicate. This, in turn, causes a further breakdown in self-esteem and family structure. An informal random study of chronic pain patients at the Pain Assessment and Rehabilitation Center (Minneapolis, Minnesota) shows a 75% divorce rate, as compared to an overall 50% divorce rate in the Minneapolis area.

As stated before, activity levels are substantially curtailed for a chronic pain patient. This is due to a lack of understanding of the problem itself, on the part of either the patient or the treating physician. Decreased activity not only diminishes body capability but also tends to significantly influence psychological state.

Exhibit 9-1 Results of Chronic Pain Syndrome

Loss of:
Self-esteem
Communication
Family structure
Activity
Goals
Group support

The patient's loss of goals leads to additional destruction of self-esteem. It has been assumed in the past that patients afflicted with this syndrome are influenced by various factors such as litigation, the dream of third-party reimbursement, or some other form of secondary gain.[18] Although these factors sometimes are true, it has been the experience of the Pain Assessment and Rehabilitation Center that these factors are present in a low percentage of people involved in injuries resulting in the chronic pain syndrome. Most patients at the center have suffered significant financial setbacks as a result of the chronic pain syndrome. This has substantially reduced their ability to achieve their goals, short-term or long-term.

If the patient has been restricted from work or is unable to perform occupationally, group support is lost. If communication between friends and family has been destroyed, additional group support is lost. With the loss of group support, self-esteem, activity levels, and goals all are negatively influenced.

Role reversal resulting from chronic pain is at the root of many family problems. Role reversal takes place if the injured family member cannot adequately carry out his or her role. This, then, reduces the patient's perceived self-image. Role reversal adds to the problems related to self-esteem, communication, and family structure, as well as to activity levels and goals.

At this point in the process one can assume that the patient may suffer a significant setback in life relative not only to financial status but also to overall psychological functioning. Only thorough evaluation and diagnosis will lead to the establishment of a proper treatment plan that takes into account all of the above factors.

DIAGNOSIS

It has been the experience of the authors that many patients have been misdiagnosed and have been inappropriately and inadequately treated. Patients should undergo a very thorough diagnostic examination, particularly if there is any indication of spinal instability, degenerative joint or disc disease, chronic tendinitis or myositis, or any intervening systemic disease. Full psychological assessment should be carried out, with emphasis on effecting possible changes by enhancing understanding through counseling, family therapy, or bibliotherapy. The individual's ability to function in the job should be assessed, particularly as it relates to both physical and psychological status. If the history indicates a possible head injury, the patient should be evaluated as to mild closed head injury complications.

TREATMENT

Exercise should be a mainstay of the rehabilitation plan for every patient. When the Pain Assessment and Rehabilitation Center was first established in 1979, the exercise equipment available was comparatively unsophisticated. Fortunately, since that time technology has substantially improved, allowing us to work on specific muscle groups and also to facilitate a more specific graded exercise program. This is extremely helpful for patients who have low levels of motivation as a result of the chronic pain complex. Placing a patient into an exercise program can lead to the patient's participation in an exercise support group. Activity levels may increase, interests may diversify, and wellness may come to be emphasized more than illness.

Certain activities in the circuit training routine need to be rigidly monitored. Initially the injured muscle and ligamentous apparatus should be subjected to very low weights and few repetitions. Gradually, over an extended period, additional activity and stress can be applied to the muscle and ligamentous apparatus as the body adapts and is strengthened. Exercising a chronic pain patient should be seen as akin to rehabilitating a million-dollar athlete. Certainly, every effort should be made to supply the patient with physical therapy modalities and supervision by a trained health care provider. Manipulation, ultrasound, massage, cool-and-stretch techniques, as well as modalities geared toward improvement of spinal stability, should be employed.

Biofeedback is a most helpful tool in a comprehensive approach to treating chronic pain. Today's biofeedback electronics can measure and display a wide variety of physiological functions. These physiological functions include activity at various muscle sites (electromyography), the brain waves (electroencephalography), peripheral skin temperature, the skin conductance response, the peripheral pulse volume, and the heart rate. Alterations of any given one of these functions will have a unique effect on the physiological state, serving to treat specific disorders and symptoms. The true breadth of the usefulness and traditions of biofeedback can be realized by reviewing the literature, noting its inclusion by the Commission on Accreditation of Rehabilitation Facilities as a required component of pain programs,[19] and reviewing the ''blueprint'' for achieving certification in biofeedback with the Biofeedback Certification Institute of America.[20] Both the literature and the blueprint reflect biofeedback's interdisciplinary origins in the psychology of operant conditioning and rehabilitative medicine and the interdisciplinary nature of its effective use.

Definitions of biofeedback reflect a variety of nonexclusive theoretical models, including goal components (regulation or self-control of physiological processes) and process components (feedback or cybernetics). For a detailed discussion of definitions, Schwartz et al. should be consulted.[21] Biofeedback is most simply, if somewhat inadequately, described as an electronic mirror reflecting information back to an active, responsive patient in real time. Given adequate information and reinforcers, the patient can learn to control a wide variety of autonomic ("involuntary") and voluntary physiological functions, including those affecting pain.

A comprehensive pain program will use the biofeedback tool and ancillary techniques to evaluate and document physiological function and dysfunction in both static states (no movement or relaxed) and dynamic states (in range of motion). As evaluation occurs, biofeedback can be used to create the kind of change that will reduce or eliminate pain. Examples include the teaching of a general relaxation response in the smooth and skeletal muscle systems to reduce pain; the deepening of the general relaxation response into a light trancelike state that eliminates pain, either with or without specific visualizations;[13(pp13–23)] the relaxing of peripheral arteries (as in autogenic training[7]) to prevent or abort migraine or vascular headaches; the relaxing of specific skeletal muscles to reduce pain in specific areas where over-recruitment takes place (as in muscle contracture headaches, temporomandibular joint–related pain, cervical pain, or back pain[22]); and the teaching of appropriate tensing or utilization patterns in areas where under-recruitment is identified as problematic.[23]

The above-mentioned problems are commonly encountered in pain patients. Less commonly encountered problems can also be effectively evaluated and treated with biofeedback. Incontinence (fecal and urinary) is a common disorder occasionally related to injury and pain. In cases where tissue damage due to surgery or accident leads to a neurologically induced or a classically conditioned inappropriate relaxation response in the pelvic floor, fecal or urinary incontinence may result. The retraining of the weakened response to an appropriately tense, properly focused muscular response can be accomplished by means of biofeedback, according to Kegel,[24] Middaugh, Whitehead, Burgio, and Engel,[25] and Perry and Talcott.[26] It should be noted that Kegel, an obstetrician and gynecologist, was the first to use biofeedback in clinical practice or otherwise.[26] A related problem occurs in the case of levatorani syndrome, where a high level of tension in the pelvic floor region creates pain therein and may cause or exacerbate low back pain.

Another interesting pain problem amenable to treatment by biofeedback is patellofemoral pain syndrome. Sophisticated biofeedback equipment will allow for the identification of the inappropriate muscle recruitment in this syndrome and then the teaching of appropriate muscle recruitment. It should be noted that there is at least one electromyographic biofeedback device on the market that will provide home practice feedback, save the home practice data for downloading in the clinic, and provide for compliance monitoring.[27] Home practice enhances the effectiveness of the biofeedback program and reduces the need for surgery for patellofemoral pain.

The overall success of biofeedback in reducing pain depends to a great extent upon a number of factors, some of which are under the physician's control, some of which are under the patient's control, and some of which, albeit few, are basically uncontrollable in a pain program, such as thought disorders or organic brain syndrome. It should be noted that intelligence is *not* a factor related to the success of biofeedback in pain control, at least not patient intelligence. Success with biofeedback requires a patient who is willing to accept the responsibility to practice, a doctor or practitioner who teaches well, and equipment sophisticated enough to meet the demands of the physiological situation.

Biofeedback services should be preceded by a psychological evaluation to determine if the patient is an appropriate candidate for such training. An interview should be completed, and a Minnesota Multiphasic Personality Inventory (MMPI) should be administered. Individuals who are schizophrenic, thought-disordered, or under severe emotional distress may not have to be excluded; however, they will need careful monitoring.

Psychological evaluation is important in the treatment of these patients for other reasons as well. The existence of depression and its severity and the presence of suicidal ideation are important to recognize prior to establishing a comprehensive treatment plan. With this knowledge, appropriate psychotherapy and/or medication plans can be implemented. For objective data, the MMPI can be relied upon. It provides an objective measure of depression as well as of other disorders, tendencies, and general emotional distress.

The interpretation of the statistical data provided by the MMPI is always a critical issue; however, it is more critical in the case of chronic pain patients. This is so because there are no norms for the very changeable chronic pain patients. Vague neurological symptoms such as appear in MMPI statements do not allow one to distinguish between psychosomatic and physical conditions.[28] Just as it is grossly inappropriate to diagnose neuroticism in chronic pain patients by the apparent absence of physical signs, so is it equally inappropriate to diagnose "real" physical pain or injury on the basis of lack of neuroticism. Hypochondriasis, psychogenic pain disorder, somatization disorder, and conversion disorder are not diagnosed by exclusion. That is to say, the lack of objective physical evidence does not lead to these psychological diagnoses. It is the clear presence of all of the factors as listed in the *Diagnostic and Statistical Manual of Mental Disorders Revised*[29] (DSM-III-R) that leads to psychological diagnoses.

Examination of pre- and postinjury MMPIs of chronic pain patients as seen by the authors in the small number of cases where they have been available indicates normal or at least not clinically significant preinjury profiles. Typically, postinjury profiles in these cases show elevations on the scales labeled hypochondriasis, depression, and hysteria. How should these elevations in injured patients be interpreted? Caldwell indicates (written communication, September 1988) that elevations of the hypochondriasis scale should be interpreted as an indication of "body breakdown fear" and hysteria elevation as an indication of "pain fear." For a careful explication of this position, the 1977 Caldwell and Chase article in *Clinical Orthopaedics and Related Research* should be consulted.[30] For a thorough discussion of issues related to braininjured patients—a frequently met chronic pain subgroup—Mack[31] should be consulted, as well as the previously cited work by Alfano and others.[28]

Neuroticism is not the only controversial psychological issue brought up in regard to chronic pain patients. Malingering occasionally is suspected. This is especially the case when a patient's subjective pain complaints are out of proportion to objective physical findings. DSM-III-R defines malingering as the "intentional production of false or grossly exaggerated physical or psychological symptoms, motivated by external incentives."[29] This should be investigated in the presence of an antisocial personality disorder or an uncooperative patient. As in the case of neuroticism, the diagnosis is not arrived at by a process of exclusion but rather by the identification of objective supportive data.

The process of diagnosis is especially difficult in the case of mild head injury, where cognitive dysfunction as identified a few months postconcussion may be very subtle on neuropsychological evaluation but nevertheless very disturbing of daily routines at work and elsewhere. Additionally, many of the symptoms of mild closed head injury, postconcussion syndrome, or organic brain syndrome are the same as those of chronic pain patients in general. To add to the complexity of this picture, it should be noted that some of the symptoms of chronic pain are similar to those of mild head injury, and some can exacerbate head injury symptoms. Sorting all of this out is a long, arduous process. For a neuropsychological approach to this diagnostic problem, see Binder.[32] In general, there are few data to support the view that malingering, compensation neurosis, or a combination thereof is to be suspected without the existence of clear objective data.[33]

The comments above only hint at how fascinating the psychological study of chronic pain patients with or without mild head injury can be. Psychological evaluation of chronic pain patients is of value to the chronic pain treatment team for many reasons: first, to determine suitability for biofeedback; second, to determine the extent of emotional distress and the extent to which chronic pain and the ensuing functional loss has led to psychological disorders requiring treatment either psychotherapeutically, chemotherapeutically, or by other means such as exercise[34]; third, to establish a baseline for monitoring change in the emotional state; and fourth, to screen for postconcussion syndrome or organic brain syndrome related to mild closed head injury, which is a commonly overlooked diagnosis.[35]

For the more severe chronic pain patients, additional services such as those supplied by a social worker or occupational therapist should be provided to help the patient regain a foothold in life. However, even this may not be enough.

The spiritual aspect of the patient's life also should be encouraged. The chronic pain patient needs every type of support. Religion and spiritual guidance can help many patients through the trials and tribulations of anger, resentment, depression, and guilt.

Dietary regulation should be encouraged. Patients who tend to eat as a means of coping with their loss of self-esteem and depression can gain significant amounts of weight. The old joke about the "seafood diet"—when you see food, you eat it—describes the eating patterns of many of these patients. Poor diet can result in significant weight gain and substantial alteration of body mechanics. The purpose of nutritional counseling for pain patients is to attain optimal weight. As this occurs, body mechanics can improve, endurance can be enhanced, and pain can be reduced. A nutritional program must be implemented in conjunction with a carefully structured exercise program if these results are to be achieved.

Group support should be provided for the more severe chronic pain patients. This is especially true for patients in an inpatient chronic pain program. Inpatient chronic pain programs are most appropriately reserved for patients with premorbid psychological disorders or strongly dependent personalities, or for patients with poor coping skills. Rehabilitation groups can provide support and encouragement in the development of self-confidence and self-esteem. These can lead to a continuing interest in physical fitness and better health. If health maintenance, employability, and social activity are to be attained, it is essential that appropriate support groups be instituted and continued on an intermittent basis after inpatient programs end. These aftercare groups need not meet frequently, since the goal is self-sufficiency.

Families often are included in the counseling component of pain programs to help improve the relationship of the patient to the family nucleus. These activities should be conducted by a qualified professional, who can frequently supply the "glue" that is necessary for the family to remain intact.

Many patients with chronic pain need to be vocationally rehabilitated. When this is evident, a vocational psychologist may be utilized to initiate vocational evaluations. This may consist of interviews, questionnaires, individually administered assessments, and work sample evaluations. Based upon gathered data, a vocational psychologist and/or a vocational assessment vendor can assist the treating doctor in making appropriate decisions regarding the rehabilitation. A schematic graph of the rehabilitation of a chronic pain patient is shown in Figure 9-3.

It should be noted that every effort is made to gradually enhance the endurance levels of a chronically debilitated patient. Through appropriate recreational activity, the patient can enhance endurance levels up to and exceeding his or her preaccident status. This would increase the patient's ability to tolerate extremes in activity levels. The anxiety level tends to return to normal when the patient is placed on a significant and well-directed program. In some patients, further counseling is necessary to help reduce the anxiety level or to control the fluctuation in the emotional state. Medication, such as antidepressants, should be considered for this purpose. Although medication in general is not considered entirely desirable, certain medications such as antidepressants,[36] anti-inflammatory agents,[37] and some muscle relaxants can be used to help control the flare-ups typically encountered by post-traumatic patients suffering from chronic pain. In some isolated cases where there is extraordinary pain and an underlying organic disease process, narcotics may be used on a short-term basis to help the patient through the most severe flare-ups.

Emphasis also should be placed on increasing the patient's endurance and ability to return to gainful employment. When return to gainful employment is instituted, rehabilitation efforts should be mildly reduced. If possible, return to work should be done on a graded basis—a work-hardening schedule—to help the patient back into the demands required by a previous occupation or an occupation restricted as necessary for this patient to function.

In summary, the key entities necessary in the rehabilitation of a chronic pain patient include patient cooperation and a significant amount of patient effort, which the treating doctor is responsible for obtaining. The treating physician can obtain cooperation by allocating enough time to educate the patient as to the nature of the problems associated with the chronic pain disorder. A thorough explanation of the injuries involved, as well as the parameters of the underlying organic process, must be provided. This includes reassurance that the pain the patient

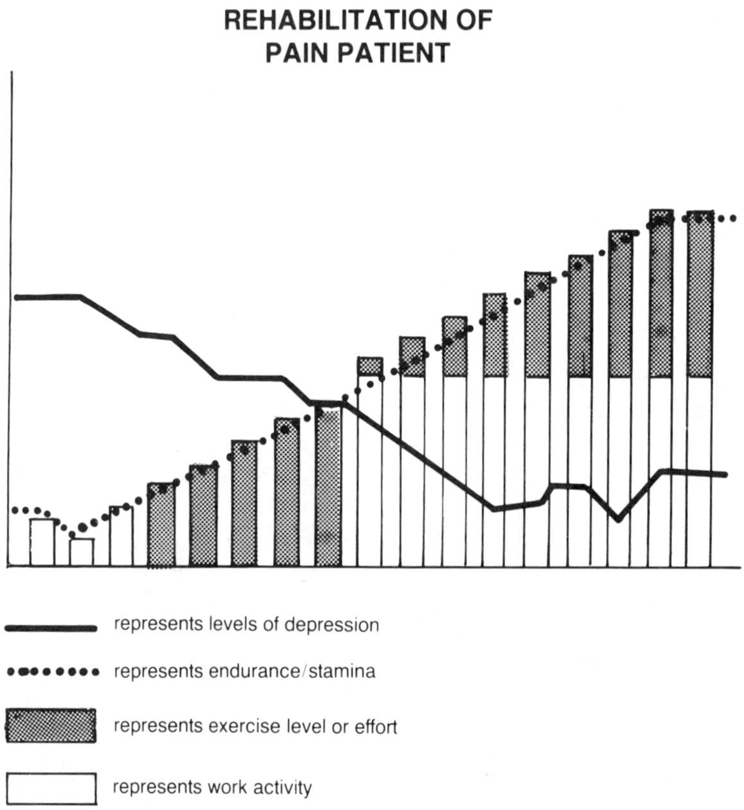

Figure 9-3 Graph depicting the rehabilitation of the pain patient.

encounters during an appropriate exercise program does not indicate additional injury but only reflects irritation of the inflamed epiphyseal joints or intervertebral discs, or recurring tendinitis or myositis. Patient education is extremely important in facilitating cooperation. The patient must be aware that in order to accomplish a return to high-level functioning, a significant amount of effort will be required. Examples can be based on previous experiences in rehabilitating injured athletes. The patient should be assured of treatment "like that for an injured athlete."

Periodic follow-up and support should be given to the patient to reinforce the need for consistent effort. Follow-up examinations are helpful to evaluate any changes relative to degenerative processes and to fully reinforce the patient's effort and cooperation. Follow-up evaluations convey the doctor's concern for the patient and play a large role in the patient's motivation to improve.

REFERENCES

1. Jackson R. *The Cervical Syndrome*. Springfield, Ill: Charles C Thomas, Pub; 1978:279–331.

2. Kirkaldy-Willis W, ed. *Managing Low Back Pain*. New York, NY: Churchill Livingstone; 1983:75–89.

3. Wedge J. The natural history of spinal degeneration. In: Kirkaldy-Willis W, ed. *Managing Low Back Pain*. New York, NY: Churchill Livingstone; 1983:3–8.

4. Paris S. Spinal manipulative therapy. *Clin Orthop*. 1983;179:55–61.

5. McNab I. Acceleration extension injuries of the cervical spine. In: Rothman R, Simeone F, eds. *The Spine*. 2nd ed. Philadelphia, Pa: WB Saunders Co; 1975.

6. Hohl M. Soft tissue neck injuries. In: *The Cervical Spine*. Philadelphia, Pa: JB Lippincott Co; 1983:282–287.

7. Cram JR. Diagnostic uses of surface EMG. In: *Clinical EMG for Surface Recordings*. Vol. 2. Nevada City, Calif.: Clinical Resources; 1990:7–13.

8. McNab, I. Acceleration injuries of the cervical spine. *J Bone and Joint Surg*. 1964;46A:1797–1799.

9. Markey RJ, Potter BE, Moffett BC. Condylar trauma and facial asymmetry; an experimental study. *J Maxillofac Surg*. 1980;8:38–51.

10. Wilkes CH. Internal derangement of the temporomandibular joint. Pathological variances. *Arch Otolaryngol Head Neck Surg*. 1989;115:469–477.

11. Schellhas KP, Wilkes CH, Fritts HM, Omlie MR, Heithoff KB, Jahn JA. Temporomandibular joint; MR imaging of internal derangements and postoperative changes. *AJR*. 1988;150:381–389.

12. Turel S. *Orthopedics; Principles and Their Application*. 2nd ed. Philadelphia, Pa: JB Lippincott Co; 1967:499.

13. Catalano EM et al. *The Chronic Pain Control Workbook*. Oakland, Calif: New Harbinger Publications; 1987:59–71.

14. McCain GA, Bell D, Mai FM, Halliday PD. A controlled study of the effects of a supervised cardiovascular fitness training program on the manifestations of primary fibromyalgia. *Arthritis Rheum*. 1988;31:1135–1147.

15. Buerger AA, Tobis JS. *Approaches to the Validation of Spinal Manipulation*. Springfield, Ill: Charles C Thomas, Pub; 1977:236–270.

16. Ahles TA, Yunus MB, Riley SO, Bradley JM, Masi AT. Physiological factors associated with primary fibromyalgia syndrome. *Arthritis Rheum*. 1984;27:1101–1106.

17. Luthe W, ed. *Autogenic Therapy*. Vols 1-6. New York, NY: Grune & Stratton, 1969.

18. Gotten N. Survey of 100 cases of whiplash injury after settlement of litigation. *JAMA*. 1956;162:856.

19. Commission on Accreditation of Rehabilitation Facilities. *Standards Manual for Organizations Serving People with Disabilities*. Tucson, Ariz: Commission on Accreditation of Rehabilitation Facilities; 1987:53.

20. Biofeedback Certification Institute of America. *Blueprint Tasks and Knowledge Statements*. Wheatridge, Colo: Biofeedback Certification Institute of America, 1980.

21. Schwartz MS et al. *Biofeedback: A Practitioner's Guide*. New York, NY: Guilford Press; 1987:33–37, 518.

22. Klasman G. Use of integrated electromyography for the assessment and treatment of musculoskeletal pain; guidelines for physical medicine practitioners. In: Cram JR et al. *Clinical EMG for Surface Recordings*. Vol 2. Nevada City, Calif: Clinical Resources; 1990:255–302.

23. Donaldson S, Donaldson M. Multi-channel EMG assessment and treatment techniques. In: Cram JR et al. *Clinical EMG for Surface Recordings*. Vol 2. Nevada City, Calif: Clinical Resources; 1990:143–174.

24. Kegel A. Progressive resistance exercise in the functional restoration of the perineal muscles. *Am J Obstet Gynecol*. 1948;56:236–248.

25. Middaugh SJ, Whitehead WE, Burgio KL, Engel BT. Biofeedback in treatment of urinary incontinence in stroke patients. *Biofeedback Self-Regul*. 1989;14:3–19.

26. Perry J, Talcott L. EMG diagnosis and treatment of pelvic muscle disorders. In: Cram JR et al. *Clinical EMG for Surface Recordings*. Vol 2. Nevada City, Calif: Clinical Resources; 1990:353–369.

27. King A, Ahles T, Martin J, White R. *EMG Biofeedback—Controlled Exercise in Chronic Arthritic Knee Pain*. Handout discussing the Myoexerciser II. Available from: Verimed, 1001 NW 62nd Street, Suite 212, Fort Lauderdale, Fla 33309.

28. Alfano DP, Finlayson MAJ, Stearns GM, Neilson PM. The MMPI and neurologic dysfunction: profile configuration and analysis. *Clinical Neuropsychol*. 1990;4:69–79.

29. American Psychiatric Association. *Diagnostic and Statistical Manual of Mental Disorders*. 3rd ed, rev. Washington, DC: American Psychiatric Association, 1987.

30. Caldwell AB, Chase C. Diagnosis and treatment of personality factors in chronic low back pain. *Clinical Orthop Rel Res*. 1977;129:141–149.

31. Mack JL. The MMPI and neurological dysfunction. In: Newmark CS, ed. *MMPI: Clinical and Research Trends*. New York, NY: Praeger Publishers; 1979:53–79.

32. Binder LM. Malingering following minor head trauma. *Clinical Neuropsychol*. 1990;4:25–36.

33. Binder LM. Persisting symptoms after mild head injury: a review of the post-concussive syndrome. *J Clin Exp Neuropsychol*. 1986;8:323–346.

34. Mellion MB. Exercise therapy for anxiety and depression. *Postgrad Med*. 1985;77:59–66.

35. Kay T. *Minor Head Injury: An Introduction for Professionals*. Southboro, Me: National Head Injury Foundation; 1986:12.

36. Carette S, McCain GA, Bell OA, Fam AG. Evaluation of amitriptyline in primary fibrositis. *Arthritis Rheum*. 1986;29:655–659.

37. Goldenberg DL, Felson DT, Dinnerman H. Randomized controlled clinical trial of amitriptyline and naproxen in the treatment of patients with primary fibromyalgia. *Arthritis Rheum*. 1986;29:1371–1377.

chapter **10**

Neural Ischemia and Cervical Spinal Manipulation

Any textbook of chiropractic neurology would be notably incomplete without a detailed discussion of the ischemic brain disorders that have reportedly occurred following cervical spinal adjustment. Without question, this is the most catastrophic iatrogenic injury that can occur in the office of any practitioner of manipulative therapy. Neural ischemia following cervical spinal manipulative therapy (CSMT) appears to be a reality. Case after documented case continues to surface[1-4] (three previously unpublished cases are described at the conclusion of this chapter). In 1987 Terrett[5] reported on 107 cases that have appeared in the international literature. It is extremely difficult to unequivocally postulate a direct causal relationship between CSMT and the subsequent neural ischemia in any of these cases, because it is entirely possible that the head and/or neck complaint or injury that prompted the patient to seek care from a practitioner of manual therapy may well have been a reflection of underlying vascular pathology. In fact, descriptions of nonmanipulated patients who suffer posterior circulation disease have been reported. Most of these nonmanipulated cases parallel their postmanipulated counterparts strikingly, especially regarding onset, type, and location of pain, as well as occurrence in patients of similar ages. The only difference appears to be the fact that one group presented for manipulation and the other did not. Ladermann[6] discusses this subject thoroughly and properly reports that it is only the temporal relationship between the cervical adjustment and the onset of ischemia that is so incriminating toward chiropractic, and that at times a reasonable temporal relationship does not exist.

After personally reviewing many cases, as well as reviewing related available literature, it is my opinion that there is, at least, an exacerbating relationship. That is to say, even if the initial arterial damage predated the manipulation, manual manipulation advances the process by indirectly traumatizing the already compromised artery. It is further my opinion that manipulation far more often plays this exacerbating role than it does a causative role. The relatively consistent temporal profile and the characteristic symptomatic profile of so many of these cases appear to clearly establish the link.

Both transient and permanent effects may result from neural ischemia due to cervical manipulation. As a consultant in chiropractic neurology, I have been contacted by chiropractic doctors, insurance carriers, and legal counsel who have brought to my attention cases of both transient neural ischemia post-CSMT and documented postmanipulative strokes. One syndrome of temporary impairment of neural function following CSMT, benign lateral medullary syndrome, has been described in the literature.[7]

The actual reported number of cases is still remarkably low, considering the number of cervical manipulations that are probably administered annually. The true incidence rate has not yet been established, since a precise calculation of the number of cervical adjustments and the number of vascular injuries has not yet been undertaken. Estimates of the incidence of cases of serious neural damage from cervical manipulation range from as few as one in several tens of millions[8] to as many as 1 in 300,000[9] cervical manipulations. It is my considered opinion that due to under-reporting or lack of recognition, or both, transient and permanent neural derangement following manipulation actually occurs with greater frequency than commonly estimated.

Fortunately, death following CSMT is quite rare. Personally, I have reviewed only one such case, which happened to be related to the carotid artery circulation. Estimates of 1 in 20 million[10] deaths from cervical manipulation have been made, and it has been likened to the chances of dying from a bee sting or from being hit by lightning.[10] Compared to the "intolerable specter"[11] of the death toll from chymopapain injection for intervertebral discopathy, which is estimated to occur in 1 in 700 procedures, the chances are really quite small. This translates to well over 28,000 dead bodies, enough to fill many professional sports arenas, produced by chymopapain injection for each manipulation-related death.

CEREBROVASCULAR ANATOMY AND HEMODYNAMICS

Anatomy

An understanding of cerebrovascular anatomy and blood flow is prerequisite for total comprehension of neural ischemia. Off of the aortic arch branches the brachiocephalic artery, on the right, and the common carotid and subclavian arteries, on the left. The first branch of the right subclavian, which branches off of the brachiocephalic on the right side, is the vertebral artery (see Figure 10-1).

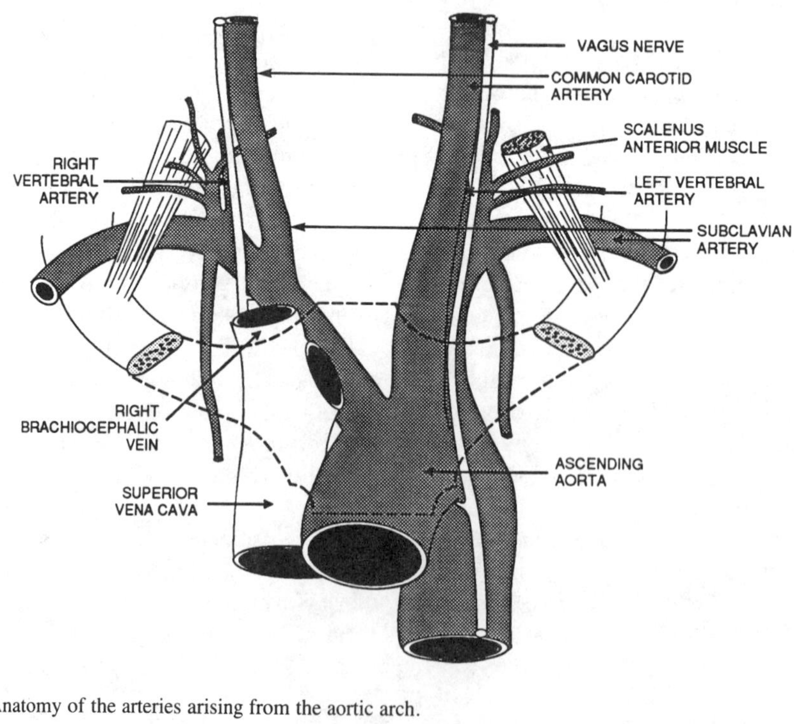

Figure 10-1 Anatomy of the arteries arising from the aortic arch.

Anatomists discuss the vertebral artery as possessing four parts. The first part of the vertebral artery ascends through tightly binding[12] myofascial tissues to eventually pass through tendinous slips of the scalenus anterior and medius muscles, as well as the longus colli[13] as they insert on along the edge of the vertebrae, after it enters the transverse foramen of the sixth, or sometimes the seventh, cervical vertebra.

The second part of the vertebral artery ascends through the transverse foraminae of cervical vertebrae C-6 to C-3; on this portion of its journey it lies adjacent to the uncovertebral joints, anterior to the exiting cervical spinal nerve roots, and medial to the intertransverse muscles. The artery is not pulled taught between these vertebrae but remains relatively lax, to allow for movements between the cervical vertebrae without its being damaged. The artery is joined here by the vertebral plexus of veins and the sympathetic vertebral nerve originating from the inferior cervical sympathetic ganglion, and between C-3 and C-2 they together begin a slightly posterior course, due to the more oblique-facing C-2 transverse foramina. After passing through C-2 a very sharp lateral course is taken, heading for the transverse foramina of C-1.

After passing through the lateral foramen of the atlas, the third part of the artery takes another sharp deflection, as it must travel almost directly posterior to run medially around the lateral mass of C-1, deep to the obliquus capitus inferior and the intertransversarius[14] muscles. Here, it lies in a groove of highly variable depth, along with the first cervical nerve.

Finally, the fourth part of the vertebral artery passes through the lower border of the posterior atlanto-occipital membrane and through the arcuate foramen, piercing the dura mater and moving upward through the foramen magnum. At this point, a branch drops off of the right and left vertebral arteries, unites, and forms the anterior spinal artery, which promptly descends to nourish the anterior surface of the cervical and upper thoracic spinal cord to about the T-4 level. The largest and most clinically significant branch, the posterior inferior cerebellar artery, takes its origin just prior to the union of the two vertebral arteries. This branch gives off branches to the lateral aspect of the medulla (hence the term "lateral medullary syndrome," describing a vascular disorder of this artery); it ultimately nourishes the anterior portion of the cerebellum.

Just beyond the origin of the posterior inferior cerebellar arteries, the right and left vertebral arteries unite to form the basilar artery. The basilar artery runs a short course along the pons, giving off numerous pontine branches, prior to splitting into the posterior portion of the circle of Willis (see Figure 10-2).

The common carotid arteries originate off of the aortic arch on the left and off of the brachiocephalic artery on the right. The right and left internal carotid arteries split off of the common carotids in the upper neck and lie in very close approximation to the anterolateral aspect of the atlas. It should be noted that damage to an internal carotid has rarely been linked to neural ischemia post-manipulation.[15] The terminal branch of the internal carotid is the middle cerebral artery, the other main contributor to the circle of Willis.

Hemodynamics

Blood coursing through the vertebral arteries is responsible for nourishing relatively specific brain areas. This is true even in light of the fact that the vertebral arteries join with the internal carotid arteries in the unusual anastomosis known as the circle of Willis. Brain structures primarily receiving a vertebral artery blood supply include

- bone and dura of the posterior cranial fossa
- facet joint structures
- cervical nerve roots
- dorsal root ganglia
- spinal cord
- much of the cerebellum
- medulla oblongata
- choroid plexus of the fourth ventricle
- posterior cerebrum (visual cortex)
- pons
- internal ear
- thalamus
- midbrain

Knowledge of the function of these brain areas, coupled with knowledge of their arterial supply,

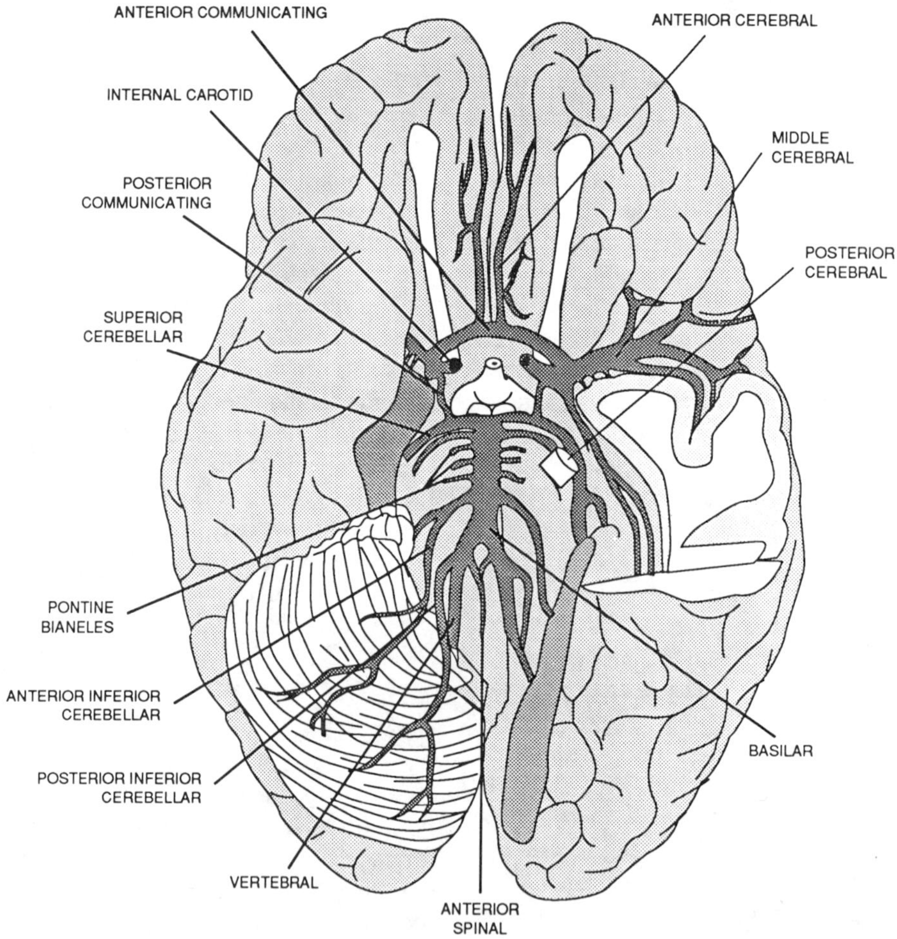

Figure 10-2 Anatomy of the major arteries of the base of the brain.

helps give one a clear understanding of the syndromes seen with vertebrobasilar ischemia. When graphically depicted, the reason for the term "posterior circulation" becomes obvious.

Studies on 20 cadavers who had cannulated major neck vessels showed that water flow may be reduced by more than 90% by movements well within the normal range of head motion.[16] With rotation it was the vertebral artery contralateral to the direction of chin deviation that was not occluded (e.g., chin to left caused right artery occlusion). When rotation was combined with extension, the ipsilateral artery was affected about as frequently as the contralateral. Rotation combined with flexion caused unpredictable results. Lateral flexion had little effect in most cases, and extension did not significantly alter flow in any case. Rotation was the single most likely movement to cause occlusion. Numerous other studies have corroborated contralateral and ipsilateral vertebral artery occlusion with head movement. One study used electromagnetic flow meters during radical neck surgery in two patients,[17] and another used retrograde brachial arteriography on 43 asymptomatic volunteers.[18]

Various authors have outlined possible locations and mechanisms for extraluminal vertebral artery obstruction associated with head movement. The first possible site corresponds to the first part of the vertebral artery. Arteriograms performed with forced contralateral cervical rotation revealed vertebral artery occlusion prior to the artery's entrance into the transverse foramen of C-6.[13] After surgical division of "tendinous interdigitations" of the scalenus anterior and medius, as well as the longus colli muscles, the occlusion was no longer present.[19] A second possible location relates to the second portion of the vertebral artery; it is proposed that ischemia results from compression by degenerative vertebral spurs along its course through the transverse foramen. A "washboard" angiographic appearance indicated displacement, with and without stenosis, caused by osteophytes, which are usually visible on plain films. Rotation and hyperextension of the neck have been associated with increased compression of the vertebral arteries adjacent to the spondylophyte.[20] The third possible site of vertebral artery obstruction is the third part of its course to the basilar artery; numerous authors have proposed that this third portion is the most susceptible to extraluminal occlusion, especially as it passes over the lateral mass of the atlas. This finding is so common and reproducible that some authorities consider this extraluminal occlusion to be "within normal limits."[21]

PATHOPHYSIOLOGICAL MECHANISMS IN VASCULAR INJURIES

It appears that the only tenable mechanism by which CSMT may be responsible for neurovascular insufficiency is indirect trauma to the arterial wall. This precipitating trauma, apparently, may constitute either frank damage, such as a tear, or vasospasm, or both. In any event, the damage leads to a clot that can occlude the artery or embolize and occlude a distal segment of the artery (see Figure 10-3). Hence involvement of the posterior inferior cerebellar artery (largest branch of the vertebral artery) is frequently seen. Many authors[22,23] believe that transient vasospasm may play a significant role, and this seems to be borne out by several case reports suggesting a link to migraine headache, as well as the reports of transient vascular phenomena.[7] The ultimate result of vasospasm may be a change in flow due to a decrease in vessel diameter or an increase in turbulence. A long enough duration of vasospasm may produce ischemic infarction. Additionally, decreased and/or turbulent flow may activate the cascade mechanism, resulting in the deposition of fibrin, which may also lead to thrombus formation and possible subsequent artery-to-artery embolization. Most cases I have reviewed have demonstrated arteriographic evidence consistent with thrombus formation.

Tearing of the intimal lining of the blood vessel may directly cause a clot or lead to dissection. In the latter case the blood acts as a lever, prying the intimal lining away from the outer layers of the artery (see Figure 10-4). A portion of the intima may then embolize, or the intima

Figure 10-3 The genesis of an arterial embolus.

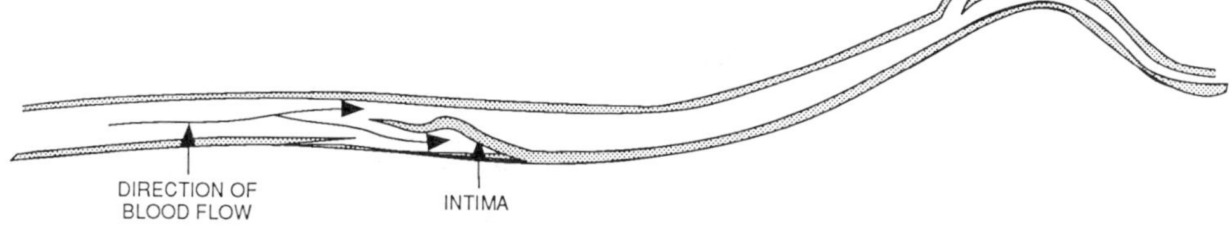

Figure 10-4 Arterial dissection.

may occlude a branch, such as the posterior inferior cerebellar artery. I have reviewed several cases where vertebral artery dissection was demonstrated arteriographically.

PATIENT ASSESSMENT: PREDISPOSITION AND CLINICAL TESTING

The question of whether or not screening procedures or tests to adequately detect patients at increased risk of neural ischemia related to CSMT are currently available is of paramount concern for the practitioner of manual cervical spinal manipulation. Actually, the unreliability of such tests has been pointed out in papers dealing with vertebrobasilar insufficiency tests.[5] Terrett identified many reasons why the testing procedures described by George[24] and others are inadequate or inaccurate. Bolton and associates[25] discuss a patient who underwent four separate provocative clinical tests, all of which failed to elicit symptoms to help detect an angiographically proven vertebral artery occlusion. The areas previously accepted as standards in patient prescreening are discussed below.

Case History

It has been noted by Terrett[5] that "a review of the major presenting complaints of patients who subsequently suffered a manipulation-induced vertebral-basilar accident reveals little which could alert the astute practitioner to an impending accident." These complaints include

- headache
- neck pain
- head and neck pain
- neck and arm pain
- headache, dizziness, and neck stiffness
- headache, giddiness, and nausea
- neck pain and stiffness
- neck stiffness
- strained shoulder, headache, and tension
- shoulder and neck pain
- chest, arm, and head pain
- a "catch in the neck"

Obviously, this is extremely typical of the average patient presenting to the office of a chiropractic physician. Previously held beliefs that pre-existing atherosclerosis, cervical spondylosis, oral contraceptives, and neck bruits may be predisposing factors are simply not borne out by the evidence at hand.[5] Available literature, and personal experience, show no preponderance in regard to the above-mentioned areas in patients who have apparently suffered from postadjustive neural ischemia. I have observed a preponderance of long-term or chronic headaches in patients who ultimately suffer neural ischemia. Many of these had previously been diagnosed as migraines. Since this appears to be present in such a high percentage of spontaneous and manipulation-related ischemic reactions, further investigation is warranted.

Bilateral Blood Pressure and Auscultation

While bilateral blood pressure measurement and cervical auscultation may seem to be appropriate tools in the identification of patients at increased risk, again, the facts are at odds with this. Terrett[5] states that "the taking of blood pressure bilaterally, does not appear to be particularly useful, as the victims are usually young and neither hypo- nor hypertension is consistently found" and "the reliability of a bruit in predicting susceptibility to vascular accident must be considered highly unreliable." Taking the blood pressure bilaterally is usually done to help diagnose a stenotic lesion distal to the aortic arch. Indeed, a stenotic lesion proximal to the origin of the vertebral artery might cause a subclavian steal syndrome. That is where blood travels up one vertebral artery and right back down the other, due to the decreased blood pressure distal to the stenotic lesion. With greater demand for blood, as in exercise, enough blood may be "stolen" to cause brainstem ischemia. This specific etiology of brainstem ischemia has not, however, appeared in the literature in any cases and therefore does not appear to be germane to this particular topic.

This author has noted, however, several cases where a sudden increase in blood pressure did occur during the course of manipulative treatment, prior to the onset of neural ischemia. Therefore, a sudden jump in blood pressure may have some significance, but the exact mechanism and relevance are unknown.

Vertebrobasilar Insufficiency Testing

Numerous authors have suggested that extension and rotation of the cervical spine should be performed as a provocative test for symptoms of ischemia.[8,24,26,27] Originally devised in 1962 by Smith and Estridge,[26] who used the term "momentarily" to describe the amount of time this maneuver was to be carried out, this test has inappropriately become a yardstick to gauge chiropractic malpractice in cases of neural ischemia.

Three variations of this test are currently in use; they differ in terms of patient position and what constitutes a positive finding of vertebrobasilar system incompetence.

1. Performed in the supine position, with hyperextension and rotation.
2. Performed in the seated position with both arms outstretched and hands supinated. Dropping of the hand is considered to be a positive sign.
3. Performed in the standing posture.

Bilateral testing is usually recommended. If positive findings occur, the test should be immediately discontinued and no manipulations performed on that patient in that direction. What is not agreed upon is exactly how long to perform the test, and exactly what is a positive finding. Estimates range from 10 to 60 seconds, with dizziness, nausea, vomiting, motor or sensory loss, or nystagmoid movements of the eye comprising a positive test.

No evidence conclusively shows that this maneuver has any correlation to impending neural ischemia related to CSMT. False-positive tests may occur due to stimulation of the vestibular apparatus, cervical sympathetics, carotid sinus receptors, and other vertebrogenic causes.[28]

Neither the exact mechanics of test performance nor the interpretation of findings is clearly delineated or universally accepted, raising the question of just what a positive test would be. It has even been proposed that reproduction of the patient's complaint might be an indication to perform CSMT in the opposite direction.[24] If "lightheadedness" or "faintness" occurs after 40 seconds[26] of extreme cervical rotation and extension, is that really a clear contraindication to CSMT? This author has performed hundreds of these tests using various amounts of time and various postures and has noted an unacceptably high percentage of patients who experience some variety of symptomatology, usually pain, dizziness, or nausea, all which may possibly be associated with neural ischemia. Most of these patient's complaints ultimately respond quite favorably to cervical adjustments, and none have experienced neural ischemia. False-negatives, on the other hand, have been expected[8] and documented.[25,29] Smith and Estridge[26] went on to state, "in spite of these precautionary steps, a few people, no doubt, will suffer brainstem injury."

An additional point of concern is the notion that since neural ischemia may not occur during the first episode of CSMT, this test should be performed on each visit[5] prior to CSMT. The clear possibility that the provocative test described by some may be more dangerous than a skilled cervical adjustment,[30] in addition to the discomfort experienced by so many and the sheer impracticality of routinely administering the test, leads me to seriously question the logic of this practice.

RECOGNITION OF POSTADJUSTIVE VERTEBROBASILAR INSUFFICIENCY

In order for the competent doctor of chiropractic to properly manage a patient who has suffered a vascular accident post–cervical adjustment, it is obviously essential that he or she recognize it at its earliest stages. I have noted that many lawsuits brought against chiropractors actually hinge not on the cause-effect relationship between the adjustment and the vascular accident but on the doctor's apparent lack of recognition of it, and on his or her apparently inappropriate subsequent actions.

In view of the rarity of postadjustive vertebral artery damage, it is no wonder that many chiropractors do not have a sufficient plan of action to deal with it. While patients and juries are able to understand the concept of an acceptable risk,[31] they may be less able to understand, or forgive, the doctor's lack of ability to detect or appropriately manage the damage he or she has apparently inflicted.[32]

Recognition

Signs and symptoms of vertebrobasilar ischemia usually occur immediately after the first few cervical adjustments, although it is possible for symptoms to begin minutes to days[5] later, and after any number of treatments. Signs and symptoms to be concerned about include

- nausea
- vertigo
- vomiting
- difficulty walking
- incoordination of extremities
- numbness or other sensory complaint
- loss of consciousness
- visual problems (double, blurred)
- tinnitus
- speech problems

Most postadjustive vertebral artery injuries result in almost complete recovery, or at least minimal residual neurological deficit. However, some result in long-term damage or death. Long-term effects are often due to the following syndromes.

Wallenberg's Syndrome

Wallenberg's syndrome, or the dorsolateral medullary syndrome,[33] derives its name from infarction of the dorsolateral area of the medulla oblongata (see Figure 10-5). This is due to occlusion of either the vertebral artery or the posterior inferior cerebellar artery, which branches off the right and left vertebral arteries just prior to their joining to form the basilar artery. The posterior inferior cerebellar artery gives off small branches as it wraps around the medulla oblongata on its way to the portion of the cerebellum for which it is named.

This syndrome involves damage of the following structures:

1. the inferior cerebellar peduncle and cerebellum, producing ipsilateral dysmetria, hypotonia, and slurred speech
2. the descending spinal tract and nucleus of cranial nerve V, producing loss of pain and temperature on the ipsilateral side of the face
3. the ascending lateral spinothalamic tract, producing pain and temperature loss on the contralateral side of the body
4. the descending sympathetic tract, producing an ipsilateral Horner's syndrome
5. the lower vestibular nuclei, producing nystagmus, vertigo, nausea, and vomiting
6. the nucleus ambiguus and the glossopharyngeal and vagus nerves and/or nuclei, producing hoarseness, difficulty swallowing, or intractable hiccups

Figure 10-6 shows the distribution of the pathological effects of Wallenberg's syndrome.

"Locked-In" Syndrome

Another syndrome, far less frequently and perhaps inappropriately reported with postadjustive vertebrobasilar ischemia, is known as the "locked-in" syndrome. This syndrome derives its name from the combination of completely normal consciousness with impaired sensation and total loss of voluntary movement other than blinking and vertical and converging eye move-

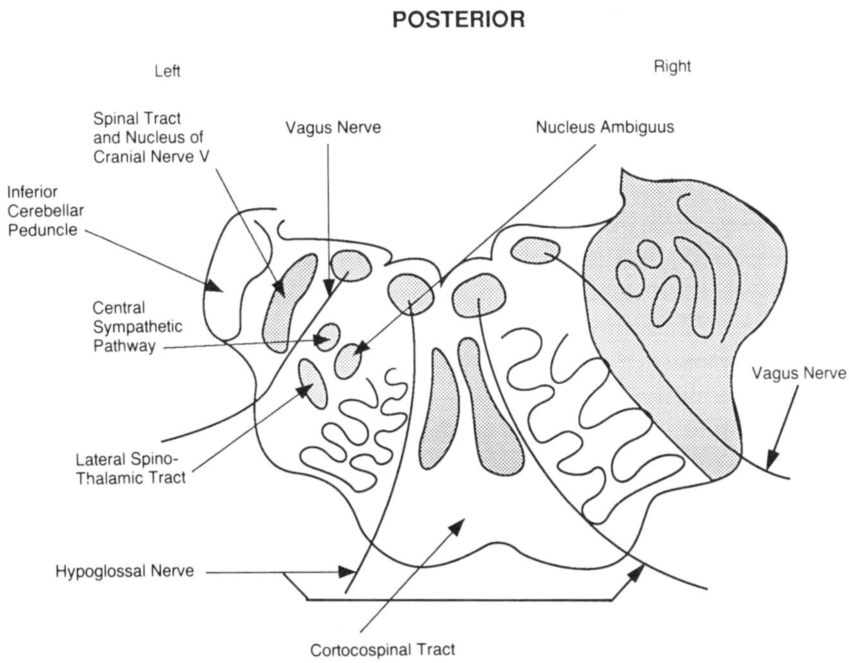

Figure 10-5 Structures in the lower medulla often involved in Wallenberg's syndrome. Shaded area on the right shows typical lesion distribution.

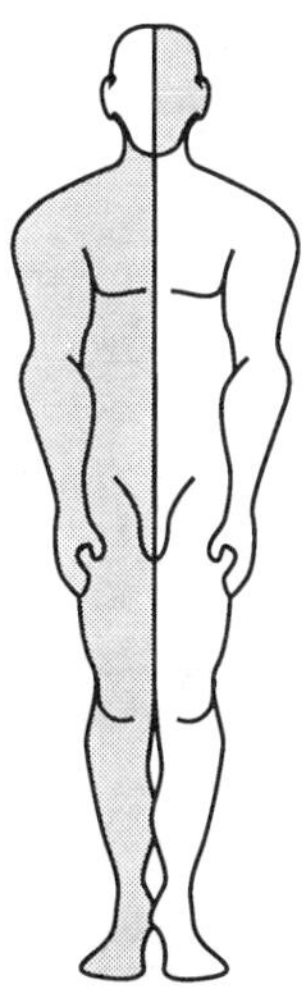

Figure 10-6 Distribution of areas of pain and temperature loss affected by Wallenberg's syndrome.

ments. The affected patient has been described as "a corpse with living eyes."[34] It is often caused by bilateral infarction of the ventral pons, usually secondary to basilar artery thrombosis (see Figure 10-7), but it also occurs in acute multiple sclerosis and some pontine gliomas.[35] Clinically, the locked-in syndrome is characterized by the sudden onset of hemiparesis, which rapidly progresses to quadriparesis. Eventually mutism occurs, along with complete loss of all functions supplied by cranial nerves V to XII bilaterally. Patients are often misdiagnosed as being comatose. Highly variable outcomes have been reported, ranging from mild residual neurological deficits to death. While the "locked-in" syndrome has been reported as related to CSMT, it is difficult to visualize a small vertebral artery embolus occluding the entire larger basilar artery. This complete basilar occlusion is necessary for a "locked-in" syndrome to occur. This inconsistency might lend more credence to the possibility of exacerbation or coincidence and not as a cause in relation to CSMT.

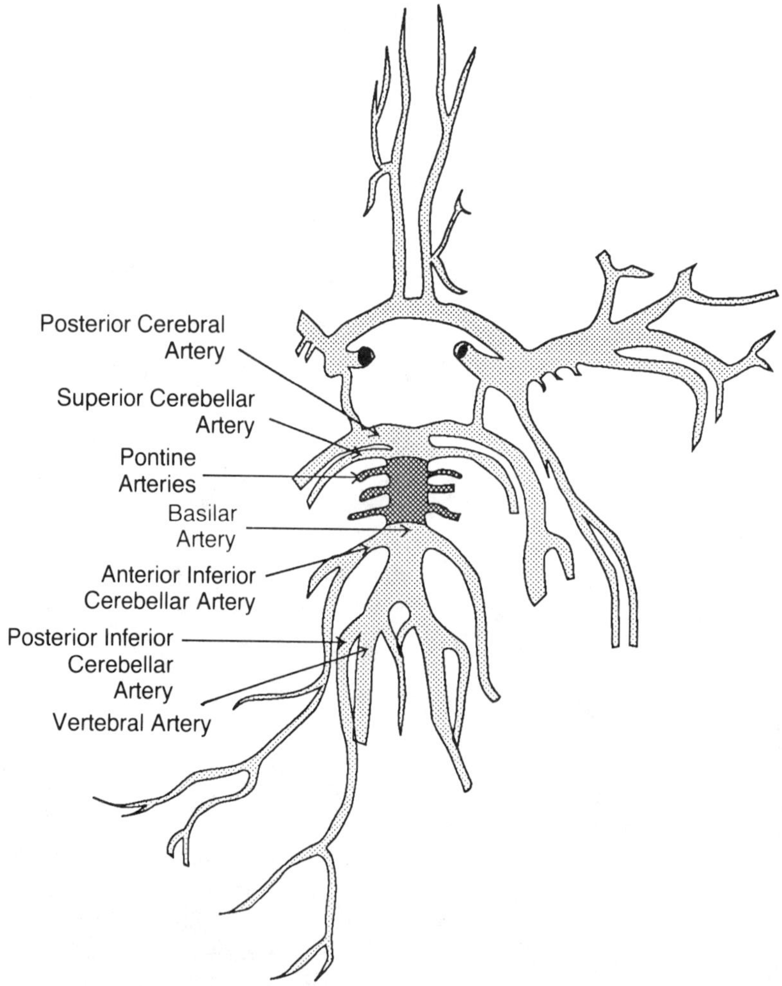

Figure 10-7 The circle of Willis with shaded basilar artery showing distribution of basilar occlusion.

Action Steps

Once your patient has reported adverse effects of a cervical adjustment possibly consistent with the syndromes outlined above, it may not be necessary to immediately call for an ambulance. Most emergency room physicians are completely unfamiliar with postadjustive vertebrobasilar ischemia anyway and are likely to misdiagnose the condition. Careful observation in the office is in order, as you should be most familiar with the condition and capable of making the preliminary diagnosis and initiating whatever referral may be necessary. A myriad of disorders will produce symptomatology identical to that of vertebrobasilar ischemia. Many of these other disorders are not serious and will clear spontaneously. If, indeed, a vascular injury has occurred, little can be done at a hospital to minimize the damage in the acute stage anyway.

Following these simple steps will enable you to provide the best possible care for your patient:

1. Do not administer another cervical adjustment.
2. Do not allow the patient to ambulate. Keep him or her comfortable.

3. Note all physical and vital signs (pallor, sweating, vomiting, heart and respiratory rate, blood pressure, body temperature, etc.).
4. Check the pupils for size, shape, and equality.
5. Check eye light and accommodation reflexes.
6. Test the lower cranial nerves, looking for facial numbness or paresis, swallowing, gag reflex, slurred speech, palatal elevation, etc.
7. Test cerebellar function, looking for dysmetria of extremities, nystagmus, tremor, etc.
8. Test the strength and tone of the somatic musculature.
9. Test for somatic sensation to pinprick.
10. Test the muscle stretch reflex and for the presence of pathological reflexes.
11. Completely immobilize the neck. A soft cervical support may be used. Take care not to cause excessive neck movements while placing the device on the patient. Any therapy involving neck movement, including neck traction or flexion, is inappropriate as it may cause further injury.

Remember, should any non–pre-existing neurological abnormality exist, make a prompt medical referral. Should the symptoms be unaccompanied by any new neurological anomaly and clear quickly and spontaneously, then it is unlikely that the patient has suffered any significant vascular insult. Remember, however, it is possible for all symptoms to clear and for a full-blown stroke to occur at a later date, as pointed out in the case histories detailed later in this chapter.

Whether or not this patient is a candidate for future cervical adjustments is often up to the confidence of the doctor as to his or her diagnosis. I suggest that no additional manipulations be performed on that visit. The patient must be instructed to contact you immediately in the event that any of these symptoms reappear. Future gentle manipulative techniques should only be undertaken after the risks are discussed with the patient. You may want him or her to sign some form of consent form (see Exhibit 10-1).

If similar symptomatology occurs a second time, I would not continue with osseous cervical adjustments on that patient and would strongly recommend a referral to a chiropractic or medical neurologist.

Exhibit 10-1 Sample Chiropractic Consent Form

Any procedure intended to help may also do harm. While chiropractic examination and therapeutic procedures (including spinal adjustment, ultrasound, heat application, electrotherapy, and manual muscle therapy) are usually considered remarkably safe and effective, please understand that occasionally there are complications. While the chances of experiencing any of these complications are extremely small, it is the practice of this chiropractic office to fully inform and educate all of our patients about them. These complications include but are not limited to:

Pain	Disc injury	Burns
Swelling	Sensory changes	Soft tissue injury
Bruising	Bleeding	Stroke (CVA)
Discoloration	Bone fracture	Dizziness
Inflammation	Nausea	Weakness

Worsening of the condition—spinal cord damage

I understand that there is no guarantee or warranty for a specific cure or result. I understand that I can request further explanation regarding any and all possible risks attendant to my care.

Signature ____________________

Date ____________________

CONCLUSION

Since it appears that cervical movements are indeed very capable of causing vertebral and carotid artery blood flow alterations, an obvious question arises: Why do not all people who fall asleep on their abdomen or turn to look over their shoulder suffer brain ischemia? Let us remember that we cannot always draw logical clinical conclusions from what appears to be basic scientific fact. Some authors have suggested[5,26,36] that the answer lies in the fact that some individuals have congenitally asymmetrical vertebral arteries and therefore are left more susceptible to the extraluminal occlusion that appears to occur with cervical movements. This argument is seen to be severely flawed, however, in light of the fact that it is actually quite common for normal asymptomatic patients to possess only one patent vertebral artery,[37] or have significant vertebral artery asymmetry such that one is twice the size of the other.[38,39] Yet it is not these patients who actually suffer the ischemia, as available angiographic data show an absence of significant asymmetry in 9 of 13 cases reported at the Mayo Clinic.[40]

It should carefully be noted, then, that head movement can cause vertebral artery compression but that the clinical significance of that compression is not clear. This is true both in those with normal or previously existing vertebral artery asymmetry.

With the above facts clearly in mind, one may consider the question of whether or not to completely or partially abandon CSMT. There are those who suggest that CSMT should be completely abandoned[41]—that it is better for 1,000 people to suffer with their minor complaints than for 1 patient to be permanently damaged by cervical manipulative therapy.

This argument is simply unacceptable and completely impractical in light of modern medical practice. If such an attitude were generally accepted, it would eliminate all nonemergency intervention, thus wiping out dozens of medical specialties and subspecialties, including any medication or surgery for similar musculoskeletal complaints. This would leave no viable therapy available for the hundreds of millions who suffer from musculoskeletal pain. I do not imagine that there are many cosmetic surgeons who would support this notion.

Much more disturbing is the assertion that thrust,[42] or rotary,[5] or other types of manipulation should be abandoned. Terrett[5] states that "the chiropractic profession should lead the field of manual medicine by abandoning those techniques which appear to carry the greatest risk." Modde[43] takes this alarmist posture to the extreme when he states that "adjustments in this position (supine or sitting cervical) should be made illegal for everyone except neurosurgeons."

In response to these arguments, it should be stated that there is no agreement as to what type of cervical manipulation is most dangerous. While numerous authors have concluded that rotation appears to be the most effective single movement producing alteration of blood flow,[16] it is not clear on which side the arterial occlusion may occur, nor what is the exact mechanism of occlusion, nor that this phenomenon is abnormal or even indirectly related to the unfortunate occurrence of neural ischemia. If cervical rotation is such a culprit, neural ischemia would certainly occur in every person who has slept on his or her abdomen or looked over his or her shoulder.

It has been theorized that improper blood perfusion through the vertebral arteries is a possible cause of head and neck pain, as well as other common symptoms presented to the chiropractic doctor.[44] Allow me to postulate that careful, educated cervical adjusting, aimed at normalizing segmental articular biomechanical function, may well improve abnormal forces applied to the vertebral artery, thereby preventing far more episodes of neural ischemia than it causes. While this may or may not be the actual case, this is just as tenable as is the suggestion that extension-rotation testing will predetermine those at increased risk. Indeed, based upon extremely common empirical evidence in chiropractic practice, where many of the classic symptoms of neural ischemia (nausea, tinnitus, lightheadedness, visual problems, etc.) are actually relieved by cervical adjustment, improvement of vertebral blood flow does not at all seem very far fetched.

An Acceptable Risk

It has been said that "if you can cure it, you can cause it." In light of the fact that the disastrous complication of permanent neurological damage is such a rare event, is the term "acceptable risk" suitable in this instance? It is my opinion that no other health care profession can match the humanity shown by ours. The fact that vertebrobasilar ischemia has received such great attention in the chiropractic literature and that testing for such a rare and elusive malady has become so emphasized documents the profession's unequaled concern for the welfare of the chiropractic patient. I contend that by grasping at straws in relation to testing for neural ischemia, we may well wind up depriving a significant number of those same patients of a safe and reliable way to relieve their suffering.

Recommendations

What needs to be clarified is the difference between nontraumatic stroke and postmanipulative stroke. It is my opinion that confusion between these two distinct entities has led to over-reliance on warning signs and overutilization of testing procedures. Screening patients for oral contraceptive use, osteophytosis, hypertension and other cardiovascular disease, family predisposition, etc., is valid in the context of stroke. It may not, however, be valid in the context of postmanipulative stroke.

The author suggests the following screening procedure. The investigation may require nothing more than a good case history upon a patient's initial presentation. It is not necessary, or prudent, to routinely perform any extension/rotation test procedures for vertebrobasilar ischemia prior to cervical manipulation. What is essential is that you, as a chiropractic doctor, be cognizant of the gravity of the procedure you are about to perform, and that the lines of communication between you and your patient remain wide open. It is good practice to talk to the patient prior and during palpation of the neck and ask him or her to be certain to immediately inform you should any uncomfortable sensation or nausea arise. It may be prudent to then hold the patient's head for about 2 to 5 seconds in the preadjustive position prior to administering an adjustment. If no discomfort is reported, the adjustment may be administered. If the patient reports pain, this is important, because an adjustment should not be synonymous with the infliction of pain. A properly administered adjustment is not painful. If the preadjustive position continues to be painful on another attempt, other nonforce techniques should be utilized on that patient on that visit.

Should the patient report dizziness or nausea, the neck should be returned to the neutral position and further discussion of the patient's sensations should be undertaken. If it is determined that the sensation was more due to apprehension than to vertigo, the neck is returned to the preadjustive posture. If the sensation returns, no manipulation should be administered to the neck of that patient on that visit.

While at face value this appears to be just another extension/rotation test, it has multiple advantages. First, this procedure takes absolutely no additional time, as the neck should always be palpated prior to adjustment. Therefore, it may be repeated on every patient on every visit that involves cervical manipulation, without added time or financial expense. Second, it involves no increased risk to the patient, as may be expected from the positions of extreme hyperextension and rotation required by the above-detailed extension/rotation testing procedures. Finally, it reminds the doctor of the magnitude of the impending manipulation and allows the patient to play an active role in helping stem a possible manipulative accident.

CASE STUDIES AND SPECIFIC PROCEDURES

It is my opinion that there is perhaps no better way to learn clinical skills than through case studies. The following examples are not written as typical case studies, in that certain areas especially relevant to the discussion have been elaborated upon. During this discussion, many readers may think that they would never have acted this way, and that this would never happen to them. Others will be thinking, "There but for the grace of God go I." In the heat of the moment, actions may be done that, in retrospect, seem unreasonable. One or more important lessons may be learned from each of these cases, principally the necessity to be prepared.

Case One

A right-handed 38-year-old married white female presented to a doctor of chiropractic with a 3-day-old complaint of left-sided neck and head pain. She was examined, and range of motion, orthopaedic, and neurological tests and a George's test were performed, and cervical radiographs were obtained.

A diagnosis of "wry neck" was made, and treatment was initiated, including positive galvanism to the cervicothoracic area and a home traction unit for use twice daily with 12 pounds of pressure. She was seen again the next day and showed slight improvement in the muscle spasms but no change in her complaint of head and neck pain. The C-5 was adjusted using the Pierce technique, C-1 was adjusted on the right, and C-5 was adjusted on the left. Positive galvanism was again used. Later that day she telephoned to report that her complaints were markedly reduced and asked if she should still continue with the traction. She was advised to continue, with a reduction in the pounds of pressure.

Her next visit was 3 days later, and she reported that she continued to feel better for one and a half days after the treatment but began to experience a return of signs and symptoms the previous afternoon. Using her traction unit made the pain worse. C-5 was adjusted with the Pierce technique, C-2 on the left, and C-7 on the right. Within 10 minutes of this treatment she complained of dizziness and nausea. She was instructed to return to the treatment room, and C-2 was adjusted. When the table was raised up, she felt "very, very dizzy." While she stood her nausea increased, and she vomited into a trash container. She was instructed to lie back down on the table. Her eye light reflexes were examined and determined to be normal, as was her pulse rate of 70, and her palpatory temperature appeared normal. Blood pressure measurement was attempted, but the electronic device was unable to give an accurate reading due to a dead battery. Ice was placed on the base of the patient's skull, and the doctor noted that her speech was slurred.

The patient requested that her husband be contacted, and he was telephoned at home. When the husband arrived, he requested that an ambulance be called, and this was done. By the time the ambulance arrived, she was sitting up, and her speech was improving. The ambulance personnel recorded her blood pressure at 80/60. The attending medical physician in the emergency room reported marked dysarthria, left gaze palsy with possible superimposed left sixth nerve palsy, tongue deviation to the right, a "possibly mild, early peripheral seventh—though this is not definite," moderate to marked left upper extremity dysmetria, and muscle stretch reflexes 3+ on the right and 1+ on the left. His assessment was "acute left cerebellar infarction, rule out dissection." A computed tomography (CT) scan and angiography were performed, and then the patient was transferred to the intensive care unit.

The CT was normal. Angiography revealed a "long segment of narrowed to absent left vertebral artery beginning a couple of centimeters distal to its origin and then being reconstituted by muscular collaterals just prior to its course over C-1." This finding was consistent with dissection. Anticoagulation with heparin was begun. During the next few days she developed some drowsiness and dysarthria. The CT was repeated 2 days later and revealed bilateral cerebellar hemisphere infarcts, left worse than right. The infarcts caused compression of the fourth ventricle and resultant enlargement of the third and lateral ventricles. Several follow-up CT scans showed continued improvement, and approximately 1 month after admission, her CT and clinical picture showed marked improvement. She is presently doing well and has minimal hard neurological deficits.

Case Two

This patient was a right-handed 36-year-old single white female organist and computer/typewriter operator with a history of birth control pill use, hypertension, and ulcers. In August 1986 she presented to her family physician with a complaint of pain in the left upper shoulder, radiating to the elbow. She was prescribed Parafon Forte and Tolectin, but since the Tolectin made her sick, she was switched to Tylenol No. 3 and advised to rest. Physical therapy was prescribed. The physical therapy and medications were not helpful after 15 outpatient visits, and in November 1986 she presented to a doctor of chiropractic. She had received chiropractic care on occasion since 1975, but this was the first time for this complaint.

It appears that the patient was not examined, outside of applied kinesiological muscle tests. No findings were recorded, other than weakness of the left levator scapulae, left deltoid, and left teres major. C-5 and C-6 were adjusted using the Gonstead technique (seated cervical). The next day she was treated with an activator for her pelvis, and posteroanterior prone adjustments of T-3, T-4, T-6, T-7, T-8, and T-9 were performed. Radiographs were obtained, including an anteroposterior full spine and a lateral cervical-thoracic view. The next day she returned, and the same procedures were followed, without radiographs, and the patient reported improvement in her arm symptoms. She was seen 2 days later, and some upper extremity exercises were initiated.

She was seen again the next day, and C-4 and C-5 were adjusted as above. Two days later she presented to the local hospital with complaints of headache, facial pain about the ear, and feeling sick "to her stomach," which she had developed that night. An ear infection was diagnosed, and antibiotics were prescribed. She presented to her chiropractor the next morning with the same symptoms. She had had similar symptoms about 6 years earlier, and adjustments appeared to help, so she was discouraged from taking the antibiotics, and C-3 was adjusted. Immediately following the adjustment she developed a "burning pain" from her jaw to just below her eye on the right. This lasted about 2 or 3 minutes. She was dizzy and felt faint for another 10 minutes. She was instructed to lie down, and after a few minutes she felt "a bit" better, but the area behind her ear was getting "sorer and sorer."

She drove to her aunt's house after leaving the chiropractor's office. She continued to experience episodes of "stabbing, searing, sharp pains." She returned to her chiropractor the next day, and only activator treatment to the cervical spine was administered. That evening the pain intensified and the patient "had some kind of seizure" wherein she pulled some drapery from a window. Her mother noted that the patient had slurred speech at that point. Her face was hot and flushed, and she continued to complain of "burning, searing" pain. After applying ice to the patient's face, the patient's mother took her to the hospital emergency room. The emergency room doctor suspected shingles.

In the emergency room she began experiencing projectile vomiting and was ataxic, falling to the right, so she was admitted and was evaluated by a neurosurgeon. Her temperature was 98°F; pulse rate, 100 beats per minute; respiration rate, 20/min; and blood pressure, 150/110. Her right eye was slightly miotic, with a sluggish reaction to light. She vomited over a period of 4 hours, as the pains waxed and waned, and the hospital nurses put ice on her face. A CT was performed; the patient was then transferred to another hospital where another CT was performed. Both CT scans revealed hydrocephalus—"massive dilatation of all compartments of the ventricular system . . . with no pathologically increased intracranial pressure . . . probably long standing . . . clinical correlation is recommended." At this time she was ataxic, with minimal ptosis and medial deviation of the right eye (now found to be present since childhood). Cerebellar tests were "not grossly abnormal," but the neurosurgeon noted some difficulty with coordination without mention of side. Strength and motor function were normal, and there was a "negative Babinski's."

She was transferred to a third hospital for a magnetic resonance imaging (MRI) scan. While lying down for the MRI, she experienced a "terrible throbbing'' in her head. She could not walk without support after the test. The original MRI report mentioned only ''severe hydrocephalus,'' although ''three to four focal areas of increased T2 signal'' were mentioned, ''of questionable significance . . . better evaluated after the patient has been shunted.'' Her neurosurgeon told her that if she did not have surgery, she would be dead by noon. A shunt was inserted.

Two days later she was evaluated by a neurologist. He believed that the increased T2 area on the MRI might be consistent with multiple sclerosis but wanted to talk to the radiologist. She was recovering from surgery and somewhat nauseated. Her speech was slurred, she displayed some nystagmus, and decreased left gaze was noted with severe weakness and dysmetria of the left upper extremity, and moderate weakness and dysmetria in all other extremities. Muscle stretch reflexes were all increased, and plantar responses were extended bilaterally with three beats of clonus at both ankles.

Four days after her surgery, an addendum to the report on the brain MRI revealed ''an abnormality involving the basilar artery . . . suggesting clot'' and stated ''the possibility of basilar artery thrombosis should be considered.'' Ten days after her surgery, a second addendum to the brain MRI stated ''increased signal in the right vertebral artery distally, suggesting thrombosis of this vessel as well.''

Presently this patient is doing well and has minimal hard neurological findings. Her current complaints are of fatigue and psychiatric problems.

Case Three

A 38-year-old white male meat plant worker with a history of cigarette smoking, hypothyroidism, controlled hypertension, and diagnosed hyperventilation presented to his doctor of chiropractic on January 24, 1985, with a complaint of neck pain. He had seen this doctor for a total of 13 prior office visits, beginning in July 1982, for five separate episodes of neck discomfort. Formal orthopaedic, neurological, and radiographic examinations were never performed. The initial four episodes responded well to chiropractic therapy, including infrared heat and cervicothoracic manipulation, with diversified technique.

On the 14th visit, after the application of infrared heat, the patient's neck was massaged for about 5 minutes and a supine cervical adjustment was administered. Immediate neck pain, followed by nausea and vertigo, was experienced by the patient as he attempted to rise from the adjustment table. His left arm felt weak and numb. The doctor observed the patient's eyes and inquired about chest pains. The patient asked if he was having a heart attack or stroke, and the doctor replied that he did not think so. The patient developed headache, sweating, dizziness, and nausea.

The patient was then placed prone on the table and an activator thrust was applied to the cervical spine. The patient's symptoms worsened. The patient was led to a back office, where he vomited. He was checked on periodically by the doctor and by an employee over a period of 2 hours. The patient's parents were called, and the doctor placed the patient in a wheelchair and helped him into his parent's car. The doctor suspected a ''flu.''

That evening the patient presented to the emergency room at a local hospital complaining of nausea and dizziness. Acute gastroenteritis was diagnosed, and the patient was sent home. He presented to his family physician 2 days later, who sent the patient to a neurologist. ''End point nystagmus'' bilaterally on left lateral gaze, ''incomplete homonymous scotomata'' with macular sparing on the left, ''left facial droop,'' ''numbness'' in the left upper extremity, and ''clear ataxia'' were noted. A CT scan showed ''two small posterior circulation'' left cerebellar lobe infarctions.

The patient has recovered well and has minimal hard neurological residua, including a small scotoma not noticed by the patient and occasional ''bouts of dizziness.'' (The author personally testified in this case, which went to court. A jury verdict came back as no negligence, and no monies were awarded.)

REFERENCES

1. Caplan LR, Zarnis CK, Hemmati M. Spontaneous dissection of the extracranial vertebral arteries. *Stroke*. 1985;16:1030–1038.

2. Chen J, Smith R, Keller A, Kucharczyk W. Spontaneous dissection of the vertebral artery: MR findings. *J Computer Assist Tomogr*. 1989;13:326–329.

3. Levine SR, Quint DJ, Pessin MS, Boulos RS, Welch KMA. Intraluminal clot in the vertebrobasilar circulation: clinical and radiographic features. *Neurology*. 1989;39:515–522.

4. Pessin MS, Daneault N, Kwan ES, Eisengart MA, Caplan LR. Local embolism from vertebral artery occlusion. *Stroke*. 1988;19(1):112–115.

5. Terrett AGJ. Vascular accidents from cervical spinal manipulation: report on 107 cases. *J Aust Chiropractors' Assoc*. 1987;17:15–24.

6. Ladermann JP. Cerebrovascular accidents related to chiropractic care: further considerations. *Eur J Chiropractic*. 1990;38:63–68.

7. Bernat JL, Hunter RW. The benign lateral medullary syndrome. *Arch Neurol*. 1978;35:112–113.

8. Maigne R. *Orthopedic Medicine. A New Approach to Vertebral Manipulations*. Springfield, Ill: Charles C Thomas, Publisher; 1972:2, 169.

9. Gutmann G. Injuries to the vertebral artery caused by manual therapy. *Manuelle Medizin*. 1983;21:2–14.

10. Chapman-Smith D. Cervical adjustment—the risk of vertebral artery injury. *J Chiropractic*. 1987:12–15.

11. Fager C. The age old back problem: new fad, same fallacies. *Spine*. 1984;9:329.

12. Carpenter S. Injury of neck as cause of vertebral artery thrombosis. *J Neurosurg*. 1961;18:849–853.

13. Husni EA, Bell HS, Storer J. Mechanical occlusion of the vertebral artery: a new concept. *JAMA*. 1966;196:475–478.

14. Okawara S, Nibbelink D. Vertebral artery occlusion following hyperextension and rotation of the head. *Stroke*. 1974;5:640–642.

15. Beatty RA. Dissecting hematoma of the internal carotid artery following chiropractic cervical manipulation. *J Trauma*. 1977;17:248–249.

16. Toole JF, Tucker SH. Influence of head position upon cerebral circulation. Studies on blood flow in cadavers. *Arch Neurol*. 1960;2:616–623.

17. Hardesty WH, Witacre WB, Toole JF, Randall P, Royster HP. Studies on vertebral artery blood flow in man. *Surg Gynecol Obstet*. 1963;116:662–664.

18. Farris AA, Posner CM, Wilmore DW, Agnew CH. Radiologic visualization of neck vessels in healthy men. *Neurology*. 1963;13:386–396.

19. Husni EA, Storer J. The syndrome of mechanical occlusion of the vertebral artery: further observations. *Angiology*. 1967;18:106–116.

20. Sheehan S, Bauer RB, Meyer JS. Vertebral artery compression in cervical spondylosis: arteriographic demonstration during life of vertebral artery insufficiency due to rotation and extension of the neck. *Neurology*. 1960;10:968–986.

21. Bauer R, Sheehan S, Meyer JS. Arteriographic study of cerebrovascular disease, II: cerebral symptoms due to kinking, tortuosity, and compression of carotid and vertebral arteries in the neck. *Arch Neurol*. 1961;4:119–131.

22. Ford FR, Clark D. Thrombosis of the basilar artery with softenings in the cerebellum and brainstem due to manipulation of the neck: a report of two cases with one postmortem examination; reasons are given to prove that damage to the vertebral arteries is responsible. *Bull Johns Hopkins Hosp*. 1956;98:37–42.

23. Kanshepolsky J, Danielson H, Flynn RE. Vertebral artery insufficiency and cerebellar infarct due to manipulation of the neck: report of a case. *Bull Los Angeles Neurol Soc*. 1972;37:62–66.

24. George PE. Identification of high risk pre-stroke patient. *J Chiropractic*. 1981;15:26–28.

25. Bolton PS, Stick PE, Lord RSA. Failure of clinical tests to predict cerebral ischemia before neck manipulation. *J Manipulative Physiol Ther*. 1989;12:304–307.

26. Smith RA, Estridge MN. Neurologic complications of head and neck manipulations: report of two cases. *JAMA*. 1962;192:528–531.

27. Kleynhans AM, Terrett AGJ. *Aspects of Manipulative Therapy*. New York: Churchill Livingstone; 1985;161–175.

28. Terrett AGJ. Importance and interpretation of tests designed to predict susceptibility to neurocirculatory accidents from manipulation. *J Am Chiropractic Assoc*. 1983;13:29–34.

29. Parkin PJ, Wallis WE, Wilson JL. Vertebral artery occlusion following manipulation of the neck. *N Z Med J*. 1978;88:441–443.

30. Schellas KP, Latchaw RE, Wendling LR, Gold LHA. Vertebrobasilar injuries following cervical manipulation. *JAMA*. 1980;244:1450–1453.

31. Ferezy JS. Neural ischemia and cervical manipulation: an acceptable risk. *J Am Chiropractic Assoc*. 1988; 22:61–63, 67.

32. Ferezy JS. Vertebrobasilar ischemia: assessment and action. *Minnesota Chiropractic Association Journal*. 1989;14–23.

33. Chusid JG. *Correlative Neuroanatomy and Functional Neurology*. Norwalk, Conn: Lange Medical Publications; 1985.

34. Plum F, Posner JB. *The Diagnosis of Stupor and Coma*. 3rd ed. Philadelphia, Pa: FA Davis & Co; 1982.

35. Gilroy J. *Basic Neurology*. New York, NY: Macmillan; 1982.

36. Green D, Joynt RJ. Vascular accidents to the brainstem associated with neck manipulation. *JAMA*. 1959;170:522–524.

37. Falconer MA. The surgical treatment of bleeding intracranial aneurysms. *J Neurol Neurosurg Psychiatry*. 1951;14:153–186.

38. Stopford JSB. The arteries of the pons and medulla oblongata. *J Anat*. 1916;50:131–164.

39. Brown BSJ, Tatlow WFT. Radiographic studies of the vertebral artery in cadavers: effects of position and traction on the head. *Radiology*. 1963;81:80–88.

40. Kruger BR, Okazaki H. Vertebral-basilar distribution infarction following chiropractic cervical manipulation. *Mayo Clin Proc*. 1980;55:322–332.

41. Boyd-Wilson J. Testimony in the New Zealand inquiry into chiropractic. *New Zealand*. 1978.

42. Grieve GP. *Modern Manual Therapy of the Vertebral Column*. London: Churchill Livingstone; 1986:873–884.

43. Modde PJ. *Chiropractic Malpractice*. Columbia: Hanrow Press; 1985:98–100.

44. Leach RA: *The Chiropractic Theories. A Synopsis of Scientific Research*. Baltimore, Md: Williams & Wilkins; 1980:109–119.

chapter 11

Record Maintenance and Narrative Writing

Leo J. Bronston

Documentation of patient care is extremely important. Accurate, concise medical records provide

- a way for physicians to manage individual cases
- the information required by the third-party payer system validating the medical necessity for ongoing therapeutic care
- detailed information regarding a patient to other health care providers
- legal documentation
- a method of monitoring quality
- a system for structuring thinking for problem solving

The intent of this chapter is to provide a workable framework for the recording of information so that it can be easily retrieved by any health care professional when he or she is evaluating or continuing the care of a given individual.

Information pertaining to the patient's initial history, objective evaluation data, the assessment of clinical condition, and any treatment that is rendered is recorded within the record. It is necessary to have appropriate written information in case a physician relinquishes care of a given patient for whatever reason. Other health care providers then can pick up where the provider left off and provide appropriate care and be able to communicate with the patient. The health record is therefore a valuable document during follow-up of the treatment process. Third-party payers are demanding increased documentation to support the rationale for continued reimbursement. The decisions made by third-party payers can be influenced by the completeness and quality of the particular notations found within the patient file. For quality assurance, one can plan a treatment program and then make a determination relative to whether the preset criteria have been met. SOAP (Subjective Objective Assessment Plan) notes, in themselves, can be utilized for research purposes by gathering the information and drawing conclusions about particular treatment patterns of patient care. When utilizing any type of record keeping system, it is important to formulate and organize your thought processes. By thinking in an organized manner, one can make better decisions regarding patient care.

Very few individuals can remember the comprehensive medical history obtained during an evaluation; it must be written down during the procedure. Jotting down short phrases, words, and dates can aid the practitioner to formulate his or her thoughts at a later time when dictation of the record is indicated. Using a written questionnaire can be additionally helpful; written questionnaires help ensure a thorough and complete clinical record. The recording of data during the intake interview should not distract the physician's attention from the patient. Equally, the written form or questionnaire should not distract the doctor from following a patient's lead during the informational stage of the history.

During the subsequent physical or neurological assessment, the physician may utilize various forms in order to follow a prescribed format during the extensive examination. For example, it is extremely important for the beginning neurologist to perform a thorough neurological examination. Until the physician becomes experienced in performing an evaluation, he or she is not actually capable of determining the tests that can be omitted. These inadvertently omitted tests may be just the ones required to produce pertinent information associated with the patient's presentation. The reasons for following a prescribed format in conducting an extensive neurological examination is to

1. determine a baseline for a particular patient
2. develop familiarity with normal responses so that one may understand and appreciate pathological responses

It is extremely important for the physician to perform a thorough evaluation and to have specific guidelines to refer to during the recording process. A physician who continually performs an examination will develop his or her own way of determining the information required. It is that level of skill and expertise, developed through repetitive evaluations, that enables a physician to gather appropriate information. A physician should never record that a test is normal unless he or she actually finds this to be the case during the evaluation. If a clinician has forgotten to evaluate a particular item, he or she should weigh the importance of the test against the inconvenience to the patient of having to undress and undergo the segment of the examination not performed.

Discussion regarding grading and recording of testing procedures will be found within the appropriate chapters of this book. While this chapter will not provide the doctor with all the various methods of recording used during the clinical assessment, some information on recording methods will be provided to assist the physician in developing his or her own recording scheme.

The patient's history can be recorded on blank sheets of paper or on a form. There should be space for a free-flow description concerning the observations within the record. A checklist is incomplete without a free-written description of those items tested; an explanation as to what was observed when a positive response is recorded must also be included.

Record maintenance involves creating a standard of practice. The patient has the right to have information recorded in a manner to establish the necessity and effectiveness of care. The information should address the quality of care rendered, the outcome, and how well the process worked. Daily records should justify the type and duration of clinical care provided through recording in objective format findings regarding the patient's condition that are supportive of decisions about therapy.

Depending on the clinical care facility, medical notations can either be directly written on the record or transcribed from dictated material. Abbreviations should be used to keep the medical record brief. Each health care facility has a list of abbreviations acceptable for use in its records, available upon request; acceptable abbreviations vary from one health care facility to another. Since others will be using abbreviations in their notations in patient records, familiarity with them will also help one keep up with the findings and diagnoses of other health care personnel involved in patient care. Appendix A lists commonly used abbreviations; definitions for abbreviations used in this chapter may be found in this appendix. In addition, Appendix B includes a compendium of common neurological terms.

THE PROBLEM-ORIENTED MEDICAL RECORD

The SOAP note format, initially devised by Lawrence L. Weed, MD, is part of a system of organizing the medical record called the problem-oriented medical record. Dr. Weed's contention was that the physician, as director of the health care team, needed a means to communicate with all members of the team. This need is more acute when the team is composed of doctors in group practice. He related the efficiency of health care and the accuracy of chart-based clinical research to the quality of medical records generated. The goal of the problem-oriented medical record system is to improve patient care while assisting clinical research investigation. More objective records also assist in monitoring physician performance by objectively accounting for it. Without specific rules to follow during record keeping, there is no way to judge a doctor's performance, or for the doctor to judge it either. The problem-oriented medical record provides for achievement of excellence by:

1. establishing a standard of care
2. providing a logical system to patient care
3. defining clinical problems one by one
4. organizing medical problems for solution
5. enabling assessment of quality of care provided.

Although many health care facilities today do not utilize the problem-oriented medical record, they do use a similar type of medical record format. Each specialty field within medicine, as well as each health care facility, has its own standards of record keeping, secondary to the fact that databases vary among disciplines.

The problem-oriented medical record lists the patient's problems in the front of the chart, and each health care provider is expected to record a separate SOAP note relative to each of the patient's problems.

Subjective

The SOAP format provides a structural, written framework for problem solving. Relative to the decision-making process, the physician initially records within the chart the patient's problem or diagnosis. Information is then gathered from the patient during the history portion of the examination. Symptomatology elicited from the patient is described in terms of frequency, duration, character, and intensity of pain patterns. The information gathered during the history comprises the subjective or "S" portion of the SOAP format.

The patient history is the most important part of an evaluation. It begins with observation of the patient during the recording process. Once the patient's problems have been stated, it is up to the physician to gather appropriate information in order to begin to formulate the differential diagnosis. The patient's current complaint should be written down as accurately as possible. When creating a problem or diagnostic impression list, one should include chief complaints as they relate to the loss of function or physiological pathology. The etiology for each complaint needs to be defined, as to whether it is due to illness or injury. One should record the intensity, frequency, duration, and pain character of each particular complaint. Various grading systems have been devised for the recording of pain intensity:

1. mild, moderate, considerable, severe
2. 0 to 10 scale, with 10 representing the most pain imaginable
3. 0 to 100 scale, with 100 representing the most pain imaginable

If the patient's problem has been caused by trauma, information regarding the mechanism of injury needs to be recorded.

It is important to ascertain the response to prior treatment and diagnostic evaluations. Any accidents or injuries postdating the original illness or injury need to be thoroughly documented. Any surgical intervention or hospitalization, whether related to the problem at hand or antedating it, must be recorded. The patient's psychosocial inventory should include current medications, alcohol intake, smoking history, hobbies, recreational activities, current exercise program, diet, emotional well-being or attitudes, goals, marital status, ages and number of children. Vocational activities can play an important role in determining a cause-and-effect relationship or perpetuating a patient's musculoskeletal or neurological complaint. Prior diseases, other than general childhood ones, should be recorded. The biological family history of diabetes, hypertension, cancer, arthritis, genetic disease, heart disease, and allergies should be addressed. Anything the patient tells the physician relative to the present condition and that is pertinent to patient management is important to record.

Any information taken from a family member should be identified as such. For example, when someone presents with symptoms secondary to a cerebral vascular accident of left hemiparesis and aphasia, the subjective portion of the notes should indicate that information received was taken from the patient's wife, as the patient was unable to verbalize secondary to aphasia.

A comprehensive questionnaire (patient-answer list) is sometimes utilized and is notably less exhausting for the physician. It also cuts down on time spent collecting the initial comprehensive history. If such questionnaires are utilized, they should be readily available to the physician at the time of the examination. An excellent comprehensive medical history questionnaire for utilization in neurological or family practice is shown in Exhibit 11-1. At times, the entire history can be dictated, after the completion of record keeping, in the presence of the patient. This procedure gives the patient an opportunity to correct any misunderstandings that may have resulted and allows the patient to know precisely what the examiner understands about each problem.

When recording the history, one should not list irrelevant information. Subjective information should demonstrate the need for therapeutics. Complaints should be brief and to the point. The patient should rate his or her subjective complaints on a scale of 0 to 100, with 100 representing the most pain an individual could ever imagine. Functional abilities can be rated by the amount of assistance needed to perform given tasks at home, on the job, etc. A physician needs to avoid listing nonspecific complaints within progress notes or during the initial intake interview. Nonspecific complaints might be a result of normal patient depression or discouragement, and without clinical significance.

Objective

After information is gathered for the medical record during the initial consultation with the patient, a physician requests or implements various types of testing procedures. The results of these tests are always recorded under the objective or "O" portion of the SOAP format.

Objective information is the measurable data that can be recorded within the clinical record. Objective data gathering requires various methods of recording and measuring objective data. Some specific data to be gathered during the objective evaluation include:

- appearance
- cranial nerve evaluation
- edema
- endurance
- gait
- height
- mental alertness
- muscle strength
- muscle tone
- posture
- pulse
- range of motion
- reflexes
- respiration
- sensation
- vital signs
- weight

Objective observations serve as valuable comparative information within written documentation. Measurements taken during one session can be compared to past measurements. Objective data are usually organized in categories. In general, categories or headings for various types of objective information depend on specific patient deficits and/or diagnostic entities. Depending on the health care practitioner or facility, one might base headings or categories on the types of tests and measurements performed, but usually headings and categories are based on areas of body evaluated and functional skills. The list below gives an idea of sample categories to use:

- ROM
- motor
- strength
- sensation
- gait
- upper extremities
- lower extremities
- trunk
- neck
- head

Placing objective data into categories is dependent on the diagnosis and deficits of an individual patient. A patient with lower back pain may have deficits in gait and lower extremity and trunk function. Information gathered would be placed in separate categories.

- trunk: considerable to severe paraspinal spasm
- lower extremity: radicular pain ending BK absent AJ
- gait: slow, deliberate, guarded

In summary, information within the SOAP note can be arranged in different ways. Within an individual category, information is listed in the most logical order possible. Usually, one joint at a time is addressed, from proximal to distal. Using the example of data obtained from examining a right lower extremity that is demonstrating a deficit, one might write the following.

- ®LE
- sensation: L4 dermatome ↓ pinprick
- motor: KJ absent (quadriceps, minimal atrophy)
- AAROM: hip flexion 60 degrees
- orthopaedic: SLR—pos. 40 degrees LBP; Braggard—neg.
- strength: quadriceps 4+ +/5

On occasion, a standard range of motion or muscle testing chart or flow sheet can be utilized. It is recommended that a standard charting method be utilized during the initial evaluation in order to gather the most comprehensive information that one can until one becomes an experienced examiner. This final document should be dated, signed, and attached to a portion of the file.

Common mistakes made in recording objective information include

- inability to record the anatomical part affected
- inadequate recording in measurable terms
- inability to state the function as having been measured or observed
- inappropriate recording of positive orthopaedic tests without regard to specific location of pain, character, etc.

The objective section of the SOAP note is very important and should be included whenever recording initial, interim, or discharge notations. This information should be well organized under headings, be written in a clear, concise manner, and list the results of the objective measurement procedures.

Objective evaluation may be performed during each office visit, depending on the patient's diagnosis and the need for continual modification of the treatment plan. Frequent objective monitoring provides the clinical findings to substantiate the necessity for continuing care. Periodic office monitoring should include but not be limited to

- spinal range of motion
- postural or gait analysis
- presence or absence of palpable paraspinal spasm or hypertonicity
- location of trigger points, whether active or latent
- presence of vertebral tenderness, reproduced by palpation
- loss of joint play, if applicable
- motor status
- sensory changes

Exhibit 11-1 An Example of a Medical History Questionnaire

Name ________ Age ________ Single / Married ____ Divorced / Widow(er) ____ Date ________

Occupation ________ All Previous Occupations ________

Birth Place ________ Birthdate ________ List all States in which you have lived ________

Education: ______ years High School ______ years College ______ years Post Grad.

Date of last physical examination ________ Please list all Symptoms	**P.I.** Please do not write in this space
1. ________	
2. ________	
3. ________	
4. ________	
5. ________	
Routine Check-up - No Symptoms ☐	

	If Living: Age	If Living: Health	If Deceased: Age at death	If Deceased: Cause	Has any blood relative ever had:	Please encircle No or Yes	Who
Father					Cancer	No Yes	
Mother					Tuberculosis	No Yes	
Brother or Sister 1.					Diabetes	No Yes	
2.					Heart Trouble	No Yes	
3.					High Blood		
4.					Pressure	No Yes	
5.					Stroke	No Yes	
Husband or Wife					Epilepsy	No Yes	
Son or Daughter 1.					Insanity	No Yes	
2.					Suicide	No Yes	
3.							
4.							
5.							
6.							

NOTE: This is a confidential record of your medical history and will be kept in this office. Information contained here will not be released to any person except when you have authorized us to do so.

PERSONAL HISTORY

ILLNESSES: Have your ever had

PLEASE ENCIRCLE ALL ANSWERS No Yes

Measles ____ No Yes
German Measles ____ No Yes
Mumps ____ No Yes
Chicken Pox ____ No Yes
Whooping Cough ____ No Yes
Scarlet fever or Scarlatina ____ No Yes
Diphtheria ____ No Yes
Smallpox ____ No Yes
Pneumonia ____ No Yes
Influenza ____ No Yes
Pleurisy ____ No Yes
Rheumatic Fever or Heart Disease ____ No Yes
Arthritis or Rheumatism ____ No Yes
Any bone or joint disease ____ No Yes
Neuritis or Neuralgia ____ No Yes
Bursitis, Sciatica or Lumbago ____ No Yes
Polio or Meningitis ____ No Yes
Nephritis ____ No Yes
Gonorrhea or Syphilis ____ No Yes
Gallbladder disease ____ No Yes
Anemia ____ No Yes
Jaundice ____ No Yes
Bladder disease ____ No Yes
Epilepsy ____ No Yes
Migraine headaches ____ No Yes
Tuberculosis ____ No Yes
Diabetes ____ No Yes
Cancer ____ No Yes

High or low blood pressure ____ No Yes
Colitis or other bowel disease ____ No Yes
Hemorrhoids or any rectal disease ____ No Yes
Nervous Breakdown ____ No Yes
Food, chemical or drug poisoning ____ No Yes
Hay fever or Asthma ____ No Yes
Hives or Eczema ____ No Yes
Frequent infections or boils ____ No Yes
AIDS ____ No Yes
Any other disease ____ No Yes

ALLERGIES: Are you allergic to

Penicillin or Sulfa ____ No Yes
Aspirin, Codeine or Morphine ____ No Yes
Mycins or other Antibiotics ____ No Yes
Merthiolate or Mercurochrome ____ No Yes
Any other drug ____ No Yes
Any foods ____ No Yes
Adhesive Tape ____ No Yes
Nail polish or other cosmetics ____ No Yes
Tetanus Antitoxin or Serums ____ No Yes

INJURIES: Have you had any

Broken or cracked bones ____ No Yes
Sprains ____ No Yes
Lacerations ____ No Yes
Dislocations ____ No Yes
Concussion, or head injury ____ No Yes
Ever been knocked unconscious ____ No Yes

WEIGHT: Now ____ One Year Ago ____
Maximum ____ When ____

TRANSFUSIONS: Have you ever had

Blood or Plasma Transfusion ____ No Yes

SURGERY: Have you had

Tonsillectomy ____ No Yes
Appendectomy ____ No Yes
Any other operation ____ No Yes
Type ____ Year ____
Type ____ Year ____
Type ____ Year ____

Do you smoke? No Yes
How many per day ____

Have you ever been advised to have any surgical operation which has not been done ____ No Yes

Have you been hospitalized for any illness ____ No Yes

Give details:

FORM 9878 COLWELL SYSTEMS, INC., CHAMPAIGN, IL 61820

continues

Exhibit 11-1 continued

DO YOU NOW HAVE OR HAVE YOU HAD WITHIN THE PAST YEAR:

Frequent or severe headaches	No	Yes
Fainting spells	No	Yes
Dizziness on change of position	No	Yes
Unconscious Spells	No	Yes
Blurred Vision	No	Yes
Double Vision	No	Yes
Spots before eyes	No	Yes
Infected eyes	No	Yes
Pain behind eyes	No	Yes
Any change in vision	No	Yes
Do you wear glasses	No	Yes
When were they last checked ______		
Earaches	No	Yes
Discharge from Ears	No	Yes
Ringing in ears	No	Yes
Decrease in hearing	No	Yes
Recurrent nose bleeds	No	Yes
Recurrent head colds	No	Yes
Sinus Trouble	No	Yes
Hay fever	No	Yes
Strange persistent odors	No	Yes
Strange taste or loss in taste	No	Yes
Persistent hoarseness	No	Yes
Difficulty swallowing	No	Yes
Enlarged glands	No	Yes
Recurrent sore throats	No	Yes
Recurrent sores in mouth	No	Yes
Soreness or bleeding of gums on brushing	No	Yes
Chest pain	No	Yes
Angina pectoris	No	Yes
Coughed up blood	No	Yes
Pain in arm(s)	No	Yes
Night sweats	No	Yes
Chronic or frequent cough	No	Yes
Chronic or frequent cough on laying down	No	Yes
Wake up at night short of breath	No	Yes
How many bed pillows do you use ______	______	

Lose urine on coughing or sneezing	No	Yes
Discharge from penis	No	Yes
Recurrent back pains	No	Yes
Backaches	No	Yes
Joint pains	No	Yes
Swelling of any joints	No	Yes
Redness or heat of any joint	No	Yes
Tingling or weakness of hands or feet	No	Yes
Muscle Spasms	No	Yes
Loss or change in sensation of hands or feet	No	Yes
Trembling of any extremity	No	Yes
Growth in neck or throat	No	Yes
Hot flashes	No	Yes
Tiredness without apparent reason	No	Yes
Brittleness of nails	No	Yes
Dryness of skin	No	Yes
Easy bruising	No	Yes
Inability to stand heat	No	Yes
Inability to stand cold	No	Yes
Change in hair texture	No	Yes
Change in skin texture	No	Yes
Any skin rash	No	Yes
X-RAYS: Have you ever had x-rays of		
Chest	No	Yes
Stomach or colon	No	Yes
Gall bladder	No	Yes
Extremities	No	Yes
Back	No	Yes
Teeth	No	Yes
Other	No	Yes
EKG: Ever had an electrocardiogram?	No	Yes
IMMUNIZATIONS: Have you had		
Smallpox vaccination within last 7 years	No	Yes
Tetanus shots (not antitoxin which lasts only 2 weeks)	No	Yes
Polio shots within last 2 years	No	Yes

DRUGS: Laxatives;	never ☐	occ. ☐	freq. ☐	daily ☐
Vitamins;	never ☐	occ. ☐	freq. ☐	daily ☐
Sedatives;	never ☐	occ. ☐	freq. ☐	daily ☐

Shortness of breath on:
- Walking several blocks ________ No Yes
- One flight of stairs ________ No Yes
- On laying down ________ No Yes

Purple lips or fingers ________ No Yes
Palpitations or fluttering of heart ________ No Yes
High blood pressure ________ No Yes
Swelling of hands, feet or ankles ________ No Yes
    At what time of day ________
Leg cramps on walking or at night ________ No Yes
Enlarged veins in legs ________ No Yes
Recurrent stomach pain ________ No Yes
Belching or heartburn ________ No Yes
    Relieved by food or medication ________ No Yes
Appetite - Good ☐ Fair ☐ Poor ☐
Nausea or vomiting ________ No Yes
Vomited blood ________ No Yes
Avoid some foods ________ No Yes
    What kinds ________
Avoid spices ________ No Yes
Abdominal cramping ________ No Yes
Color of bowel movement ________
Any blood in BM ________ No Yes
Rectal pain with bowel movement ________ No Yes

DO YOU NOW HAVE OR HAVE YOU HAD WITHIN THE PAST YEAR:

Change in size, shape or texture of BM ________ No Yes
    Describe ________
Pain on urinating ________ No Yes
Difficulty in starting urination ________ No Yes
Do you get up at night to urinate ________ No Yes
    How many times ________
Urinate more than before ________ No Yes
Urinate less than before ________ No Yes
Any blood in urine ________ No Yes
How many times per day do you urinate ________
Full feeling of bladder, but only small
    amount of urination ________ No Yes

Source: Courtesy of Colwell Systems, Champaign, IL.

Tranquilizers:	never ☐	occ. ☐	freq. ☐	daily ☐
Sleeping pills, etc.;	never ☐	occ. ☐	freq. ☐	daily ☐
Aspirin, etc;	never ☐	occ. ☐	freq. ☐	daily ☐
Cortisone, ACTH;	never ☐	occ. ☐	freq. ☐	daily ☐
Thyroid;	never ☐	yes, in past, none now ☐		
	daily ☐	now on ____ gr. day		
Appetite depressants	never ☐	occ. ☐	freq. ☐	daily ☐

Have you ever been treated for drug habits ________ No Yes
Have you ever taken insulin or tablets for diabetes ________ No Yes
Have you ever taken hormone tablets or injections ________ No Yes
SEX: Entirely satisfactory? ________ No Yes

WOMEN ONLY - MENSTRUAL HISTORY

Age at onset ________
Regular? ☐ Yes ☐ No ☐ Varies
Cycle ________ days (from start to finish)
Flow: Heavy ☐ Medium ☐ Light ☐
Number of pads used per period ________
Any clots passed ________ No Yes
Pains or cramps ________ No Yes
Date of last period ________
Date of last pelvic exam ________
Date of last Pap Test ________
    Results: ☐ Neg. ☐ Pos.
Any discharge from vagina ________ No Yes
    If so, color ________
        amount ________
Any itching of vaginal area ________ No Yes
Do you take birth control pills ________ No Yes
    How long have you taken them ________
Pregnancies:
    How many children born alive ________
    How many still births ________
    How many premature births ________
    How many Cesarean Sections ________
How many miscarriages ________
Any complications with pregnancy ________ No Yes
    Describe ________
Other ________

Assessment

Once the physician has gathered the subjective and objective data, he or she is then able to provide his or her written assessment. The assessment portion is valuable as a reference point for third-party payers, other health care professionals, and anyone else who may retrieve a medical record to obtain an overview of the patient's progress and/or summary of the patient's significant medical history. The assessment, which is generally written in a problem list format, is performed only after thoroughly reviewing the subjective findings and objective evaluations.

The physician records deficits or abnormal findings of the objective assessment as they correlate with the subjective findings. It is from this point that a problem list can be developed. The problem list includes the actual pathologies involved, any loss of range of motion, strength deficits, abnormal sensory findings, loss of flexibility, and/or other pertinent information of clinical interest. This problem list becomes part of the assessment portion of the notes. It is the actual summary and/or impression of the examination that forms the working diagnosis for each problem. Once a problem list is established, the physician can address the problem areas as to the need for rehabilitation, referral, and/or therapeutic intervention in order to improve the pathological states present.

The physician's working or initial diagnosis is formulated by abstract correlation of his or her knowledge with the database. The information gathered is then entered as separate subheadings within the assessment record (see Figure 11-1). The date of onset of the diagnosed condition and the date that therapy begins, if applicable, is essential to the record. One can highlight items that do not fall within normal limits by listing them within the assessment section of the note. It is important to set priorities as to which of the pathologies detected is the most important. List that pathology as number one; then follow with enumeration of other problematic areas. The

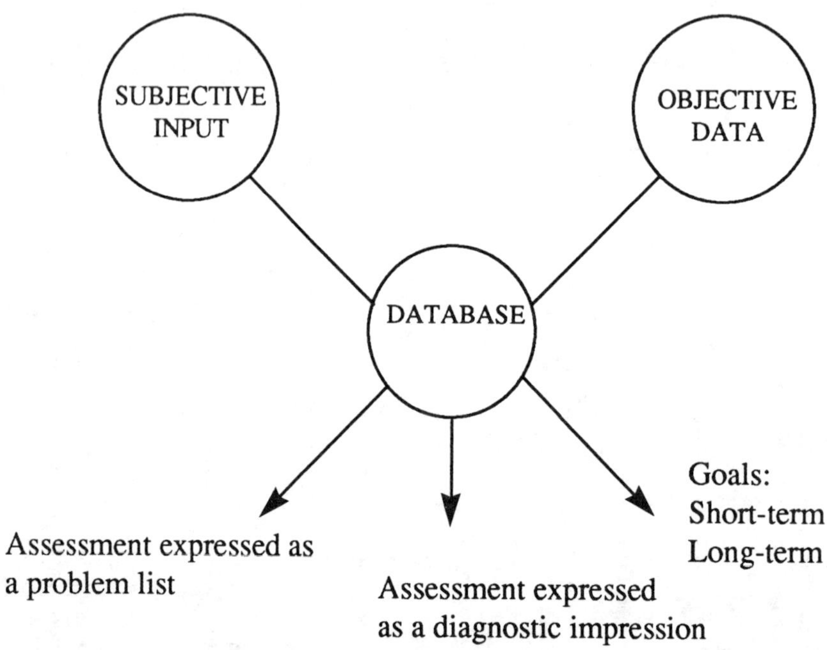

Figure 11-1 Formulating the diagnostic impression.

problem list is recorded in functional terms but should have some specificity regarding anatomical area. For example, the physician should not simply state "ROM is increased, 'feeling better.'" He or she should instead write "lumbar flexion AROM is increased to 90°; patient feeling better, as observed from increased household activity during ADL." The problem list will help the physician set priorities and serve as a basis for goal setting. Goal orientation is important to note within the assessment portion of documentation. Setting goals requires professional expertise. A physician who sets goals provides a system for identifying and solving problems. Table 11-1 demonstrates the relationship between the problem list and goals.

Prioritizing the treatment and continually measuring the effectiveness of therapeutics provides assistance when communicating with third-party payers and other health care professionals as to the response to care. Short- and long-term goals are actually pieces of objective information that can be measured over the treatment process.

When writing short-term goals, the degree of performance must be realistic and measurable or observable. Each goal should name a specific time span in which it will be achieved. It should also be expressed in terms of function, when possible. Subsequent follow-up evaluations will focus primarily on immediate short-term goals based on deficits. Short-term goals are prioritized just as the clinical problems list is. Specific physician goals are set up for those existing clinical problems. Therefore, the assessment contains the analysis of desired plans for the patient (see Table 11-2). When recording assessment data, one can indicate any inconsistency between patient's complaints and the objective findings. Justifications specified for treatment goals can be discussed. Comments regarding the patient's anticipated progress and/or rehabilitation potential must be discussed. The need for further testing or diagnostic intervention should be addressed within the assessment.

Short-term goals are written within the assessment portion. They are based on long-term goals, which are stated as the intended outcome of therapy in the long range. Short-term goals deal with particular pathological functioning that can be improved. They direct the immediate course of the treatment plan. Revision of short-term goals as the patient makes progress is done on a regular basis. Once the physician has determined decisions regarding the treatment of a particular individual, he or she can then formulate impressions as to those pathological states

Table 11-1 The Problem List and Goals

Problem List

1. ↓ cervical AROM
   a. extension 20°
   b. Ⓡ lateral bending 15°
2. severe cervical paraspinal myospasm
3. radicular pain ending AE
4. bicep reflex 1+
5. Ⓡ deltoid muscle 4++/5
6. loss of joint play C5–C6

Short-Term Goals

1. ↑ cervical ROM
2. ↓ pain
3. ↓ spasm
4. ↓ inflammation
5. re-evaluation 5–7 days
6. consider MRI diagnostic imaging
7. consider EMG 10–14 days

Long-Term Goals

1. restore deltoid strength
2. restore bicep reflex
3. vocational posture education
4. evaluate for residual deficits

Diagnostic Impression

1. Ⓡ C5 cervical radiculopathy
2. suspect acute cervical discopathy

Table 11-2 Goal Setting

Dx: cervical hyperflexion-extension strain
S: c/o neck pain 8/10 c̄ movement, stiffness continuous
O: AROM: 0–20° cervical rotation Ⓛ and Ⓡ
0–15° cervical extension
A: short-term goal: ↑ cervical rotation AROM 0–45° bilaterally c̄ in 10 days
↑ cervical extension AROM 0–30° c̄ in 10 days
long-term goal: ↑ neck AROM to WNL and pain free within 2 mo.

that cannot be treated or goals that would be unusual for treatment. After the goals are set, the treatment plan is then outlined and listed as a plan, "P" of the SOAP format.

Plan

The immediate treatment plan is guided by short-term goals and periodically needs to be reassessed in order to realize progress, if evident. When setting up the treatment plan, one must describe the application of various interventions addressing each of the short-term goals. When writing the plan, the physician should use specific time estimates for achieving goals. If a patient's progress is slower than that of another patient with the same diagnosis, this should be explained. Goals should focus on the patient's abilities, stating specific exhibited patient behavior and any special conditions or equipment needed to help with the patient's care, such as orthotics or assistive devices. Goals should be measurable and include time frames. Explaining the impact of deficits, such as strength related to function, can be valuable. Explanations should be clear, concise, and directed toward the problem list. Be sure to continually justify treatment as you near the completion of your goals, to point out progress the patient has made toward the goal, and to identify problems requiring further therapeutic intervention.

A treatment plan is extremely important and should include information such as

- frequency of anticipated visits
- anticipated time frame for specified goal achievement
- treatment progression
- plans for further assessment or reassessment
- planned discharge
- referral for other services
- plans for consultation, if indicated
- types of therapeutic intervention

Recording the treatment modalities requires precision. Which modality, where applied, for how long, at what intensity, and in what position should be included:

P: will be seen 3×/wk. for the following: continuous US to ® shoulder at 1.0 w/cm^2 for 6 min; ® glenohumeral mobilization with stabilization of scapulae; ice cup 10 min. Instruct pt. in home exercise program (attached).

or

P: will be seen twice daily and will be progressed through attached knee exercise program.

Exercise, if prescribed, needs to be specifically described in terms of repetitions, positions, equipment used, application to extremity or trunk, modification, and/or amount of resistance utilized. Home exercise programs should be described in a brief statement that includes goal or rationale, illustrations, position, and directions. Keep the language simple. When discharging the patient, one should note whether or not goals were achieved and any recommendations for follow-up treatment.

PROGRESS NOTES

The progress of a patient undergoing treatment should be followed with notes expressed in the SOAP format. These notes should include mention of continuation of the treatment plan, changes relative to the assessment, the patient's subjective response to treatment (whether unresponsive or responsive), and other factors and/or new developments. Updated objective evaluation data should be provided pursuant to the initial treatment plan at prescribed intervals. The treatment plan may constantly change, depending on the diagnosis, the acuteness of the condition, and/or complicating factors. It is important to have a continual knowledge of the patient's symptoms in order to change the treatment plan or to determine the necessity for a re-evaluation earlier than prescribed in the plan. It is equally important to understand or monitor the responsiveness to therapeutics utilized.

There are individuals who feel that customizing daily records by providing a flow chart or a consistent "canned" statement regarding a particular service is a "cookbook" version of a written record. Customizing can be of benefit, however, by creating less paperwork and reducing secretarial time spent recording daily information. After the initial office visit, each and every office visit thereafter may yield customized progress notes until the next specified updated evaluation. If the initial record keeping clearly states the assessment and plan, certainly it may not always be necessary to re-evaluate your patient on a daily basis or to reiterate the plan of treatment, as long as it is following that which had been prescribed prior. Customization of your records at this point is accepatable.

Such customization of records may take the form of stating that your assessment is "as noted within record" and your plan "as per treatment plan." Any modification of the treatment plan made during subsequent visits should be reflected within the new progress note. Coding your notes according to a glossary developed by you is not an acceptable procedure. Internally, the office or clinic may understand a particular code, but others reviewing your work will not. Nor should they be expected to educate themselves to your methods for recording patient information.

"Canned" verbiage may reflect procedures already in place or common symptom description. This method of recording is employed solely for the sake of brevity, and it takes away from the thoroughness of note taking. Recording the patient's actual subjective symptoms should not be replaced by a cold "canned" response, as this would reflect poorly on the concern you have for your patient. The patient's subjective complaints are definitely a valuable part of daily clinical assessment regarding the need for continual or ongoing care. Subjective symptoms should be expressed in terms having to do with loss of function or with physiological changes, such as pain rating—for example, "Pt. states that she is feeling better, as observed with her increased functional activity around the house, described as light housekeeping 2 hours per day s̄ tiring. Constant LBP ↓ 5/10 from 7/10."

The "S" portion of progress notes does not have to be recorded during every office visit if the symptoms remain unchanged. The physician may not expect subjective symptomatology to readily improve, as reflected by goals previously discussed within the written record. Subjective statements should be related to objective changes in function and meaningful subjective patient expression regarding pain. Complaints should be briefly worded and to the point. They should demonstrate the need for therapy. The patient should rate his or her subjective pain complaints on a pain scale. Functional abilities can be rated by the amount of assistance needed to perform given tasks, at home, on the job, etc. Avoid listing nonspecific complaints within the progress notes. They may be a result of a "normal" patient's depression or discouragement regarding their clinical condition. Putting in statements like "I don't think I'm doing very well" may serve as a red flag to reviewers and may not validate the objective data.

Do list the patient's level of functioning prior to the onset of his or her current diagnosis, and briefly describe the patient's response to care based on the level of function obtained. Certainly, each and every visit may not show significant enough improvement relative to function to require the need for documentation. But during the next scheduled evaluation, subjective functional activity and pain need to be thoroughly addressed.

The subjective information within progress notes should include any exacerbations, indicating their dates of onset, severity, and mechanisms of injury. New injuries and missed appointments (other than vacations, illness, or other) also should be recorded, as well as any additional illness that may prevent the patient from further care. Other treatment the patient may be receiving, the level of the patient's cooperation, and any other contributing factors or information pertinent to the patient's care should be recorded on a daily basis.

All objective observations should be measured; estimates should be avoided. Initially, all clinical findings should be quantified where appropriate and exhibit progress when re-evaluated later. Be sure to make baseline measurements of any activity or deficit. Be careful when reporting mental status; if in doubt, do not guess, and do not emphasize the negative. It is better to refer the patient to an allied health care professional for further assessment. Re-evaluate and remeasure on a regular basis. If one is to send information to a third-party payer, it may be better to write out ratios. For example, express muscle strength as "moderately reduced" rather than as "4+ +/5."

The diagnosis should continually change to reflect the patient's progress or, if such is the case, lack of progress or complications. The level of care rendered should be appropriate for the given diagnosis. Short-term goals, if reached, need to be expressed within the assessment. Furthermore, if new goals are to be met, these goals are to be addressed appropriately.

A discussion of the patient's progress and therapy in the progress note could include further explanation of why there is a failure to progress as quickly as previous goals had predicted. One can indicate whether or not an individual has rehabilitation potential and why. If there is difficulty in obtaining necessary information (e.g., secondary to patient psychological status), this is the place to document it, as well as such things as lack of patient cooperation in positioning for a manual adjustment procedure.

The plan provided for a patient may include numerous notations pertaining to ancillary therapies, types of adjustment or manipulations, the exercise program, orthopaedic supports, reevaluation examinations, work restrictions, referrals, physician opinions, radiographs or other diagnostic tests, and/or nutrition advice. When describing your plan, documenting the frequency of patient care is important. One needs to be specific and to describe the treatment provided. Justify the amount of time spent with the patient by stating the type and amount of treatment the patient receives.

The portion of the progress note covering changes in previously assessed subjective findings should be expressed in the same terms used to quantify the subjective findings in the initial assessment. For example, if pain was rated on a scale, one should utilize this pain scale in determining whether goals are decreasing the patient's pain. The subjective response to treatment can be generally noted—whether pain is experienced following exercise or with movement, or whether there is fatigue.

Compliance with the treatment program needs to be addressed within the interim progress note. So should any additional medical problems. On occasion, the patient may develop illnesses, such as viral infections, which may delay progress in attaining goals.

It is good to note a patient's level of functioning at home within the interim progress note. On occasion, one may find no objective improvement. However, subjectively the patient may reveal great gains relative to functional activity at work or home. When writing the discharge notation, the physician definitely needs to relate any subjective information regarding functional activity gains or remaining deficits.

NARRATIVE REPORT

Each clinical site may offer variations on the form of notes used. The formulation of a narrative report depends on the same information found within SOAP notes. The narrative is important because it compiles all the information obtained into a sequence of events. Whereas the SOAP note is a method of identifying, working through, and solving the patient's problems, the narrative report is a summary of pertinent information obtained.

A narrative report freely expresses information, but in a logical manner. The opening statement of a narrative report should reflect your involvement with the patient, i.e., whether or not you are an independent examining physician or the treating physician, or both. The patient's marital status, age and date of birth, and the location and date of examination need to be indicated within the first paragraph. The rationale for writing the report, such as to determine residual impairment, if applicable, or to respond to a recent request for an update regarding the patient's therapeutic care, should be included within the opening paragraph.

Narrative reporting should address the etiology of specific incidents, injuries, and/or illnesses. When injury is involved, it is critically important to give specific information detailing the mechanics or mechanism of injury. State whether loss of consciousness occurred. Any safety precautions being observed by the patient at the time of an injury should be detailed (e.g., seat belts).

After the physician has explained the historical information leading up to the patient's illness and/or injury, a thorough explanation of the medical or chiropractic care subsequently rendered should be provided. This would be followed, if applicable, by any current therapeutic intervention being provided by your health care facility.

The portion of the report devoted to the psychosocial history is of importance; it should include the patient's marital status, number and age of children in the family, vocational activity (including a description of the current occupational status), and certainly prior educational achievements.

The health history inventory should include the biological family history, a listing of diseases other than the general childhood ones, the patient's habits as related to smoking and alcohol intake, along with current medications utilized. An inventory of exercise activity, hobbies, and/or recreational interests are also discussed.

When discussing the patient's current symptomatology, each problem should be discussed according to its subjective symptoms. The description should cover the character, frequency, duration, and intensity of symptoms. It is important to use a pain scale, to establish a point of reference. The physician should detail what pain control and/or extent of relief is currently provided for.

All medical records within possession that the physician consulted to document the patient's past medical history should be summarized within the narrative report. Any psychological assessment tools, such as pain drawings, disability pain scales, Minnesota Multiphasic Personality Inventory (MMPI), and/or Oswestry scales, can be discussed briefly. The physician should record within the narrative report his or her most current physical/neurological examination. The report can cover the examination in detail or can briefly summarize the positive findings. Other diagnostic tests, if applicable, should detail results. After recording the objective physical examination, the physician should then summarize his or her assessment relating the patient's subjective complaints to the objective findings. The discussion should indicate whether any of the patient's subjective symptomatology is unrelated to the accident or incident. The prognosis or plan for this patient should be briefly discussed, relative to the need for further intervention, if necessary. If maximum medical-chiropractic improvement has been reached, certainly this needs to be expressed within the conclusion of the report. Furthermore, any residual impairment relating to an injury for which treatment was provided needs to be discussed. Impairment rating percentages are not necessarily included in a narrative report unless specifically requested. Usually, such percentages of impairment are provided on a state workers' compensation form, when requested. A separate document recording your impairment rating and how you achieved it, if applicable to state law, is suggested.

CONCLUSION

In conclusion, in order for the physician to establish a standard of care, he or she needs a logical system of recording patient care. Defining clinical problems one by one and organizing them for a solution is of paramount importance. The problem-oriented format provides such a logical system. The narrative report is the document derived from the medical file. The narrative summarizes the clinical information recorded as found within the problem-oriented format. The basic components of a problem-oriented record are as follows:

1. The database, which includes chief complaint, present illness, patient profile, review of systems, physical examination, and laboratory report.
2. A complete, numbered problem list generated from the database. This can be written on a sheet of paper and placed in the front of the chart. A problem is defined as any-

thing that requires management or diagnostic work-up. This list is added to or changed as new problems are identified and active problems are cleared and resolved.

3. The assessment, which is a compilation of subjective information gathered during the history portion of the examination and objective information gathered by the physician. It will initially state the short-term and long-term goals, based on a list of identified problems. The emphasis is on unresponsive problems; problems that have been resolved are written up very briefly. A plan of action is developed based on analysis of the subjective and objective information.
4. The plan, which should include what the patient will be told about the illness, how he or she will be advised, medications to be prescribed, therapeutics to be performed, and/or where and when the patient is to be sent for work-up if comprehensive care is warranted.

The progress notes also reflect the SOAP format for recording the patient's progressive course of therapy. They should contain no irrelevant information. Subjective information need not be recorded on each and every visit, depending on the initial therapeutic care determined as necessary to achieve short-term goals.

The SOAP format provides a comprehensive, well-organized method for recording patient information and serves as a guideline to help the physician to think through problems. This information forms a part of the patient's permanent medical file and should be easy for allied health care providers and third-party payers to interpret. Record keeping is considered legal documentation, as are all parts of the medical file. The patient's care needs initial assessment, reassessment at predetermined intervals, and a final assessment offered upon discharge. Variations of the SOAP format are used by various medical institutions.

Accuracy is extremely important to ensure within the medical record. Incorrect spelling, punctuation, or grammar can lead to misleading information. Information should be concisely expressed; abbreviations can help in achieving brevity. One should avoid vague terminology.

If one handwrites the note, it needs to be legible. Illegible notes defeat the purpose of the recording process. Hyphens should be avoided in notes; they might be confused with minus and plus signs used in recording muscle grades or orthopaedic tests. Errors should not be erased or covered with correction fluid. Rather, if an error is made, it should be crossed out, initialed, and dated. One should definitely sign the notes, whether they are dictated or in written form, after reviewing them for accuracy.

SUGGESTED READING

Bates B, Hoekelman RA. *Examination and History Taking*. Philadelphia, Pa: JB Lippincott Co; 1987.

Griffith J, Ignatavicius D. *The Writer's Handbook: The Complete Guide to Clinical Documentation, Professional Writing and Research Papers*. Baltimore, Md: Resource Applications, Inc; 1986.

Hurst JW. How to implement the Weed system. *Arch Intern Med*. 1971;128:456.

Hurst, JW. The art and science of presenting a patient's problems. *Arch Intern Med*. 1971;128:463.

Hurst JW, Walker HK, eds. *The Problem-Oriented System*. Chicago, Ill.: Medcom Press, 1972.

Kettenbach, G. *Writing S.O.A.P. Notes*. Philadelphia, Pa: FA Davis Co; 1990.

Lewis CB. *Documentation: The Patient's Course on Successful Reimbursement*. Bethesda, Md: Professional Health Educators, Inc; 1987.

Logan C. *Medical and Scientific Abbreviations*. Philadelphia, Pa: JB Lippincott Co; 1987.

Mayo Clinic and Mayo Foundation. *Clinical Examinations in Neurology*. Philadelphia, Pa: WB Saunders Co; 1963.

Walter JB, Pardee GP, Molbo DM, eds. *Dynamics of Problem-Oriented Approaches: Patient Care and Documentation*. Philadelphia, Pa: JB Lippincott Co; 1976.

chapter **12**

Neurological Procedures and Flow

To aid in the practical understanding of chiropractic/neurological examination procedures, this chapter presents outlines for several different ways of organizing the brief neurological examination. The outlines describe what to do, in what order, as well as what to look for, for fundamental examination procedures. A good screening exam should take only about 10 to 15 minutes.

FUNDAMENTAL PROCEDURES

The following outline details fundamental procedures for performing a complete neurological examination. Like the examination itself, the outline is divided into mental status, motor, sensory, reflex, and cerebellar components. Tests relative to each examination area are listed.

I. Mental status examination: Performed during the history

A. Behavior and appearance
   1. Socioeconomic
   2. Body language
   3. Cleanliness

B. Stream of talk
   1. Speed
   2. Inflection
   3. Slurring
   4. Stuttering

C. Mood and affective responses
   1. Emotional lability
   2. Emotional indifference
   3. Anxiety
   4. Anger

D. Content of thought
   1. Illusions
   2. Delusions
   3. Hallucinations
   4. Fear
   5. Anger

E. Intellectual capacity
   1. Great
   2. Within normal limits
   3. Retarded

F. Sensorium
   1. Consciousness
   2. Attention span
   3. Orientation to time, place, and person
   4. Short- and long-term memory
   5. Fund of information
   6. Insight and judgment
   7. Calculation

II. Cranial nerve examination

A. Cranial nerve I
   1. Use nonoffensive odors.
   2. Test each nostril separately.
   3. "Fake out" the patient.

B. Cranial nerves II, III, IV, VI (ocular system)
   1. Observe eyes (What do the eyes look like to you?)
      a. Corneal light reflection
      b. Limbus-to-lid and limbus-to-canthi distances
   2. Cover-uncover test (may be omitted)
      a. Intermittent
      b. Alternating
   3. Central (acuity) (What do the eyes see?)
      a. Snellen chart
      b. Newsprint
      c. Direction of bars in E chart
      d. Number of fingers
      e. Light perception
   4. Peripheral fields by confrontation
      a. Confront patient (approximately 50 cm).
      b. Test all four quadrants of each eye.
      c. Compare patient vision to yours.
      d. Test bilateral stimulus inattention.
   5. Ocular motility
      a. Six cardinal fields of gaze
      b. Diplopia
      c. Nystagmus
      d. Accommodation
         i. Cormiosis
         ii. Convergence
         iii. Lens thickening (near vision)
   6. Pupillary light reflexes (and ciliospinal reflex)
      a. Direct
         i. Subdued light: focus on distant object.
         ii. Pupil size
         iii. Illuminate retina: ipsilateral constriction.
      b. Consensual
         i. Subdued light: focus on distant object.
         ii. Illuminate retina: contralateral constriction.
      c. Ciliospinal (sympathetic)
         i. Subdued light: focus on distant object.
         ii. Pinch over face or neck.
         iii. Observe bilateral pupil dilation.
   7. Ophthalmoscopy
      a. Use good technique.
      b. Red reflex
      c. Fundus
         i. Disc
         ii. Vessels
         iii. General background
         iv. Macula

C. Cranial nerve V
   1. Motor
      a. Inspect temporalis, masseter.
      b. Palpate temporalis, masseter.
      c. Oppose jaw closure.
      d. Note alignment on forced open.
      e. Move and resist lateral jaw motions.
   2. Sensory
      a. Alternatc pin and touch.
      b. Test mandibular, maxillary, and ophthalmic division.
   3. Reflex
      a. Jaw jerk
      b. Corneal (sensory)

D. Cranial nerve VII
   1. Motor
      a. Inspect face during history.
      b. Test strength of
         i. Frontalis
         ii. Orbicularis oculi
         iii. Buccinator
         iv. Platysma
   2. Sensory
      a. Test taste of anterior two-thirds of tongue, to salt, sugar, and quinine.
      b. Test half of tongue; rinse in between.
      c. Test hyperacusis.

3. Reflex
    a. Corneal (motor)

E. Cranial nerve VIII
    1. Sensory (cochlea)
        a. Otoscopy
        b. Watch tick or finger rustle
        c. Rinne, Weber, Schwabach tests
        d. Auditopalpebral reflex
    2. Sensory (vestibular)
        a. Ataxia (vertigo)
        b. Nystagmus (positional)
        c. Caloric irrigation (usually omitted)

F. Cranial nerves IX and X
    1. Motor
        a. Speech
        b. Palatal elevation
    2. Sensory
        a. Test taste on posterior third of tongue.

G. Cranial nerve XI
    1. Motor
        a. Inspect sternocleidomastoid and trap.
        b. Palpate sternocleidomastoid and trap.
        c. Test strength of sternocleidomastoid and trap.

H. Cranial nerve XII
    1. Motor
        a. Inspect tongue and palate (atrophy or fasciculation).
        b. Test tongue motility.
            i. Out (deviation)
            ii. Against cheek (strength)

III. Somatic motor examination

A. Inspection
    1. Somatotype
    2. Cutaneous lesions
    3. Muscles
        a. Atrophy, hypertrophy
        b. Asymmetry
        c. Joint malalignments
        d. Fasciculations, tremors, involuntary movements
    4. Chiropractic spinal analysis
        a. Alignment
        b. Kyphosis, scoliosis
        c. Pelvic height
        d. Plumb line
        e. Range of motion of joints
        f. Others
    5. Gait analysis
        a. Free walking
        b. Toe and heel walk
        c. Tandem
        d. Deep knee bend
        e. Hop on toes

B. Palpation
    1. Hypertonia
        a. Clasp-knife spasticity
        b. Lead pipe rigidity
    2. Hypotonia
        a. Reflex arc
        b. Cerebral or brainstem
        c. Cerebellar
        d. Neural shock (cerebral or spinal)
    3. Atrophy (aplasia, hypoplasia)
        a. Lower motor neuron (denervation)
        b. Myopathic
        c. Disuse
    4. Hypertrophy
        a. Use
        b. Myotonias
        c. Muscular dystrophy ("pseudohypertrophy")
    5. Chiropractic motion exam
    6. Tenderness

C. Muscle strength tests
    1. General rules
        a. Muscle strength approximates doctor's.
        b. Muscles are strongest when shortest.
        c. Antigravity muscles are stronger.
    2. Muscles to test (rostrocaudal, sans cranial nerves)
        a. Neck flexors and extensors
        b. Scapular abductors and adductors
        c. Arm abductors and adductors
        d. Triceps
        e. Biceps
        f. Wrist flexors and extensors
        g. Pronators and supinators

h. Thenar, hypothenar, and interossei muscles
i. Finger flexors, abductors, and extensors
j. Abdominal muscles
k. Spinal muscles
l. Hip flexors and extensors
m. Hip abductors and adductors
n. Medial and lateral rotators
o. Hamstrings
p. Toe extensors
q. Anal sphincter (tone)

D. Muscle percussion
1. Biceps
2. Thenar eminence
3. Tongue
4. Myotonic grip

E. Muscle tone (range of motion)
1. Spasticity
2. Rigidity
3. Clonus (patella, wrist, ankle)

F. Muscle stretch reflexes
1. Technique
a. Crisp blow (double whiplash)
b. Joint in neutral position
2. Test
a. Jaw
b. Biceps
c. Triceps
d. Brachioradialis
e. Medial hamstring
f. Pectorals
g. Finger and toe flexors (Hoffmann's and Trömner's)
h. Quadriceps
i. Achilles
3. Reinforcement
a. Jendrassik
b. Counterpressure
c. Tension on tendon

G. Superficial and pathological reflexes
1. Extensor toe sign
a. Forewarn patient.
b. Hold patient's leg.
c. Length, pressure, and velocity
d. Flexion synergy
2. Abdominal
3. Cremasteric
4. Bulbocavernosus
5. Anal pucker

IV. Sensory examination

A. Superficial sensation
1. Light touch (anterior spinothalamic)
a. Use cotton wisp.
b. "Fake out" patient.
2. Pain (lateral spinothalamic)
a. Alternate between sharp and dull stimuli.
b. Move from area of greater to area of lesser sensation.
c. "Fake out" patient.
3. Temperature (lateral spinothalamic)
a. Use if indicated.
b. Use hot and cold test tubes.
c. Use sensitive indicator.

B. Deep sensation (posterior columns)
1. Vibration
a. Test sensitivity to 128 or 256 Hz.
b. Use bony eminence.
c. "Fake out" patient.
2. Joint sense (statesthesia)
a. Romberg (crude)
i. Narrow base
ii. Note swaying with closed eyes.
b. Position sense
i. Use digits 2, 3, or 4.
ii. Separate toes or fingers.
iii. Patient reports "up or down."
iv. Do several times.
3. Two-point discrimination
4. Others

C. Association cortex (combined)
1. Astereognosis
a. Have patient identify coin, key, button, etc.
2. Topagnosia and autotopagnosia
a. Touch digits 1 to 5.
3. Graphognosia
a. Write numbers or letters on skin.
4. Anosognosia
5. Tactile inattention

V. Cerebellar examination

A. Stance and gait dystaxia
1. Tandem stance
2. Tandem walk

B. Arm dystaxia (dysmetria)
   1. Arms in front
   2. Finger to nose
   3. Inspect for tremor.
   4. Observe overshooting and undershooting.
C. Dysdiadochokinesia
   1. Have patient pronate and supinate hands as fast as possible.
   2. Test separate and together.
   3. Observe overshooting and undershooting.
   4. Thigh slap
   5. Toe tap
D. Leg dystaxia
   1. Heel to shin
E. Hypotonia
   1. "Rag-doll" posture and gait
   2. Passive movements
   3. Pendular reflexes
F. Overshooting and checking tests
   1. Wrist slap
   2. Rebound sign of Holmes
G. Additional features
   1. Decomposition of movement
   2. Weakness, fatigability
   3. Nystagmus

NERVOUS SYSTEM EXAMINATION—CLINICAL COMPONENTS

The following outline discusses general test procedures for neurological examination areas and the effects a lesion would have on the areas being tested.

I. Motor

A. Strength: Doctor must overcome muscle tested.
B. Tone: Test when passive range of motion is checked, and during palpation.
C. Volume: Inspect for bilateral symmetry, mensuration.
D. Implications of findings
   1. Upper motor neuron disease: decreased strength (paresis/paralysis); increased tone (spasticity); mildly decreased or normal volume (spastic atrophy)
   2. Lower motor neuron disease: decreased strength (paresis/paralysis); decreased tone (flaccidity); decreased volume (denervation atrophy)
   3. Extrapyramidal disease: decreased strength (paresis); increased tone (rigidity); normal volume, involuntary movements
   4. Cerebellar disease: decreased strength (paresis); decreased tone (hypotonia); normal volume, lack of coordination

II. Sensory

A. Superficial: Use cotton wisp for light touch. Use pin for pain. Hot and cold test tubes for temperature only if indicated.
B. Deep: Use Romberg for crude test. Use tuning fork for vibration and/or joint sense position, if indicated.
C. Implications of findings
   1. Brain disease: unusual and vague sensory impairment, rarely complete loss (anesthesia), usually associated with agnosia or hyperpathia
   2. Cord disease: loss of involved modalities below level of lesion, depending on which district of cord is involved (anterior and lateral = contralateral; posterior = ipsilateral)
   3. Peripheral disease: loss of all modalities in nerve distribution, though possibly on a different gradient (radicular, peripheral, etc.)

III. Reflex

A. Superficial: Test plantar and abdominal reflexes routinely, others if indicated.
B. Deep: Test biceps, triceps, brachioradialis, patella, and Achilles reflexes routinely.
C. Pathological: If present, Babinski reflex is a variable of plantar reflex.
D. Visceral: Test pupillary reflex and others if indicated.

- E. Implications of findings
    1. Upper motor neuron disease: absent superficial reflexes, increased deep reflexes, pathological reflexes
    2. Lower motor neuron disease: normal superficial reflexes, decreased or absent deep reflexes, no pathological reflexes
    3. Extrapyramidal disease: usually related to abnormal reflexes
    4. Cerebellar disease: hypotonia, causing pendular patella

IV. Cerebellar

- A. Truncal: Test free walk and tandem stance routinely.
- B. Upper: Perform finger-to-nose test if indicated.
- C. Lower: Perform heel-to-shin test if indicated.
- D. Implications of findings: Use tests of coordination to determine site of pathological involvement.

NEUROLOGICAL EXAM FLOW

The following outline suggests a possible sequence of screening examination procedures for a central nervous system evaluation, organized in terms of patient position. It may be useful for the typical chiropractic patient who presents with spinal and/or head pain. A patient who can perform well on all of the tests below is not likely to be suffering from serious neurological disease. Positive findings must be followed up with more testing, including possible referral. Please remember that only part of the neurological portion of a complete chiropractic, neurological, orthopaedic, and physical examination is represented below. Mental status should be assessed in all patients, as well as physical examination of the head, neck, and spine.

I. Standing

- A. Free, heel, and tandem walking
- B. Hop on toes
- C. Shallow knee bend
- D. Romberg
- E. Postural assessment (observe for postural tremor)
- F. Normal thoracic-lumbar ranges of motion

II. Sitting

- A. Upper extremity strength, tone, and volume
- B. Knee flexors
- C. Hip flexors, abductors and adductors, and rotators
- D. Feet and toe flexors and extensors
- E. Muscle strength reflexes
- F. Cranial nerves
- G. Finger to nose and finger
- H. Rapid alternating movements of hands
- I. Heel to shin
- J. Drift
- K. Vertebrobasilar insufficiency test
- L. Intrathecal tests

III. Supine

- A. Sensory tests (pain, vibration, light touch)
- B. Abdominal and plantar reflexes
- C. Anterior flexors strength, tone, and volume
- D. Mensuration
- E. Meninges test for imitation

IV. Prone

- A. Posterior extensors strength, tone, and volume
- B. Hamstring monosynaptic reflexes
- C. Spinal palpation

COMPLETE NEUROLOGICAL EXAM

Exhibit 12-1 is a sample examination form that contains references to tests performed in a comprehensive neurological examination and contains space for charting the examination's findings. Some items, such as Chvostek's sign, are not specific neurological tests and are therefore not included in this chapter's discussion even though they have been included on the form.

Exhibit 12-1 Complete Neurological Exam (Adult)

A. Mental status
- General behavior and appearance ________
- Stream of talk ________
- Mood and affective responses ________
- Content of thought ________
- Intellectual capacity ________
- Sensorium ________

B. Speech
- Dysphonia ________
- Dysarthria ________
- Dysprosody ________
- Dysphasia ________

C. Head and face

Inspect:
- Facial gestalt ________
- Contours ________
- Hair, scalp, eyebrows, beard ________
- Head ________

Palpate:
- Skull ________
- Carotid arteries ________
- Temporal arteries ________

Percuss:
- Sinuses ________
- Mastoid ________

Auscultate:
- Eyes ________
- Temples ________
- Mastoids ________

Transilluminate:
- Sinuses ________

COMMENTS

____

____

____

D. Cranial nerves

I. Olfactory

anosmia ____/____ ______ (odor used)

II. Optic

(ophthalmoscope)	*o'clock*	*disc diameter*
	____/____	____/____
a. disc		
pigment crescent	____/____	____/____
scleral crescent	____/____	____/____
myelinated nerve fibers	____/____	____/____
hemorrhagic or blurred margins	____/____	____/____
pallor	____/____	____/____
hyperemia	____/____	____/____
cup/disc ratio	____/____	____/____
disc at diopters	____/____	____/____
b. vessels		
tortuosity	____/____	____/____
general size	____/____	____/____
occlusion	____/____	____/____
artery/vein ratio	____/____	____/____
constriction or plaques	____/____	____/____
light reflex/blood column	____/____	____/____
arteriovenous crossings	____/____	____/____
venous pulsations at disc	____/____	____/____
c. general background		
general pigmentation	____/____	____/____
local pigment	____/____	____/____
preretinal hemorrhages	____/____	____/____
superficial hemorrhages	____/____	____/____
deep intraretinal hemorrhages	____/____	____/____
exudates	____/____	____/____
cotton-wool	____/____	____/____
microaneurysms	____/____	____/____
edema	____/____	____/____
drusen	____/____	____/____

continues

Exhibit 12-1 continued

d. macula

pigment	____/____	____/____
hemorrhages	____/____	____/____
exudates	____/____	____/____
edema	____/____	____/____

(visual acuity): 20 /____/ 20/____
corrected vision ____________ uncorrected vision ____________
(check one)

(peripheral vision):	Lat (90°)	____/____	Med (60°)	____/____
	Sup (50°)	____/____	Infer (70°)	____/____
(light reflexes)	Direct	____/____	Consensual	____/____
(II and III)	Accommodation	____/____	Pupil Size	____/____

COMMENTS:

____
____
____

III. Oculomotor (globe movements)

nystagmus	____/____ (position) ____/____
convergence	____/____
width of palpebral fissures	____/____
cover-uncover test	____/____
limbus-to-lid margins	____/____/____/____
interorbital distance	____________
enophthalmos	______/______
exophthalmos	______/______

COMMENTS

____
____
____

IV. Trochlear: See III

V. Trigeminal:

Corneal reflex V and VII ____/____

	ophthalmic	*maxillary*	*mandibular*
pain	____/____	____/____	____/____
light touch	____/____	____/____	____/____
heat	____/____	____/____	____/____
cold	____/____	____/____	____/____
anesthesia	____/____	____/____	____/____
hypesthesia	____/____	____/____	____/____
jaw jerk	____/____	____/____	____/____
lat. pterygoid	____/____	____/____	____/____
masseter	____/____	____/____	____/____
temporalis	____/____	____/____	____/____
medial pterygoid	____/____	____/____	____/____

VI. Abducens: See III

VII. Facial

taste (anterior 2/3 tongue)		*substance used*
sweet	____/____	____________
salty	____/____	____________
sour	____/____	____________
bitter	____/____	____________
orbicularis oculi	____/____	
wrinkle forehead	____/____	
smile, pout, frown	____/____	
show teeth	____/____	
puff cheeks	____/____	
Chvostek's sign	____/____	

COMMENTS

____
____
____

Exhibit 12-1 continued

VIII. Vestibulocochlear
- whisper test ____/____
- watch tick ____/____
- finger rustle ____/____
- Weber ____/____ ________ (equal)
- Rinne ____/____
- Schwabach ____/____
- simultaneous stimuli ____/____

otoscopy
- external ear canal ____/____
- tympanic membrane ____/____

vestibular
- nystagmus (see III) ____/____
- caloric irrigation ____/____

COMMENTS

____

____

____

IX. Glossopharyngeal

taste (posterior 1/3 tongue) — *substance used*
- sweet ____/____ ____________
- salty ____/____ ____________
- sour ____/____ ____________
- bitter ____/____ ____________

IX and X
- gag reflex ________
- phonation ____/____
- palatal reflex ____/____
- hoarseness ________
- dysphagia ________
- oculocardiac reflex ________
- carotid sinus ________
- laryngoscopy ________

COMMENTS ____

____

____

X. Vagus: See IX

COMMENTS ____

____

____

XI. Spinal accessory
- trapezius ____/____
- sternocleidomastoid ____/____

COMMENTS ____

____

____

XII. Hypoglossal
- atrophy ____/____
- fasciculations ____/____
- deviations ____/____
- lingual articulations ____/____
- strength ____/____

COMMENTS

____

____

____

E. Reflexes

superficial (mucous membrane) reflexes:
- palmar ____/____
- corneal: see V and VII
- nasal ____/____
- gag: see IX and X
- palatal: see IX and X
- interscapular ____/____
- upper abdominal ________
- lower abdominal ________
- cremasteric ____/____
- gluteal ____/____
- plantar ____/____
- anal ____/____

continues

Exhibit 12-1 continued

COMMENTS

____

____

____

muscle stretch reflexes of the upper extremities:
- jaw: see V
- biceps (muscl. cut, C-5, C-6) ____/____
- triceps (radial, C-6, C-7, C-8) ____/____
- brachioradialis (radial, C-5, C-6) ____/____
- finger flexors (median, ulnar, C-6 to T-1) ____/____
- scapulohumeral (dorsal scapular, C-4, C-5) ____/____
- deltoid (axillary, C-5, C-6) ____/____
- pectoralis (ant. thor. C-5 to T-1) ____/____
- latissimus dorsi (thoracodorsal C-6, C-7, C-8) ____/____
- clavicle (not specific) ____/____
- pronator (median, C-6, C-7, C-8, T-1) ____/____
- wrist extension (radial, C-6, C-7, C-8) ____/____
- thumb (median, C-6 to T-1) ____/____

muscle stretch reflexes of the trunk:
- costal periosteal (intercostal T-5 to T-9) ____/____
- deep abdominal (intercostal T-5 to T-12) ____/____
- iliac (intercostal T-10 to T-12) ____/____
- symphysis pubis (varies, T-8 to L-2) ____/____
- back reflexes (thoracic, lumbar, sacral) ____/____

muscles stretch reflexes of the lower extremities:
- patellar (femoral L-2, L-3, L-4) ____/____
- Achilles (tibial L-5 to S-2) ____/____
- adductor (obturator L-2, L-3, L-4) ____/____
- internal hamstring (tibial L-4 to S-2) ____/____
- external hamstring (common peroneal L-5 to S-3) ____/____
- tensor fasciae latae (sup. gluteal, L-4 to S-1) ____/____
- gluteus (inter. gluteal, L-5 to S-2) ____/____
- extensor hallucis longus (deep peroneal L-4 to S-1) ____/____
- tibialis posterior (tibial L-5 to S-1) ____/____
- peroneal (peroneal, L-4 to S-1) ____/____
- plantar muscle (tibial L-5 to S-1) ____/____

visceral reflexes:
- direct, consensual, accommodation: see cranial nerves II and III
- ciliospinal ____/____
- blink ____/____
- oculocardiac ____/____
- carotid sinus: see cranial nerves IX and X
- bulbocavernosus ________
- bladder and rectal ________
- mass reflex ____/____

COMMENTS

____

____

____

pathological reflexes of the lower extremities:
- extensor toe sign ____/____
- ankle clonus ____/____
- patellar clonus ____/____
- Neri's sign ____/____

Exhibit 12-1 continued

pathological reflexes of the upper extremities:
- Hoffmann's sign ____/____
- Klippel-Feil ____/____
- Trömner's sign ____/____
- Chaddock's sign (wrist) ____/____
- Bechterew's sign ____/____

pathological reflexes of the head:
- Babinski's platysma sign ____/____
- snout reflex ________
- head retraction ________

COMMENTS

____
____
____

F. Somatic nervous system

inspect: describe:
- tremors ________/________
- involuntary movements ________/________
- body gestalt ________/________
- cutaneous lesions ________/________
- muscular atrophy (mensurate) ________/________
- muscular hypertrophy ________/________
- asymmetry ________/________
- joint misalignments ________/________
- fasciculations ________/________
- gait ________/________
- toe walk (hop) ________/________
- heel walk ________/________
- tandem walk ________/________
- deep knee bend ________/________

palpation and joint ROMs:
- muscular hypotonia ________/________
- tenderness ________/________
- spasticity ________/________
- rigidity ________/________

strength of:
- serratus anterior ________/________
- cervical flexors ________/________
- cervical extensors ________/________
- sternocleidomastoid ________/________
- deltoid ________/________
- biceps ________/________
- wrist extensors ________/________
- triceps ________/________
- finger flexors (grip) ________/________
- supraspinatus ________/________
- abdominal ________/________
- lumbar extensors ________/________
- gluteus maximus ________/________
- hamstrings ________/________
- hip abductors ________/________
- hip adductors ________/________
- iliopsoas ________/________
- quadriceps ________/________
- tibialis anterior ________/________
- hallux extensor ________/________
- gastrocnemius ________/________

percussion and meningeal:
- thenar eminence ________/________
- myotonic grip ________/________
- Brudzinski ________________
- Kernig ________________

COMMENTS

____
____
____

G. Cerebellum
- rag doll posture and gait ________________
- broad-based gait ________________
- tandem stance ________________

continues

Exhibit 12-1 continued

tandem gait ____________
finger-to-nose ______/______
dysmetria ______/______
pronation-supination ______/______
thigh slapping ______/______
heel-to-shin ______/______
pendular reflexes ______/______
hypotonia (ROM) (see somatic nervous system) ______/______
wrist slap ______/______
arm pull (rebound) ______/______
nystagmus (see cranial nerve VIII) ______/______
decomposition of movement ______/______
general paresis ____________

H. Somatic sensory system

	hands	*trunk*	*feet*
light touch	___/___	___/___	___/___
pain	___/___	___/___	___/___
temperature	___/___	___/___	___/___
vibration	___/___	___/___	___/___
position	___/___	___/___	___/___
Romberg	____________		
stereognosis	____________		

COMMENTS

____
____
____

I. Cerebral functions

agraphognosia ____________
finger agnosia ______/______
two point—hands ______/______
trunk ______/______
feet ______/______

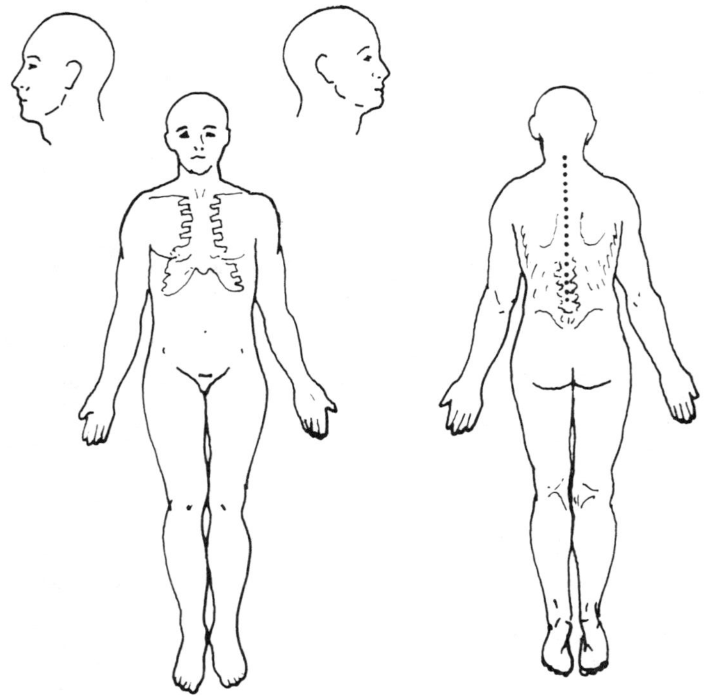

right-left disorientation ____________
atopagnosia ____________
inattention—tactile ____________
auditory ____________
visual ____________

appendix **A**

Common Abbreviations for the Medical Record

The list of acceptable abbreviations varies from one facility to the next, particularly regarding terminology specific to allied health care fields such as physical and occupational therapy. The following is a compilation of the most common abbreviations.

A:	assessment
aa:	equal amounts of each
AAROM:	active assisted range of motion
AB:	abortion
ABG:	arterial blood gas
ABR:	absolute bed rest
ac:	before meals
AC joints:	acromioclavicular joints
ACTH:	adrenocorticotrophic hormone
AD:	right ear
ADH:	antidiuretic hormone
ADL:	activities of daily living
ad lib:	as desired
ad noct:	at night
AE:	above elbow
aec:	at earliest convenience
AFB:	acid-fast bacillus
AFO:	ankle-foot orthosis
AIDS:	acquired immunodeficiency syndrome
AIIS:	anterior inferior iliac spine
AK:	above knee
AM:	before noon
AMA:	against medical advice
amb:	ambulate
amp:	ampule
A & P:	anterior and posterior
A/R:	apical/radial
AROM:	active range of motion
AS:	left ear
ASA:	acetylsalicylic acid (aspirin)
ASAP:	as soon as possible
ASHD:	arteriosclerotic heart disease
ASIS:	anterior superior iliac spine
ASO:	automatic stop order
AU:	both ears
A-V:	arteriovenous
Ba:	barium
BAER:	brain auditory evoked response
BE:	barium enema; below elbow
bid:	twice a day
BK:	below knee
BM:	bowel movement
BP:	blood pressure
BPH:	benign prostatic hypertrophy
bpm:	beats per minute
BRP:	bathroom privileges
BSO:	bilateral salpingo-oophorectomy
BUN:	blood urea nitrogen
Burd:	Burdick suction
C:	centigrade
Ca^{++}:	calcium
CA:	cancer
CAD:	coronary artery disease

Caps: capsule
CAT: computerized axial tomography
CBC: complete blood count
CBD: common bile duct
cc: cubic centimeter
CC: chief complaint
CHF: congestive heart failure
cm: centimeter
CMG: cystometrogram
c/o: complains of
COLD: chronic obstructive lung disease
Comp: compound
CO_2: carbon dioxide
CNA: certified nurse administrator
CNS: central nervous system
cont.: continue
C-1–C-7: cervical vertebrae, by number
COPD: chronic obstructive pulmonary disease
CP: cerebral palsy
CPK: creatinine phosphokinase
CPR: cardiopulmonary resuscitation
CRNA: certified registered nurse anesthetist
C & S: culture and sensitivity
CSF: cerebrospinal fluid
cu: cubic
CVA: cerebrovascular accident
CWI: crutch walking instructions
Cx: cervix
Cysto: cystoscopy
DAT: diet as tolerated (or dietary assessment)
DC: discontinue; doctor of chiropractic
D & C: dilatation and curettage
DDS: doctor of dental surgery
D_5W: 5% dextrose in water
Diff: differential
dil: dilute
DIP: distal interphalangeal joint
DM: diabetes mellitus
DNS: deviated nasal septum
DO: doctor of osteopathy
DOA: dead on arrival
DOE: dyspnea on exertion
DP: dorsalis pedis
DPM: doctor of podiatric medicine
dr: dram
DSD: dry, sterile dressing
DTR: deep tendon reflex
DTs: delirium tremens
DUB: dysfunctional uterine bleeding
D/W: dextrose in water
Dx: diagnosis
ECF: extended care facility
ECG, EKG: electrocardiogram
EEG: electroencephalogram
EENT: eyes, ears, nose, and throat
E & G: esophagogastroscopy
EG & D: esophagogastroduodenoscopy
EMG: electromyogram
EOM: extraocular movements
ER: emergency room
ESR: erythrocyte sedimentation rate
et: and
EU: etiology unknown
Ext: extract
f: female; fair (e.g., fair muscle strength)
F: Fahrenheit
FBS: fasting blood sugar
FF: force fluids
FH: family history
Fl: fluid
FUO: fever of unknown origin
Fx: fracture
g, gm: gram
G: good (muscle strength, balance)
G: gravida
GB: gallbladder
GI: gastrointestinal
gr: grain
gtt: drop
GTT: glucose tolerance test
GU: genitourinary
G/W: glucose in water
Gyn: gynecology
h, hr: hour
H: hypodermic
Ha, H/A: headache
HAV: hallux abductor valgus
HCD: herniated cervical disc
Hct: hematocrit
HEENT: head, eyes, ears, nose, and throat
Hgb, Hb: hemoglobin
H/H: hematocrit and hemoglobin
HLD: herniated lumbar disc
HNP: herniated nucleus pulposus
H & P: history and physical

HR: heart rate
hs: bedtime, hour of sleep
ht: height
Ht: hematocrit
Htn: hypertension
H_2O: water
Hx: history
ICU: intensive care unit
I & D: incision and drainage
IM: intramuscular
imp.: impression
in.: inches
I & O: intake and output
^{131}I: radioactive isotope of iodine
IPK: intractable plantar keratosis
IPPB: intermittent positive pressure breathing
IQ: intelligence quotient
IUD: intrauterine device
IV: intravenous
IV DA: IV drug abuser
IVP: intravenous pyelogram
IVU: intravenous urogram
kcal: kilocalories
Kg: kilogram
KJ: knee jerk
K_{10}: type of gastric tube
KUB: kidney, ureter, bladder
L: liter
LAH: left anterior hemiblock
lb: pound
LBBB: left bundle branch block
LBP: low back pain
LDH: lactic dehydrogenase
LE: lupus erythematosus; lower extremity
LH: luteinizing hormone
liq: liquid
LKS: liver, kidney, spleen
LLL: left lower lobe
LLQ: left lower quadrant
LMP: last menstrual period
LOA: leave of absence
LOC: level of consciousness
L-1–L-5: lumbar vertebrae, by number
LP: lumbar puncture
LPN: licensed practical nurse
LS: lumbosacral spine
LSP: lumbosacral spine and pelvis
LUL: left upper lobe
LUQ: left upper quadrant
LVH: left ventricular hypertrophy
m: meter
MD: doctor of medicine; muscular dystrophy
meds: medications
MFT: muscle function test
mg: milligram
MI: myocardial infarction
MIC: minimum inhibitory concentration
min: minutes
ml: milliliter
mm: millimeter
mo: month
MO: mineral oil
MOM: milk of magnesia
MP, MCP: metacarpophalangeal
MPJ: metatarsophalangeal joint
MS: multiple sclerosis
N: normal (e.g., normal muscle strength)
NaCl: sodium chloride
NAS: no added salt
NB: newborn
neg: negative
NKA: no known allergies
noc: night
NPO: nothing by mouth
NS: normal saline
NSR: normal sinus rhythm
NWB: non–weight bearing
O: oral; objective
OB: obstetrics
OBS: organic brain syndrome
OD: right eye
oint: ointment
OP: outpatient
OPD: outpatient department
OR: operating room
os: mouth
OS: left eye
O_2: oxygen
OU: both eyes
oz: ounce
P: phosphorus; poor (e.g., poor muscle strength); plan
PA: physician's assistant; posterior and anterior

P & A: percussion and auscultation
PAC: premature atrial contractions
PAT: paroxysmal atrial tachycardia
pc: after meals
PCN: penicillin
PE: physical examination
per os: by mouth
PERL: pupils equal, reactive to light
PERRLA: pupils equal, round, reactive to light, and accommodating
PFT: pulmonary function test
pH: hydrogen ion concentration
PH: past history
PID: pelvic inflammatory disease
PNF: proprioceptive neuromuscular facilitation
PNI: peripheral nerve injury
po: by mouth
pos: positive
poss: possible
postop: postoperative
PO_2: arterial oxygen content
PRE: progressive resistive exercise
PREG: pregnant
preop: before surgery (operation)
PRN: as necessary
PROM: passive range of motion
PSIS: posterior superior iliac spine
pt: posterior tibial; patient
PT: physical therapy; prothrombin time
PTA: prior to admission
PTT: partial thromboplastin time
PUD: peptic ulcer disease
PVC: premature ventricular contraction
PVD: peripheral vascular disease
PWB: partial weight bearing
q: every
q am: every morning
qd: every day
qh: every hour
qid: four times a day
qn: every night
QNS: quantity not sufficient
qod: every other day
qoh: every other hour
QS: quantity sufficient
qt: quart
q 2–12 h: every 2–12 hours
R: rectally
RA: rheumatoid arthritis
RBBB: right bundle branch block
RBC: red blood cell
RD: registered dietician
re: regarding
resp: respiratory, respiration
Rh: rhesus factor
RLL: right lower lobe
RLQ: right lower quadrant
RN: registered nurse
RNA: ribonucleic acid
R/O: rule out
ROM: range of motion
ROS: review of systems
R Ph: registered pharmacist
RPR: rapid plasma reagent
RROM: resistive range of motion
RUL: right upper lobe
RUQ: right upper quadrant
Rx: prescription
SCB: strictly confined to bed
SC joint: sternoclavicular joint
SCU: special care unit
sec: seconds
SGOT: serum glutamic-oxaloacetic transaminase
SGPT: serum glutamate pyruvate transaminase
SI: sacroiliac
sig: directions for use, give as follows, let it be labeled
SIJ: sacroiliac joint
SLE: systemic lupus erythematosus
SLR: straight leg raise
SOAP: subjective, objective, assessment, plan
SOB: shortness of breath
S-1–S-5: sacral vertebrae, by number
SOS: once if necessary
spec: specimen
sp. gr.: specific gravity
SSE: soap suds enema
stat: at once
STS: serological test for syphilis
subq: subcutaneous
Sx: symptoms
T: trace (e.g., trace muscle strength)
tab: tablet
TB: tuberculosis
tbsp: tablespoon

T & C,
  T & Rh: type and crossmatch
TENS, TNS: transcutaneous electrical nerve stimulator
THR: total hip replacement
TIA: transient ischemic attack
tid: three times a day
TKR: total knee replacement
TMJ: temporomandibular joint
t.o.: telephone order
T-1–T-12: thoracic vertebrae, by number
TPR: temperature, pulse, respiration
TSH: thyroid-stimulating hormone
tsp: teaspoon
tr: traction
TUR: transurethral resection
Tx: treatment
u: units
UA: urinalysis
UE: upper extremity
UGI: upper gastrointestinal
UMN: upper motor neuron
ung: ointment
UO: undetermined origin
up ad lib: ambulation as desired
URI: upper respiratory infection
US: ultrasound
USP: United States Pharmacopeia
UTI: urinary tract infection
UV: ultraviolet
VD: venereal disease
VDRL: venereal disease research laboratory
vol: volume
VS: vital signs
VTP 1: voluntary termination of pregnancy, first trimester
Wang: Wangensteen suction
WBC: white blood count
wc: wheelchair
WDWN: well developed, well nourished
wk: week
WNL: within normal limits
WR: Wassermann reaction
wt: weight
x: number of times performed
yd: yard
y/o: years old
yr: year

ā: before
c̄: with
p̄: after
s̄: without
Ⓛ: left
Ⓡ: right
♂ male
♀ female
↓ down
↑ up
~ approximately
@ at (this symbol is not exclusively used for at)
Δ change
> greater than
< less than
= equals
\+ plus, positive (positive also abbreviated pos.)
− minus, negative (negative also abbreviated neg.)
\# number, pounds
/ per
% percent
+, & and
↔ ⇄ to and from
← from
→ to, progressing forward, approaching
1° primary
2° secondary, secondary to

appendix **B**

A Compendium of Common Neurological Terms

Steven A. Mickelson

A compendium of neurological terms is a helpful addition to one's library. Many times the practicing doctor or student is faced with having to interpret a report from a medical or chiropractic specialist, e.g., a chiropractic neurologist. Anyone who has spent additional hours studying a specialty of necessity learns a phlethora of terms and descriptions to communicate his or her ideas to the referring physician. Unfortunately, it is this very wealth of knowledge that causes a failure of communication, simply because the terminology goes beyond the accepted norm for the profession. The following glossary is a compilation of some of the terms seen in 3 years of study in the very new specialty of chiropractic neurology.

The definitions, in most cases, are by no means complete explanations of the terms or phrases but rather are abbreviated versions, designed to at least get the reader on the right track as far as the term or idea is concerned. There are hundreds more signs, tests, syndromes, phenomena, etc., that could have been included, but the line had to be drawn somewhere.

abducens: Cranial nerve (VI); supplies the external rectus muscle of the eye.

acalculia: Inability to calculate.

acromegaly: Gradual enlargement of hands, feet, skull, and lower jaw, caused by a hyperfunctioning pituitary gland.

acroparesthesia: Commonly thought of as a mild type of Raynaud's disease, this condition begins with numbness, tingling, pain, and coldness of the upper extremities. Most common in middle-aged women.

action potential: The basic action unit of nerve transmission, which occurs when sodium ions move through the nerve membrane into the cell.

acute retrobulbar neuritis: A condition of inflammation of the optic nerve in which the patient experiences vision loss, but the doctor sees no abnormalities on the retina.

Addison's disease: Chronic insufficiency of the adrenal cortex, leading to weakness and a bronzed skin color due to hyperpigmentation.

adhesive arachnoiditis syndrome: Severe headaches, lower back pain, or burning pain in the lower extremities is associated with this syndrome, which can be caused by the oil-based dyes used in myelograms, which may interfere with the arachnoid mater.

adiadochokinesia: See dysdiadochokinesia.

Adie's pupil: A benign condition of the pupil in which the response to light is either very slow or absent.

adiposogenital dystrophy: See Fröhlich's syndrome.

agnosia: Refers to a failure to recognize familiar objects perceived by the primary senses.

agraphia: Inability to write.

akathisia: Motor unrest characterized by continual shifting of posture and movement, as in paralysis agitans; seen with long-term psychotropic drug use.

alacrity: A cheerful promptness noted in mental status examination.

albinism: Congenital absence of tyrosinase in the melanocytes, causing characteristic white skin and hair and red pupils and irises.

alexia: Inability to read.

Alzheimer's disease: A disease of undetermined etiology, causing diminished cognitive function.

amaurosis fugax: Transient monocular blindness caused by occlusion of the ophthalmic branch of the carotid artery. This is one form of transient ischemic attack.

amyotrophic lateral sclerosis: Also known as Lou Gehrig's disease; a progressive disease of the motor neurons with no sensory deficits. There is a mixture of upper and lower motor neuron paralysis and often an asymmetrical wasting of hands or arms. Fasciculations are commonly seen.

anisocoria: Pupils of unequal size.

anomia: Inability to name common objects, despite ability to describe them.

anterior lobe: The cerebellar lobe mediating the coordination of the trunk and lower limbs (antigravity muscles). Its involvement in the rostral vermis syndrome produces "drop attacks."

anterior median fissure: The name for the large fissure on the anterior surface of the spinal cord.

Anton's syndrome: Denial of and unawareness of blindness. Usually the patient has had an infarction of both occipital lobes following basilar artery occlusion or stenosis, leading to a double hemianopia and cortical blindness. The patient may be unaware of this blindness and may vigorously deny having it (Anton's syndrome).

aphasia: A form of language apraxia characterized by loss of motor or expressive skills, due to cerebral defect.

apraxia: Inability to carry out, on request, a complex or skilled movement, attributable to sensory changes or to deficiencies of understanding.

aqueduct of Sylvius: The communicating duct between the third and fourth ventricles of the brain.

arachnoid mater: The delicate, avascular, weblike membrane, which together with the dura mater and pia mater forms the lining for the brain and spinal cord.

arachnoid villi: Located in the dural venous sinuses, these small vascular protrusions are the main site of absorption of the cerebrospinal fluid.

archicerebellum: See posterior lobe.

Argyll-Robertson pupil: A miotic pupil that does not react to light; seen in tabes dorsalis.

Arnold-Chiari malformation: A birth defect in which part of the medulla and cerebellum extend into the cervical spinal canal.

astereognosis: Inability to recognize objects from touch alone.

astrocytoma: A noninvasive tumor involving the glial tissue of the central nervous system. It is the most common of the gliomas. Peak incidence is in 30- to 40-year-old adults and in children.

ataxia: An unsteady gait, with wide stance and difficulty balancing.

athetosis: Slow, writhing movements of the fingers and extremities.

auditory nerve: See vestibulocochlear nerve.

autonomic nervous system: A functional division of the nervous system innervating the involuntary muscles and glands of the body.

autoradiography: Radiography using radioactive amino acid solutions to trace neuronal pathways in test animals.

Avellis's syndrome: A brainstem syndrome of cranial nerves X and XI causing ipsilateral paralysis of soft palate, larynx, and pharynx and contralateral loss of pain and temperature sense.

Babinski's sign: A highly significant upper motor neuron lesion indicator; the most reliable finding is dorsiflexion of the great toe when the bottom of the foot is stroked laterally from heel to ball.

Bainbridge reflex: Reflex regulation of cardiac output by receptors in the right atrium that monitor central venous pressure.

ballism: A violent flinging motion of the body (see hemiballismus).

baroreceptors: Sensors in the carotid sinuses and aortic arch that are stimulated by changes in arterial blood pressure.

Battle's sign: A sign of head trauma and possible basilar skull fracture that includes ecchymosis over the mastoid or bleeding from the ears.

Beevor's sign: Deviation of the umbilicus toward the side of the abdomen with weakened muscles, upon sitting up. Also known as the umbilical migration test.

Bell's palsy: Paralysis of cranial nerve VII, causing a characteristic hemiparalysis of the face. This cranial neuropathy is commonly seen in the second stage of AIDS.

Bell's phenomenon: Upon trying to close the eyes, the eyeball on the affected side can be seen turning upward.

Bender Gestalt test: A test of visual-motor function.

Benedikt's syndrome: Paralysis of the nerve and tremor of the opposite arm, resulting from an intrinsic lesion of the midbrain that may involve the red nucleus and cranial nerve III fibers.

Bernard-Horner syndrome: See Horner's syndrome.

biceps reflex: The biceps reflex is predominantly an indicator of C-5 neurological integrity, although it also has a smaller C-6 component. The reflex is elicited by the examiner tapping on the biceps tendon on relaxed flexed arm.

Bikeles' sign: Resistance to extension of the forearm caused by traction on the brachial plexus.

blepharospasm: Eyelid spasms usually associated with hysteria.

blind spot: A normal physiological blind spot located on the retina where the optic nerve enters the fundus.

blinking reflex: Closure of the eyelids in response to bright indirect light, seen in infants up to 1 year old. Also known as the dazzle reflex. Absence may indicate blindness.

blood-brain barrier: The physiological barrier between the blood and the central nervous system, thought to be responsible for the immunoprivilege of the brain.

Bonnier's syndrome: Resembles Meniere's disease with the additional symptoms of contralateral hemiplegia, somnolence, tachycardia, weakness, and anxiety. Associated with a lesion in Dieter's (lateral vestibular) nuclei affecting cranial nerves VIII, IX, and X.

brachioradialis reflex: Tapping the brachioradialis tendon at the distal end of the radius causes the hand to jerk. Tests the radial nerve at C-6.

bradykinesia: Abnormal slowness in movement.

breath holding attacks: Seen most often in children, generally with an underlying psychological problem.

Broca's aphasia: Inability to speak despite knowing what to say. In a variety of Broca's aphasia, motor expressive–nonfluent aphasia, the patient understands written or verbal requests but can't repeat words or phrases.

Broca's area: The speech area, usually found in the left frontal lobe of the brain.

Brown-Séquard syndrome: An acute spinal cord lesion involving damage of the lateral half of the cord, resulting in an ipsilateral loss of position sense and contralateral loss of pain and temperature sense.

Brudzinski's sign: Flexion of the neck in the supine position causes corresponding flexion of knees. May be seen in meningitis.

bulbar palsy: Dysfunction of cranial nerves IX to XII. Often seen in the later stages of amyotrophic lateral sclerosis.

bulbocavernosus reflex: Squeezing the glans penis causes contraction of the anal sphincter and perianal muscles. If present, may indicate that reflex innervation of the bladder and bowel is intact.

caloric test: Tests each ear canal separately for inner ear disease. Cold water normally causes contralateral nystagmus, while warm water normally causes ipsilateral nystagmus.

Cannon's law: After lower motor neuron denervation, muscle percussion irritability is greatly increased. (Hyperexcitability.)

canthus dystopia: Excessive eyelid tissue, especially over the medial canthi.

carpal tunnel syndrome: Entrapment of the median nerve as it passes through the carpal tunnel (which is formed anteriorly by the transverse carpal ligament and posteriorly by the carpal bones). It manifests as tingling pain in the wrist and fingers, especially the thumb and first two fingers.

cataplexy: Sudden temporary loss of muscle tone.

cauda equina: Literally, horse's tail; the name given to the lumbosacral and coccygeal nerve roots, which occupy the subarachnoid space below where the spinal cord ends at about the first lumbar level of the bony spine.

causalgia: A painful disorder of an extremity, usually associated with median, sciatic, or tibial nerve injury and accompanied by trophic changes in the affected skin and nails.

Charcot's joints: Joints that are severely degenerated due to a lack of pain sense, as seen in tabes dorsalis.

choroid plexus: Intracranial area in which cerebrospinal fluid is produced.

ciliospinal reflex: Brisk bilateral pupil dilation seen within 5 seconds of firmly pinching the skin on the neck. Tests for integrity of the sympathetic nerve supply to the head.

circle of Willis: Blood circulatory system at the base of the brain.

clonus: A repeating muscular contraction in the ankle, wrist, or knee, seen in upper motor neuron lesions. A very brief exhaustive clonus may be normal.

clouding: A mild decrease in consciousness.

cluster headache: An excruciatingly severe headache, generally involving pain behind or in one eye, that "clusters" around certain days on the calendar and then does not occur again for months or years.

cochleovestibular nerve: See vestibulocochlear nerve.

cogwheel rigidity: Ratchet-like rigidity seen in extrapyramidal diseases such as Parkinson's disease.

coma: A complete loss of consciousness.

concomitant heterotopia: The eyes do not "line up" but move together in all fields of gaze.

confrontation: A test for visual fields made by comparing the doctor's visual field to the patient's as the doctor faces (confronts) the patient.

consensual light reflex: The contralateral eye constricts equally after shining a light in one eye.

contralateral: Opposite side.

conus medullaris: The cone-shaped end of the spinal cord before it gives rise to the filum terminale.

cordotomy: Severance of pain tracts in the cord, for the treatment of intractable pain.

corectasis: An enlarged pupil.

corectopia: An eccentric pupil.

cormiosis: An abnormally small pupil, sometimes referred to as miosis.

corneal reflex: Touching the cornea begins a sensory arc (cranial nerve V) that causes blinking via a motor arc (cranial nerve VII).

cough syncope: Loss of consciousness during or after a coughing spell.

cremasteric reflex: Elevation of the ipsilateral testicle upon stroking of the inner thigh.

delirium: A moderate decrease in consciousness.

delirium tremens: Delirium associated with alcohol withdrawal. Symptoms include insomnia, tremulousness, agitation, anxiety, hallucinations, and convulsions.

diaschisis of Monakow: Spinal (neural) shock.

dizziness: The sensation of spinning, which is correctly termed vertigo. The word is commonly used to indicate many different symptoms, such as lightheadedness or faintness.

drop attack: Sudden inability to maintain upright posture; the victim literally drops, with no loss of consciousness. Associated with the rostral vermis or anterior lobe syndrome of the cerebellum, or with cerebral lesions.

drusen: Benign yellow-white specks of hyaline bodies (uneven pigment) seen on the retina during ophthalmoscopy.

dysarthria: Difficulty articulating speech due to a motor impairment, despite knowing what one wants to say.

dyscalculia: A defect in calculatory skills with otherwise normal intelligence.

dysdiadochokinesia: An inability to perform rapid, repetitive, alternating movements, such as rapidly pronating and supinating the hands on the upper thighs; can be a sign of cerebellar disease.

dysmetria: Literally, difficult measuring. Difficulty in controlling the range of muscular movement; seen in cerebellar disorders.

dystonia: Loss of normal muscle tone with a disturbed posture.

Edinger-Westphal nucleus: The parasympathetic component of the oculomotor nucleus.

Ekbom's syndrome: See restless leg syndrome. This syndrome is characterized by a restless discomfort in the legs, especially at night.

emmetropia: Normal visual acuity.

emotional lability: Rapid and unpredictable mood swings.

engram: A vivid, lasting memory. Sometimes associated with psychic trauma.

ependymoma: A slow-growing calcific ventricular wall tumor (usually fourth ventricle), occurring most often in children. Presents with signs of increased intracranial pressure. Associated with a short average survival rate.

epilepsy: Commonly referred to as a seizure disorder.

erythema chronicum migrans (ECM): A round, reddened area usually seen where a Lyme-infected tic has bitten. May be accompanied by fever, chills, malaise, fatigue, headache, and swollen lymph nodes.

esotropia: An inward or medial heterotropia.

exophthalmos: A "bugging out" of the eyes characterized by the sclera being visualized above and below the limbus.

exotropia: An outward or lateral ocular deviation.

fasciculation: Contractions of muscle fascicles caused by depolarization of a lower motor neuron.

fibrillations: Fibrillations are spontaneous contractions of individual muscle fibers, without initiation from upper or lower motor neurons.

filum terminale: A thin extension of pia mater that attaches to the first coccygeal segment.

flocculonodular lobe: Phylogenetically the oldest part of the cerebellum, this lobe's main function is orientation of the head and upper trunk in space. It has many vestibular connections.

foramen of Monro: Cerebrospinal fluid pathway between the lateral and third ventricles.

foraminal compression: Radiating pain during compression of the cervical spine; indicates narrowing of the neural canal, facet problems, or muscle spasm.

fovea centralis: A spot on the macula lutea that is the central focus point on the retina.

Fröhlich's syndrome: Characterized by retarded development of secondary sexual characteristics and obesity. Occurs primarily in male children and may correct itself at puberty.

Froment's sign: Weak thumb adduction seen in ulnar nerve palsy.

fundus, optic: The back part of the eyeball, as visualized with ophthalmoscopy.

funiculus: Cord. The term is used in discussing the tracts of the spinal cord: dorsal, lateral, and ventral.

Gerstmann's syndrome: Characterized by acalculia, finger agnosia, right-left confusion, and agraphia.

giant polyphasic motor units: Found during electromyography in lower motor neuron disease during slight contraction of the muscle indicative of lower motor neuron disease.

glioblastoma multiforme: A malignant central nervous system tumor with a very poor prognosis.

glioma: A glial (non-neuronal tissue) cell tumor.

global aphasia: Profound expressive and receptive deficits.

globus hystericus: The feeling described as "having a lump in your throat." Usually associated with hysteria.

graphesthesia: The ability to recognize letters or numbers traced on the skin.

Green-Joynt sign: Detection of a lytic lesion in the skull by auscultation. Lytic metastatic tumors transmit the patient's vocally produced sounds in a manner distinguishable from the normal skull.

hemiballismus: A violent flinging movement of half of the body.

Hering-Breuer reflex: A reflex limiting excursion of the lungs during both inspiration and expiration.

heterophoria: A latent ocular deviation from normal ocular alignment apparent only when special tests are performed.

heterotopia: An ocular deviation from normal ocular alignment able to be visualized without additional tests.

Hoffmann's reflex: Briskly flicking one of the fingers of a hand in supination causes sudden distal finger extension, resulting in a pathological reflex flexion of all digits on that side (clawing).

Holmes-Adie pupil: See Adie's pupil.

Holmes phenomenon: See rebound sign of Holmes.

honeymoon paralysis: Paralysis of the muscles supplied by the radial nerve when the arm is abducted for a prolonged period, as may occur when supporting the weight of the head of one's new bride or groom.

Horner's syndrome: A syndrome that can include flushing of the skin, ptosis of the eyelid, miosis, and anhidrosis of one side of the face, caused by interruption of sympathetic fibers in the cervical chain.

hyperacusis: A pathological increase in the awareness of sound.

hypertelorism: Greater than normal interorbital distance.

hypotelorism: Smaller than normal interorbital distance.

insomnia: Inability to fall asleep.

ipsilateral: Same side.

Jendrassik's maneuver: A technique of distracting patients by having them interlock their fingers and try to pull them apart, while the examiner at the same time tests for a muscle stretch reflex. Reflexes tested this way can be labeled (R) for reinforced.

Kernig's test: Painful knee extension when the hip is flexed; usually associated with meningitis.

Kleine-Levin syndrome: Characterized by excessive sleeping and eating.

Klüver-Bucy syndrome: Bilateral removal of the temporal lobes leads to a syndrome characterized by voracious appetite, increased sexual activity, and generalized lassitude.

Korsakoff's syndrome: Amnesia caused by a destructive lesion in the thalamus.

leptomeninx: Undistinguishable combination of the pia and arachnoid mater.

Lhermitte's sign: A sudden electrical tingling felt in the spine and lower extremities during neck flexion. May be indicative of cervical myelopathy or multiple sclerosis.

limbus: A border; usually refers to the border between the sclera and the cornea.

limbus to lid, limbus to canthi: A phrase describing the normal appearance of the eyes, with eyes focused straight ahead. The lid covers part of the iris, but never the pupil, and the lower lid forms a tangent with the lower border (limbus), with equal amounts of medial and lateral sclera visible.

Lindau's disease: Hemangioblastoma with cysts and tumors of the liver, pancreas, and kidneys.

Lyme disease: First seen in Lyme, Connecticut, this disease is now endemic to New England, Minnesota, Wisconsin, and the Pacific Northwest. It is associated with the spirochete *Borrelia burgdorferi* and is transmitted to man via the deer tick. The acute stage includes the bite site's developing erythema chronicum migrans, with associated flulike symptoms. The second stage may present with neurological symptoms, and the third stage generally presents with rheumatological symptoms.

masked facies: Reduced facial movement, as though the patient were wearing a mask characteristic of Parkinson's disease.

masseter muscle: Closes jaw under cranial nerve V control.

medulloblastoma: Second-most common childhood central nervous system tumor. It is highly malignant, affects males more than females, and presents with ataxia and cerebellar vermis syndrome.

Meniere's disease: This disease is characterized by paroxysmal attacks of vertigo, nausea, vomiting, pallor, and cold sweats. Due to disease of the labyrinth of the inner ear.

meningioma: A slow-growing benign tumor of mesodermal origin that causes signs of compression relating to its location.

meralgia paresthetica: Sensory defect in the anterolateral upper thigh resulting from entrapment of the lateral femoral cutaneous nerve.

micturition syncope: A loss of consciousness during or after urination.

miosis: Constriction of the pupil.

myoclonic jerk: Discharge of the reticular activating system, causing a startle reaction of the whole body or of a single large muscle group.

narcolepsy: A sleep disorder characterized by an uncontrollable urge to sleep.

neologisms: Nonsense words made up by patients due to either lack of understanding or an apraxia.

neural shock: An acute state of hypotonic paralysis after onset of an acute upper motor neuron lesion.

nystagmus: Involuntary oscillation of the eyes.

obtundation: Severe decrease in level of consciousness.

oculogyric crisis: Spastic upward deviation of the head and eyes, often seen with parkinsonism.

oculomotor nerve: Cranial nerve III; controls most of the muscles that move the eye.

olfactory nerve: Cranial nerve I; governs the sense of smell.

oligodendroglioma: A slow-growing tumor of the central nervous system appearing in 30- to 40-year-olds. Chronic headache and seizures may be the only symptoms.

onion skin sensory loss: A layered sensory loss associated with hysteria.

optic nerve: Cranial nerve II; innervates the retina.

orthostatic hypotension: A sudden drop in blood pressure with faint feelings or actual syncope, associated with changing posture—usually recumbent or sitting to standing.

oscillopsia: What a person with nystagmus sees.

pacchionian granulations: Arachnoid villi are called this when they mature with age.

pachymeninx: Dura mater.

paleocerebellum: See anterior lobe.

palsy: Weakness or paralysis.

papilledema: Swelling of the optic disc due to venous engorgement.

papillitis: Inflammation at or around the site of entry of the optic nerve onto the optic fundus.

paralysis: Loss of muscular movement.

paresis: Weakness.

Parkinson's disease: Also known as paralysis agitans, this is a progressive disease of the extrapyramidal system, characterized by slow movements, masked facies, and emotional lability.

parosmia: Distortion of the sense of smell.

past pointing: When patient has trouble pointing to the examiner's finger or goes "past" it.

percussion myotonia: When the doctor processes a muscle, there is a characteristic humping of the muscle. Seen in muscle disease and disturbed potassium levels.

perseveration: Meaningless repetition of a word, response, or idea.

Phelan's test: A test in which the doctor holds the patient's wrist in sustained flexion; if this produces pain or numbness in the distribution of the median nerve, it may be indicative of carpal tunnel syndrome.

pinealoma: A central nervous system tumor seen in the area of the pineal gland.

pituitary adenoma: Enlargement of the sella turcica is the most notable result of this fairly common intracranial tumor.

posterior lobe: Lobe of the cerebellum that helps to coordinate willful muscle contractions. Also known as the neocerebellum or hemispheres.

posterior median sulcus: The small posterior sulcus of the spinal cord.

posterolateral sclerosis: A spongy degeneration of both the lateral (corticospinal) and posterior districts of the spinal cord.

pseudobulbar palsy: Paralysis of the upper motor neurons associated with the cranial nerves of the medulla, which affects speaking, swallowing, and movements of the pharynx and tongue. Caused by a bilateral cerebral lesion, it mimics bulbar palsy.

pseudopapilledema: Observed as a functional optic disc with indistinct margins and a benign central disc protrusion; caused by drusen in the nerve fiber layer.

ptosis: Prolapse or sagging of an organ or part, such as the eyelid in Horner's syndrome.

quadrantanopia: Loss of vision in one quarter of the visual field.

Quinquaud's sign: The toxic tremor of chronic alcoholism.

rabies: An acute, often fatal viral (rhabdovirus) infection generally spread by the bite of a rabid animal and characterized by fever, headache, pain, and paresthesia at the bite site, and later by muscle spasms, cyclic breathing, and hydrophobia.

radial nerve: A direct extension of the posterior cord of the brachial plexus, this nerve is often involved in injuries of the humerus.

rebound sign of Holmes: Cerebellar sign of overshooting. The examiner pulls the patient's arm away from the patient's body, against resistance. The arm is suddenly released; if it "overshoots" on its way back toward the patient's body, this is suggestive of cerebellar dysfunction.

Reye's syndrome: An acute encephalopathy occurring predominantly in children. It usually follows a viral illness and recently has been associated with the use of aspirin.

Rinne test: A hearing test to compare air to bone conduction. A vibrating tuning fork is held to the mastoid; when the sound is no longer heard, the tuning fork is held to the ear, and the sound should be heard again.

Romberg test: Assesses the patient's ability to maintain an upright posture with eyes open and then closed, while standing on a narrow base. Patients who have vestibular disease will have some trouble when they close their eyes, but patients with posterior column disease will have a great deal of difficulty even with eyes open.

Rossolimo's reflex: Flicking one of the toes causes the others to flex in a pathological reflex.

Saturday night palsy: Radial nerve paralysis caused by prolonged pressure on an arm, as might result from a long sleep after a tough "Saturday night."

scotoma: Islands of reduced vision within the visual fields.

Shy-Drager syndrome: Characterized most prominently by orthostatic hypotension; caused by a central nervous system degenerative condition.

Snellen chart: Standardized chart used for testing visual acuity.

stupor: A level of consciousness just above coma.

subclavian steal syndrome: Proximal stenosis of a subclavian artery may cause blood to flow up one vertebral artery and down the other.

suppression amblyopia: Blindness not caused by eye lesions but rather by "suppression" exerted by higher centers.

swivel chair test: A test used to differentiate between vestibular- and cervical mechanoreceptor–caused vertigo. The patient is placed on a "swivel chair" and rotated while stabilizing the head. Reproduction of the vertigo in the absence of head movement is considered a positive finding.

syncope: Sudden loss of consciousness (i.e., fainting).

tandem walking: A test for coordination in which the patient walks by placing the heel of one foot directly in front of the toe of the other.

tangent screen test: A test using a tangent screen 1 to 2 meters square to measure and chart the visual fields. It is used in detecting and monitoring papilledema, which may increase the size of the normal blind spot.

Tay-Sachs disease: A hereditary disease that strikes early in infancy, causing retarded mental development, paralysis, and blindness. Macular degeneration and a pathognomonic "cherry red spot" on the degenerated retina are seen.

tic: A quick, stereotyped movement of the face, tongue, or extremities. Usually an identical sequence of movements is seen.

tic douloureux: Excruciating paroxysmal pains associated with damage of one of the branches of the trigeminal nerve.

Tinel's sign: An "electric shock" feeling in the distal portion of a superficial nerve's distribution upon percussion. May be indicative of nerve regeneration.

Todd's paralysis: A temporary paralysis associated with some seizure disorders.

Tolosa-Hunt syndrome: Characterized by a unilateral headache with associated ophthalmoplegia.

topesthesia: The ability to localize stimuli on the skin.

transient ischemic attack: An acute, localized vascular incident involving some kind of transient motor or sensory loss with complete resolution in 24 hours or less. May be a sign of impending stroke.

uncal herniation: Herniation of the uncal portion of the temporal lobes down through the foramen magnum, caused by extremely high intracranial pressure.

uncinate fit: Uncal lesions may trigger these fits, characterized by imaginary odors that may be very disagreeable. Athetoid movements of the lips and tongue, along with clouding of the consciousness, may be seen.

Valsalva's maneuver: Forced exhalation against a closed glottis. If pain is felt in the spine during this, it can be a sign of disc herniation or a space-occupying lesion.

vertebral subluxation: A loss of normal movement or position between two segments of the spinal column, causing nerve irritation.

vertigo: The feeling that the world or oneself is spinning.

vestibulocochlear nerve: This cranial nerve (VIII) has two divisions; the cochlear division is associated with hearing, the vestibular division with equilibrium.

visual suppression: Failure to attend to a visual stimulus if it is simultaneously accompanied by a stimulus on the opposite side.

von Hippel-Lindau disease: Lindau's disease with the addition of retinal angioma.

waddling gait: Seen in conditions of proximal muscle weakness.

Wallenberg's syndrome: A brainstem and cerebellar syndrome caused by occlusion of the posterior inferior cerebellar artery.

wallerian degeneration: The degeneration that occurs in an axon when it is separated from its cell body.

Weber's sound-lateralizing test: A vibrating tuning fork placed on the vertex of the skull should be heard equally in both ears.

Weber's syndrome: A vascular lesion of the cerebral peduncle causing ipsilateral oculomotor nerve paralysis and contralateral hemiparesis of the face.

werewolf sign: Pale optic disc seen in ophthalmoscopy and associated with optic atrophy.

Wernicke's aphasia: The patient articulates spontaneously and well but uses words inappropriately or uses neologisms. Also, the patient has difficulty understanding written or verbal requests and can't repeat phrases (sensory receptive/expressive fluent aphasia).

Wernicke's encephalopathy: This disorder, seen almost exclusively in alcoholics, is due to thiamine deficiency and is characterized by paresis of the ocular muscles, nystagmus, ataxia, apathy, and, later, mental confusion.

Wilson's disease: Also known as hepatolenticular degeneration, this is a congenital defect of copper metabolism affecting both the lenticular nuclei and the liver. It generally appears in adolescence to early adulthood and presents with rigidity, tremor, and loss of voluntary movement.

wrist drop: The most common presenting complaint of radial nerve problems. It is most obvious during arm flexion.

Index

H

I

J

K

L

M

N

O

P

Q

R

S

T

U